I0878472

Living on Campus

Living on Campus

An Architectural History of the American Dormitory

CARLA YANNI

UNIVERSITY OF MINNESOTA PRESS
MINNEAPOLIS • LONDON

The University of Minnesota Press gratefully acknowledges the generous assistance provided for the publication of this book by the Rutgers University Research Council.

Copyright 2019 by the Regents of the University of Minnesota

All rights reserved. No part of this publication may be reproduced, stored in a retrieval system, or transmitted, in any form or by any means, electronic, mechanical, photocopying, recording, or otherwise, without the prior written permission of the publisher.

Published by the University of Minnesota Press
111 Third Avenue South, Suite 290
Minneapolis, MN 55401-2520
http://www.upress.umn.edu

Library of Congress Cataloging-in-Publication Data
Yanni, Carla, author.
Living on campus : an architectural history of the American dormitory / Carla Yanni.
Minneapolis : University of Minnesota Press, 2019. |
Includes bibliographical references and index. |
Identifiers: LCCN 2018037431 (print) | ISBN 978-1-5179-0455-5 (hc) |
ISBN 978-1-5179-0456-2 (pb)
Subjects: LCSH: Dormitories—United States—History. | Architecture and society—United States—History.
Classification: LCC NA6602.D6 Y36 2019 (print) | DDC 720.1/03—dc23
LC record available at https://lccn.loc.gov/2018037431

Printed in the United States of America on acid-free paper

The University of Minnesota is an equal-opportunity educator and employer.

25 24 23 22 21 20 19 10 9 8 7 6 5 4 3 2 1

To Bill,
who is in charge of funny

To Joseph,
whose laugh lights up our world

To the elder Joseph,
who takes such good care of Mom

Contents

Introduction

In Philip Roth's *Indignation,* the atheistic, lovesick, and profoundly unlucky protagonist, Marcus Messner, son of a kosher butcher from Newark, New Jersey, transfers from an urban university to a prestigious coeducational college in the boondocks of Pennsylvania. The year is 1951. Marcus's grades—all As—are beyond reproach. And yet the dean of men, Mr. Hawes Caudwell, hassles him: "You seem to be having some trouble settling into dormitory life." The falsely congenial Caudwell continues: "I'm a bit concerned about your having already resided in three different dormitory rooms in just your first weeks here. Tell me in your own words, what seems to be the trouble?"[1] The dean wants Marcus to join the Jewish fraternity, or at least to consort with other Jews. And Marcus knows it. "Why should I have to go through this interrogation," he ponders, "simply because I'd moved from one dormitory room to another to find the peace of mind I required to do my schoolwork?"[2] Marcus's question is a reasonable one. But from the dean's vantage point, college is not only for schoolwork. The objective of college, and in particular the goal of dormitory life, is to offer students practice in the fine art of getting along with their fellows, albeit while staying within socially accepted categories as determined by college leaders.

Living on Campus: An Architectural History of the American Dormitory explains why Americans have believed for so long that college students should reside in purpose-built structures that we now take for granted: dormitories. This was never inevitable, nor was it even necessary. In the chapters that follow, I will show that living on campus is a manifestation of three hundred years of American educational ideology that placed a high priority on social interaction among students. The architecture of dormitories provides a lens through which to examine the socially constructed nature of the student. Furthermore, the history of this building type illustrates that, starting before the American Revolution, student housing acted to include some and exclude others, causing inequalities that intruded on the collegiate ideal. At every step, the architecture of dormitories has participated in the establishment of the essential norms of American life. Residence halls helped universities to reinforce an elite class of men in the new republic, develop an educated cadre of Victorian wives and mothers, build up middle-class values in the Progressive Era, espouse capitalistic individualism in the face of the Cold War, and negotiate with counterculture students in the 1960s. Dorm living is one of the most widely shared experiences in modern American life. Hundreds of thousands of students pass through residence halls, and their lives are changed by their encounters with these buildings. In spite of that simple fact, the history of the buildings is not well understood.

Residence halls are not mute containers for the temporary storage of youthful bodies and emergent minds. Dormitories constitute historical evidence of the educational ideals of the people who built them. The varied designs of residence halls reflect changes in student life, as well as college officials' evolving aspirations for their institutions, the students themselves, and society at large. The ancient universities of Europe (Uppsala, Bologna, Utrecht, the Sorbonne, and others) lasted for centuries without elaborate or purpose-built housing for their students.[3] Community colleges in the United States have not historically provided residence halls, although some have recently added them. Students at four-year colleges frequently choose to live in unregulated off-campus apartments. So why have American educators believed for so long that housing students is essential to educating them? And, more specifically, what role has architecture played in legitimating that idea? In this book I explore the experiences of college students by looking closely at the material cultures and built environments of their dwellings.

Living on Campus is a social history of a building type. This allows me to analyze how architects and patrons solved similar problems in different contexts. Throughout the book, I introduce comparative building types where historically relevant. In the nineteenth century, park designers, urban reformers, prison wardens, and psychiatrists believed that the environment, including architecture, could transform behavior. By looking at the built environment, we can examine where men and women were segregated and where they were allowed (or even encouraged) to be together. In my book on the architecture of nineteenth-century mental hospitals, *The Architecture of Madness: Insane Asylums in the United States,* I employ the concept of environmental determinism to describe how Victorian psychologists believed they could improve the behavior of patients, and even cure mental illness, by housing patients in purpose-built, carefully ordered environments.[4] In his book *Huck's Raft: A History of American Childhood,* Steven Mintz makes a similar observation about the treatment of children in institutions like orphanages and reformatories. He notes that although such institutions "stand as relics of a seemingly more repressive, less enlightened past," they "were inspired, to varying degrees, by a utopian faith that it was possible to solve social problems and reshape human character by removing children from corrupting outside influence and instilling self-control through moral education, work, rigorous discipline, and an orderly environment."[5] So, too, college officials argued that it was crucial for students to live on campus in order for them to benefit from the self-improving atmosphere of the purpose-built college.

This book inhabits an intellectual space between vernacular architectural studies and traditional architectural history.[6] Some of the buildings discussed here were designed by well-known architects, but others are ordinary structures. I analyze communal dwellings over long periods and start with the assumption that the physical form of the buildings was inextricable from their social context. Dorms may be found in almost every historical style. From the seventeenth century to 1968, dormitories track architectural fashions. In most cases, one style does not carry much more meaning than another. We can find dorms in colonial and Georgian styles, Greek Revival, Gothic Revival, Richardsonian Romanesque, Colonial Revival, Elizabethan Revival, Arts and Crafts, Dutch Colonial Revival, modernist, Brutalist, and postmodernist. One could teach the entire history of style in American architecture by looking only at residence halls. Most campuses are hodgepodges of historical styles. Exceptions include the University of Colorado Boulder (Tuscan vernacular) and the University of New Mexico (Pueblo Revival), both of which had strict design covenants that required architects to build historicizing structures in one style. Although my primary concern in this book is not style per se, I do analyze moments when aesthetics generated controversy and commentary. For example, sources indicate that former presidents of Rutgers College expressed a deep sense of loss when modernism replaced historicism on that campus. Some of the case studies represented here were designed by "high art" architects, but my approach to these buildings is not fundamentally concerned with their artistry. Instead, I am interested in their social historical meanings, whether typical or extraordinary.

Although the range of styles was vast, the range of plans was more limited. To simplify a bit, two plans dominated the construction of residence halls: the double-loaded corridor and the staircase or entryway plan. (I will use the terms *staircase* and *entryway* interchangeably.) These were standardized basic layouts referred to frequently by architects and others; I did not invent the categories. A 1929 book

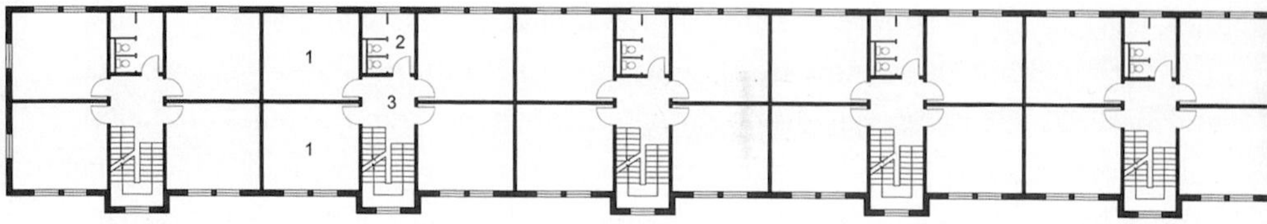

Figure I.1. The entryway (or staircase) plan, based on the residence halls at Oxford and Cambridge Universities, is one of the most common dormitory types. In this particular version, four student rooms and small bathrooms are accessible from the landing on each floor. 1 = bedroom; 2 = bathroom; 3 = staircase (on the ground floor the staircase is aligned with an entryway). Drawing by John Giganti, based on plans from Charles Z. Klauder and Herbert C. Wise, *College Architecture in America and Its Part in the Development of the Campus* (New York: Charles Scribner's Sons, 1929).

on college architecture presented the two plans as equally viable.[7] At the level of dormitory planning, the staircase plan utilized several doors that opened directly to the outdoors, granting students, usually male, the freedom to move in and out of their buildings at all hours. The permeable staircase plan was widely used for colleges but was never employed at asylums, orphanages, or jails.

A staircase-plan dormitory had no central desk or observation point. Upon entering the building, students circulated up and down the staircase, which was the center of social groupings. In contrast, a dormitory with a double-loaded corridor contained rooms on both sides of a hall, allowing for a single entrance (or two) for even a very large building. Compared with the staircase plan, this plan made it easier to track students and visitors. Because surveillance of women was a higher priority than management of men, architects and deans avoided the staircase plan for the housing of female students. In 1949, the author of a pamphlet produced by the American Institute of Architects observed, "It is noted that women's colleges

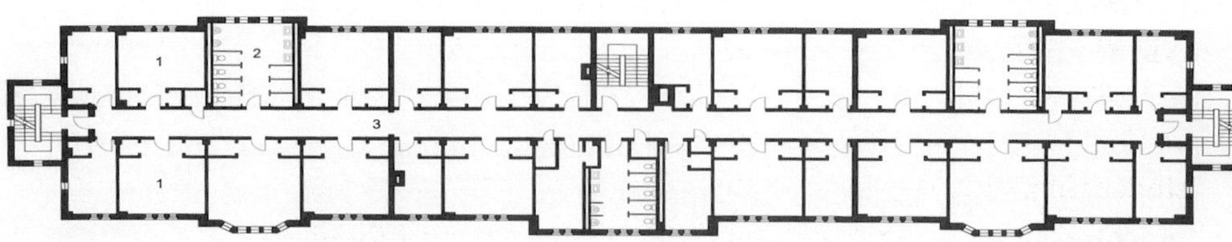

Figure I.2. The double-loaded corridor is a common arrangement for dormitory spaces. A typical configuration includes student rooms, lounges, and group bathrooms situated on both sides of a long hall. 1 = bedroom; 2 = bathroom; 3 = corridor. Drawing by John Giganti, based on plans from Charles Z. Klauder and Herbert C. Wise, *College Architecture in America and Its Part in the Development of the Campus* (New York: Charles Scribner's Sons, 1929).

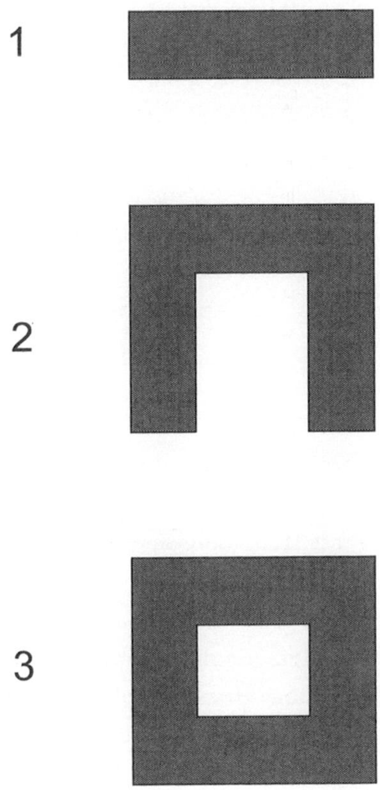

Figure I.3. Three of the most common dormitory footprints: 1 = the rectangular prism or rectangular block form; 2 = the U, C, or three-sided quadrangle; 3 = the fully enclosed quadrangle or square donut. These types can be arranged with entryways, double-loaded corridors, or other internal divisions. Drawing by John Giganti.

generally provide more supervision and therefore prefer the corridor-type plan to the entry-type plan."[8] The corridor could be used in a building that took the form of a rectangular prism, a U shape, or a square donut.

For each chapter, I have chosen case studies that fit within a confined chronological era, with periods getting shorter as we move toward 1968. I have sought to include a range of institutions: private, public, large, small, single gender, and coed. The case studies are keyed to important changes in the management of student life, such as when two important deans combined forces at the University of Chicago. In selecting the case studies, I concentrated on moments of controversy in education. If a building is still standing, I considered that a good reason to choose it over another similar example, but I include some significant buildings (such as the second Ladies' Hall at Oberlin) despite their long-ago demolition. With the growing professionalization of student deans over time, it became relatively easy to pinpoint buildings that they thought of as models, and therefore I could select examples that were admired by deans of women (such as at Howard University) and by deans of men (as at the University of Wisconsin–Madison). A deep cache of archival material (as at the University of Michigan and the Ohio State University) was an added incentive to investigate a particular building. For the sake of clarity, each chapter contains at least three discrete case studies, with comparative material included to deepen the discussion, and the examples proceed in rough chronological order. There was no way for me to assemble a scientifically perfect selection of cases, and I know that my choices of case studies will be open to debate. Another scholar who selected different examples would have written a different book, but I do not think his or her conclusions would be widely divergent from mine.

Architectural historians will miss some favorite buildings. I chose not to write about the University of Virginia, because it has been well covered elsewhere.[9] Wanting to concentrate on the undergraduate experience, particularly the transition from childhood to adulthood, I decided not to look at housing for married or graduate students. I did not, therefore, include Josep Lluís Sert's or Walter Gropius's dormitories at Harvard. Louis Kahn's Erdman at Bryn Mawr is fascinating, but it is more closely tied to Kahn's own artistic agenda than to the themes of this book. Alvar Aalto's Baker House at MIT, with its memorable *parti,* is mostly an interpretation of the single-loaded corridor, and (as charming as it is) did not yield much of a legacy.[10] An extremely rough estimate places the number of four-year colleges in the United States at about three thousand, and if each one has an average of ten dormitories, there would be thirty thousand possible case studies.[11] I focused on purpose-built structures, primarily to narrow the scope of my investigation but also because the archival records for such buildings are particularly revealing in terms of the makers' intentions.[12]

Presidents and other upper-level college officials made most of the design decisions. Student deans sometimes complained that architects and other administrators ignored their concerns. To take one example, the National Association of Women Deans and Counselors sent a questionnaire to its members in 1963. Under the heading "Extent of Staff Participation in Building Design and Decoration," one dean responded, "Deans and resident counselors meet with the architect who incorporates as few suggestions as possible."[13] At Ohio State in the 1960s, the university planner intervened on behalf of the dean of students and "his housing people" because the latter group had "known nothing whatsoever about the fact that the program was being drawn up."[14] The program in question was the architectural brief for dormitories to house four thousand students—the largest single building project ever undertaken by OSU. The upper-level administrators did eventually consult the dean of students. Students did not play a consequential role in dormitory design until the 1960s.[15]

Paul V. Turner's foundational 1984 book *Campus: An American Planning Tradition* brings to light important innovations in the development of the American college campus in a holistic sense, rather than as a single building type. In *Campus,* Turner is primarily concerned with planning history and the history of colleges as ensembles of related structures. He cares deeply about the expression of a college's values through architectural style. In contrast, my focus is on issues of inclusion, exclusion, class, and gender. Without Turner's generous and extensive scholarship, this book would have been much more difficult to write. I also benefited greatly from the work of Helen Lefkowitz Horowitz, in particular her books *Alma Mater* and *Campus Life*.[16] The latter offers a rich longitudinal study, which must be the starting point for anyone interested in the social history of students. *Alma Mater* expanded methodological horizons for many historians by combining social history and the history of place, but even that pathbreaking book contains few illustrations of plans.

WHY LIVE IN A DORMITORY? SOCIABILITY AND NETWORKING

Colonial- and Federal-era colleges, especially those in rural locations, were obligated to build housing for their students, because there were not enough boardinghouses or other dwellings nearby.[17] Educators wanted some distance between their students and the vice-filled city. Every outpost, no matter how small and isolated, fancied itself a New Athens, and town boosters optimistically assumed that an institution of higher learning was required.[18] Furthermore, many early colleges were missionary in spirit, and thus needed to be close to potential converts.[19] Each denomination had one or more of its own colleges, and, as one contemporary observer noted, America seemed to have an "excessive multiplication" of colleges of "dwarfish dimensions."[20] These numerous and small colleges differed fundamentally from European academies of higher learning. The small residential college, as developed in the United States, had no exact parallel in the Old World. Furthermore—and this is an essential argument for this book—the fixation on college as a means of didactic character forming was embedded in America's religious landscape: without a state religion, each denomination used institutions of higher learning to imprint its specific morality upon its followers. This moral guidance was easier to transmit if the students lived on campus with the faculty. As Nathaniel Hawthorne describes the fictitious Harley College, modeled on Bowdoin College in Maine, in his novel *Fanshawe*: "The local situation of the college, so far secluded from the sight and sound of the busy world, is peculiarly favorable to the moral, if not to the literary, habits of its students; and this advantage probably caused the founders to overlook the inconveniences that were inseparably connected with it."[21]

As I discuss in chapter 1, colleges were often housed in single, multipurpose structures that encompassed all the functions of a school, including the president's home, faculty apartments, student bedrooms, chapel, library, dining hall, and classrooms. There was not much opportunity for privacy, but then privacy was in short supply in houses of the period, too. Several of the college rooms, the chapel and dining hall in particular, supported assembly. Harvard's first governing board reported: "It is well known . . . what advantage to Learning accrues by the multitude of persons cohabiting for scholasticall communion, whereby to acuate the minds of one another, and other waies to promote the ends of a Colledge-Society."[22] Although the actual curriculum was limited, Christian morality was nonetheless a large part of what boys were supposed to absorb at the colonial college. This character formation was not gleaned from book study so much as from the observation of role models. As early as 1671, American college leaders were proposing that students and faculty living together in a communal setting was an "advantage to learning." Sharing living space with their professors was good for students' moral development. This attitude was an essential intellectual and emotional precondition for the American dormitory.

Benjamin Franklin, who is counted among the founders of what later became the University of Pennsylvania, saw the enhancement of social ties as a reason for going to college: "Persons of Leisure and Public spirit" will "zealously unite, and make all the Interest that can be made to establish [themselves], whether in Business, Offices, Marriages or any other thing for their advantage."[23] Franklin had a particularly pragmatic view of higher education. He recognized that many boys did not go to college solely for book learning or credentials—they also went to meet other people of their social class, who, with a little luck, had younger sisters. Although Franklin wished for a more egalitarian society than the one that gave rise to Oxford and Cambridge, he also recognized that the members of the ruling classes in the colonies had to interact and socialize. Franklin's interest in matchmaking as a by-product of collegiate life can be traced forward in time to an interview question that fraternity members used at Williams College in 1836 to help them select new brothers: "Would you allow your sister to marry him?"[24]

Who was included in, and who was excluded from, dormitory life? Enforced diversity—the ostensible raison d'être of modern-day residence halls—never entered the minds of early American college officials. In fact, antidiversity was the norm. Today residence halls are drenched in the self-congratulatory rhetoric of diversity, but the building type emerged in the service of exclusion. College life introduced men to other men like themselves. Using funds from England, Harvard built its Indian College so that whites would not have to dwell with Native Americans. While it might look like these early dormitories were nothing more than boxes for warehousing young men, they were in fact a public celebration of the importance of colleges in the colonies and nascent republic, a topic explored in the first part of chapter 1.

Chapter 1 also considers white male fraternities and the houses they lived in. Fraternities amplified the cultures of privilege and sexism that loomed over college life. From their earliest days, Greek organizations dominated social life on campus, and college administrators were aware of this imbalance. Non-Greek-affiliated students were often left without access to membership on sports teams, friendships,

Figure I.4. Old West, Dickinson College, 1803–5, Benjamin Henry Latrobe, architect, interior of student room, date of photograph unknown. Although the students were obviously posing, the photograph shows a typical men's room, with books, a tennis racket, a desk, dresser, and bed. Archives and Special Collections, Dickinson College.

and leadership positions. At the University of Michigan and Cornell University, just two of many examples from the late Victorian era, poor students lived in run-down boardinghouses while wealthy students lived in grand fraternity houses. The thousands of fraternity houses that currently dot the American landscape are a building type unto themselves, significant enough to warrant a book-length study of their own (by a different author, I hasten to add). Nonetheless, in my archival research I found that the histories of the dormitory and the fraternity are so entwined that I decided to include a few Greek houses here for comparison purposes.[25] Historian Nicholas Syrett has explored the lives of students in white fraternities, concluding that such fraternities have served to define class-based constructions of masculinity.[26] He also points out that when women began to attend college with men, fraternity brothers rejected these women students as potential mates. Many social and cultural historians are attuned to difference and discrimination in texts; in this book I provide a model for analyzing how physical structures have reinscribed the segregation of races, social classes, and genders.

The housing of women on coeducational campuses is the main subject of chapter 2. Women's residence halls were generous in their public spaces and well appointed in terms of furniture; these structures sought to keep women protected and confined, but they certainly did not resemble prisons. While every college claimed that female students were housed in homelike structures, everyone recognized this as a kind of fiction: a building with a hundred women under one roof was not a home. Nonetheless, the appearance of domesticity on the interior, especially in the common rooms, was essential. This was in accord with an educational philosophy that promoted the idea that young women were being trained for future lives as wives and mothers. Women's dormitories on coed campuses reveal the paradox of female students who braved the male-dominant atmosphere: dormitories announced their presence, but elaborate halls suggested they needed protection. Domesticity was a double-edged knife.

Where did college students live during the height of the future-loving Jazz Age? Chapter 3 shows that they lived in medieval revival quadrangles. The quad was the preferred architectural form during the 1920s and 1930s because it inspired memories of Oxbridge, created a private exterior courtyard, and offered a "traditional atmosphere of academic quiet."[27] The University of Wisconsin built two quadrangles that were considered models for other universities.[28] At Howard University, a premier African American university, an influential dean of women, Lucy Diggs Slowe, worked closely with architect Albert Cassell. In 1933 the Howard yearbook, *The Bison,* brimmed with pride at the successful completion of new women's dormitories: "Out of a sea of green, they rise in grandeur."[29]

Figure I.5. Women students at the University of Chicago, 1899. This is one of many evocative photographs in a remarkable album that documents the life of an undergraduate at the University of Chicago, Hedwig Loeb; her sister, Hannah; and their friends. Here the young women, wearing tartan skirts, are gathered on the lawn outside Green Hall for a game they called "golf ballet." Hedwig Loeb's photo album, 1899–1900, Hedwig L. Loeb Papers, Special Collections Research Center, University of Chicago Library.

Low-rise buildings were the status quo in student housing until the 1940s, but, as discussed in chapter 4, just after World War II skyscraper residence halls burst into the clouds at many universities. The Servicemen's Readjustment Act (better known as the GI Bill), which included education benefits, went into effect shortly after the war; in 1946, approximately one million veterans enrolled in U.S. colleges and universities, almost doubling the size of the student population.[30] Colleges were swamped by the massive influx of people; thousands of students dwelled in temporary and retrofitted structures. The GI Bill was the most sweeping educational legislation enacted by the federal government since the 1860s, and it catalyzed a building boom during which residence halls exploded in number and

Figure I.6. Women's Dormitory, Howard University, 1929–31, Albert Cassell, architect, photograph from 1951. Students walk through the original west gate of the quadrangle; one range of the building is visible behind them. Two more wings were built later in accordance with Cassell's plans. Today the complex is known as the Harriet Tubman Quadrangle. Scurlock Studio Records, Archives Center, National Museum of American History, Smithsonian Institution.

in size. Most state schools, and many private ones, created superblocks made up of these looming devices for storing students. At Rutgers University, which had only recently become the state university of New Jersey, three long, thin, nine-story slabs, housing a total of one thousand men, rose alongside the Raritan River in 1955; every floor had a lounge, and half of the student rooms enjoyed river views. Long hallways were lined with cookie-cutter double bedrooms. The buildings shared the Student Activities Center, which boasted floor-to-ceiling windows and a roof garden. The designers of modernist skyscrapers at many public universities knowingly rejected the application of historical styles, which smacked of privilege in those optimistic postwar days, when state funding for education was increasing and when most Americans thought of education as a public good.[31]

The Ohio State University built two octagonal towers (begun in 1962) that soared over every other building on the campus. The towers offered nice views from every room and preserved the ground area for playing fields—with 100 percent confidence in air-conditioning and fast elevators, why build low? Local politics obligated state universities to hire regional architects, and thus these high-rise

Figure I.7. Women's Dormitory, Howard University, 1929–31, Albert Cassell, architect, interior of a double room, photograph from 1951. Scurlock Studio Records, Archives Center, National Museum of American History, Smithsonian Institution.

dormitories tended not to receive much notice in the national architectural press. State universities had taxpayers to serve and used public funds sparingly, which was one reason, along with architectural taste, that modernism edged out historicism on state campuses. In 1957, a group of deans sympathetic to modernism reported: "College architects have shown commendable ingenuity in the adaptation of modern architectural styles to the functions of residence halls, and the colleges well equipped with Colonial, or Gothic halls built from 10 to 50 years ago now listen to criticism alike from envious undergraduates and from experts in neighboring colleges who built more efficient and convenient housing of glass and steel and concrete."[32]

But towers and slabs did not hold sway for long. Architects, educators, and students soon grew weary of rigid modernist urban planning and found precedents in

Figure I.8. River Dorms, Rutgers University, 1955, Kelly and Gruzen, architects. The postwar period saw a sharp increase in the number of high-rise dormitories. At Rutgers, two men look out at the Raritan River from the balcony of the lounge on one of the upper floors of the River Dorms. This photograph was taken on move-in day. Buildings and grounds, box 9, Special Collections and University Archives, Rutgers University Libraries.

Figure I.9. Morrill Tower, Ohio State University, 1963–67, Schooley, Cornelius, and Schooley, architects. The Ohio State University built high-rise dormitories despite the large amount of land available near the campus. Drawer 67, folder "Lincoln and Morrill Towers (2)," Photo Archives, The Ohio State University Archives.

much-beloved vernacular villages, which seemed to encourage casual interaction. Eero Saarinen at Yale composed a plan for two colleges that recalled the hill towns of Italy in its irregular steps, crooked street pattern, and variation of building heights. A more obvious way to reject the rigidity of the high-rise was to return to the comfort of the quadrangle. The first buildings at the University of California, Santa Cruz, were quadrangles such as Cowell College, which inspired Livingston College, a part of Rutgers. UC Santa Cruz was a brand-new university in 1965, yet its residential colleges harked back to the Middle Ages. Students would dwell, dine, and study together; a handful of faculty members would live on-site. Among students, hatred of the modernist superblock dovetailed with the upsurge of their own power within the world of higher education.[33]

Approved in 1968, Kresge College at the University of California, Santa Cruz (Charles Moore and William Turnbull, of the firm MLTW), was designed as a colorful, highly ornamented, village-like setting—an anti-institutional residential college nestled among redwood trees. When professors, staff members, and students established Kresge College, they conducted a class that was managed as a loosely run group therapy session. The members of this therapy group promoted an ideal social realm in which "straight talk" and "being authentic" would prevail. Kresge apartments opened directly onto the street. Students participated actively in the design process, and, along with administrators and instructors, shunned time-honored dormitory spaces: there were no group bathrooms, no cafeteria, and almost no corridors. The residences at Kresge College turned all previous attempts at housing students upside down and inside out; the college offers a logical concluding point and serves as the last case study in this book.

THE DORMITORY'S RELATIONSHIP TO OTHER COMMUNAL HOUSING TYPES

Medieval monasteries served as the architectural precursor to the quadrangles of Oxford and Cambridge, and hence they are the distant precedents for many American colleges.[34] Monasteries were places of study, learning, and the production of knowledge. In physical form, a monastery often included a rectangular outdoor space that was walled off from the neighboring town or countryside. In some monastic orders, brothers lived apart from the world, in sturdy, well-built structures that included dining rooms, individual cells for sleeping, and outdoor square courtyards or cloisters. Monastic churches were the precedents for the chapels at Oxbridge colleges. Convents shared many of the same characteristics. Of course, this similarity to colleges cut two ways: some viewed the monastery as a heralded

Figure I.10. Kresge College, University of California, Santa Cruz, 1967–73, MLTW, architects. The architecture is evocative of a village with a narrow street, thus rejecting both the quadrangle and the skyscraper models. Photograph by author.

and worthy predecessor, while for others it was a tainted and superstitious remnant of the Catholic past.

From the seventeenth century forward, Oxford and Cambridge dominated ideas about the proper architectural form for American colleges. Housing almost all of their students, they were oddly the exception, not the rule, among the oldest universities. The buildings at Oxford and Cambridge were designed in a variety of styles, but they were usually three or four stories tall and took the form of a series of connected square donuts. These quadrangles used the entryway plan as a means of getting boys to their rooms, which were located off of staircases. When women's dormitories began to be added in the Victorian era, they employed long corridors rather than staircases.[35] (The term *quadrangle* can also be used to refer to a series of buildings around a rectangular lawn, but in this book I use it to refer to the square donut plan.) Historian of education Alex Duke notes that college leaders were especially enamored of the English idea that faculty members should live with students to create an atmosphere of around-the-clock scholarly debate.[36] Taking these precedents from across the pond as mere examples to be improved upon, Americans creatively reinvented the British system to suit their own needs. The residential colleges at Yale and Harvard, built around 1930, were more luxurious than their English forebears.

Dormitories are related to the residential housing found in several other types of reforming institutions, many of which, in spite of possible good intentions, have inauspicious legacies. For American historians, David Rothman's *The Discovery of the Asylum,* first published in 1971, broke new ground; inspired by the writings of Michel Foucault, Rothman presents prisons, workhouses, and mental asylums as an axis of antebellum evil.[37] The depersonalization, repetitive daily regimens, and insistently orderly architecture of these institutions caused the erasure of self in the face of oppression in the early years of the American republic. The features that colleges shared with such institutions included forced interaction among strangers, harsh rules, and strict punishments, as well as regimented schedules for

Figure I.11. Old Court, Clare College, Cambridge University, 1638–1715. Clare College is a traditional quadrangle: an interior square courtyard (open to the sky) enclosed by four low-rise structures, creating a square donut. This form was the basis for many collegiate dwellings. Photograph by Ayla Lepine.

eating and praying. (Harvard professors disciplined students by beating them with birch branches until 1734, and then shifted to ear boxing; it was not until 1788 that Harvard began to use fines rather than corporal punishment to control student behavior.)[38] American colleges were not built for the purpose of punishment, or even for the strict separation of students from society, but what if upper-class people used those same devices of social control, enacted in a purpose-built structure, in the service of replication of their own elite status? What might that look like? It might look like a bit like a colonial- or Federal-era dormitory.

Asylums were sites that publicly celebrated the medical therapy then known as "moral treatment." Dormitories were a logical extension of asylums, and not just because of the drollery that ensues from comparisons of college students to madmen. These two building types are examples of communal housing; both forced architects to consider issues of fireproofing, ventilation, categorization of residents, separation of genders, and surveillance. In both cases, institutional leaders used architecture to construct cultural norms and to encourage socially acceptable forms of interaction. If the critical fortunes of the asylum led to constantly decreasing relevance, the residence hall's trajectory was toward greater importance; the asylum's negative associations meant that the hulking structures were eventually abandoned, while many dormitories (even old ones) are still in use.

Space and Childhood

In discussing the spaces of childhood, architectural historian Marta Gutman has explained, "Adults used physical spaces and changing material culture to set out and put in place their goals for childhood."[39] For historians interested in the daily lives of small children, who tend not to leave behind a treasure trove of diaries, the study of material culture enables glimpses into these lives that are unavailable any other way. Obviously, the same is not true of college students, who live among and produce texts. Even so, the physical spaces of supposedly normative late adolescence are oddly understudied; at this point, we know more about asylums and orphanages than we do about dormitories.

As Gutman notes, "Physical space is not a backdrop for childhood, but rather the two—space and childhood—are mutually constitutive."[40] The space of college dormitories can be set within this framework. However forcefully professors, deans, and architects have tried to impose corrective behavior on their charges, the students have always pushed back. Students find creative ways to undermine fuddy-duddy deans and prying professors. The grand dome of the main building at MIT was not envisioned as a pedestal for a realistic full-scale model of a fire truck, nor was the observatory at Carleton College imagined as R2-D2, but students made both of these come true. Benjamin Latrobe did not expect the storage rooms in the basement of Dickinson College's Old West to serve as a dance hall, where boys danced with each other in the middle of the night to fiddle music.[41] Beds and desks are frequently duct-taped to dorm ceilings. Occasionally roommates meet the same fate. Dormitories have been witness to sex, and lots of it: awakenings and setbacks, experiments and failures, pleasures and perils, assignations and assaults. This is all to say that college students place demands on buildings that no architect or administrator could possibly predict. The inhabitants of dormitories make their own meanings; these kinds of minor mutinies can be hard to document in the early period, but diaries, journals, and newspapers let us know that students have always transformed the dormitory's orderly spaces of control into other realms.

Hotels and Apartment Houses

Not all communal antebellum dwellings were part of coercive institutions where inmates were confined against their will. Although the nineteenth-century hotel demonstrated some of the same physical forms as the dormitory, including double-loaded corridors, bedrooms, dining rooms, parlors, and behind-the-scenes kitchens, the hotel was also different from the dormitory in many ways. The hotel, which served a mobile and ever-changing clientele, was a commercial space where liquor and entertainment (not to mention the services of sex workers) were on offer. The hotel was far more public than the college dormitory and served political uses.[42] The hotel was *of* the city; the dormitory was not. In her study of the first apartment buildings in New York City, Elizabeth Cromley locates a battle over privacy and efficient use of space in the crowded city. The row house needed so much space for circulation that it made the tasks of daily life difficult, especially for servants.[43] Middle-class New Yorkers did not want to live in tenements, either, and a whole generation of city dwellers needed to be convinced that living in French flats was socially acceptable. Richard Morris Hunt, among others, promoted apartment buildings as suitable homes rather than just pileups of houses under one roof. But other than having many people under one roof, the apartment house did not resemble the dormitory, because a dormitory did not have separate familial units and thus did not need to be subdivided into sections, each with its own kitchen, parlor, dining room, bathroom, and servants' quarters. Similarly, the plan of a tenement bore little resemblance to that of a dormitory. Many of today's residence halls lean heavily in the direction of apartment blocks. At many universities, on-campus apartments for juniors and seniors are managed by the department of student affairs; with trained university personnel on-site, this arrangement assures students' families of greater security, and yet each small group of students can live in a setting with its own kitchen.

Boardinghouses

Not all students lived in dormitories in the early years of American colleges. From the time colleges came into existence in the colonies, some students lived in boardinghouses (see chapter 1). These were not an architectural type: they were ordinary homes, usually walking distance from campus, in which students rented rooms. In some cases, the landladies provided meals (board) for a price. It was difficult to supervise students in this type of lodging, but that did not stop deans from trying. Deans of women, in particular, kept a sharp eye out for potential problems in boardinghouses. They regularly inspected the homes to make sure that the only occupants were female and that the buildings were safe from fire, outfitted with iron bedsteads, and had parlors on the first floor, so that the women would not be tempted to entertain men in their bedrooms. In 1926, when the professional society of deans of women convened for a meeting, student housing was a topic of detailed discussion. One dean tackled the unenviable task of diagnosing an outbreak of skin disease, which required her to drive around Greeley, Colorado, visiting all the boardinghouses to make sure her charges were not sharing beds.[44] Other, less itchy problems were also associated with boardinghouses, such as price gouging, lack of trained adult supervision, poor heating, and unhealthful food; in addition, deans worried about the loneliness of the student residents and the time they wasted walking long distances to campus.

Corridors

The image of the long hallway is persistent, and corridors themselves are worthy of study. Architectural historian Mark Jarzombek has written thoughtfully about corridors—especially about their downstream history, as they descended from celebratory vaulted spaces of palaces to the repetitive and banal interiors of modernist institutions: "Modern materials, abstract detailing, and the low ceilings of the post–World War II corridors put an end to the idea of corridic grandeur. Stripped of its vaults, frescoes, paintings, statues, and marble floors, the corridor, despite various claims still in its favor, slowly became a flash-point—one of many, of course—of what was wrong with modernism."[45] This sentiment can certainly be found among collegiate officials in the 1960s, who sought relief from monotonous hallways in dormitories.[46] We can find elegant and elaborate corridors in some dormitories (like the University of Michigan's Martha Cook Building, discussed in chapter 2) and gloomy concrete corridors in others (as in the River Dorms at Rutgers, addressed in chapter 4).

The endless, echoing corridor plays a central role in a story I heard many times as I pursued this research. The first version is "I lived in a dorm that was just like a prison." And the second is the dramatic (but unlikely) "I lived in a dormitory that was designed by a *prison architect*!" Like many historical myths, these two stories reveal underlying truths. Certainly, a lot of dormitories have unnerving corridors. Prison cell blocks, however, actually employ a different sort of corridor, in which the cells are stacked and each level opens onto a walkway, creating a long, thin space that is several stories tall. Another explanation for students' perceptions of the dormitory as prison might lie in the increase in the numbers of students after World War II. Many universities responded by putting up housing blocks quickly in the period after the war, and these blocks' inexpensive construction, lack of ornament, and repeated identical buildings call to mind penal architecture. Additionally, when the baby boomers began to attend college, the style known as Brutalism was in vogue, and architects used a preponderance of masonry block and concrete as exterior materials for dormitories. In reality, comparisons between dorms and jails are mostly fodder for miserable undergraduates who feel subjugated by everything, including architecture. This is not to say that their complaints are unreasonable; it is only to say that while their dorms may be uncomfortable, they are not truly equivalent to prisons.

Brutalist buildings, especially those with slit windows, have engendered another myth among students, namely, that college officials use such architecture to prevent student uprisings. This is almost always wrong, as the buildings typically predate whatever student protests are at issue, but it is such a widely disseminated myth that the fact-checking website Snopes.com lists it among urban legends in need of debunking.

COLLEGE STUDENTS: WHO WERE THEY?

The diversity of college students makes it impossible to characterize them in a few lines, and the long period discussed in this book, stretching from the eighteenth century to 1968, makes such a summary even more difficult. Childhood (or adolescence, or young adulthood) has never been a fixed state, but rather has always been under construction and reconstitution, subject to norms based on class, race, and gender. There are, however, some reliable historical developments that can be noted. One overall trend from the colonial period forward was toward increasing autonomy for youth and a related loss of control by teachers, parents, and other supervisors. Another trend: students got older. In the earlier period covered here, students were commonly as young as fourteen. Today, college students are usually between the ages of eighteen and twenty-two, and many are in their middle twenties.[47] Twenty-first-century students are also diverse in terms of race, and more women than men graduate with bachelor's degrees.[48]

We tend to think of Harvard as one continuously operating institution, and in some respects it is, but when it was founded in 1636—the first college in the English-speaking colonies—the students were nothing like present-day collegians. In the seventeenth century, adults viewed children as weak and prone to sin; they required guidelines and reprimands.[49] During the colonial period, a boy's relationship to his family was usually at least partly an economic one, in that the labor performed by children was essential for survival; sending an able-bodied boy to college was both a cost and a loss to the family.[50] During the period before the Revolutionary War, one Native American, Caleb Cheeshahteaumuck, graduated from Harvard; there were no black students.[51]

In the later eighteenth century, middle- and upper-class adults began to cherish children for their emotional and sentimental ties to the family. Families that could manage it arranged for their children to mature gradually, in calibrated steps, within institutions segregated from adult society. As adults began to see children as deserving of a happy beginning to their lives, guardians began approaching their charges with thoughtful incremental conditioning.[52] During this period fertility rates declined among the upper classes, and the intensity of family affection increased as adults centered their lives on the nuclear family.[53]

From 1870 to 1915, the numbers of female college students grew steadily. According to a report published by the National Center for Education Statistics:

> The proportion of women earning bachelor's degrees rose slowly during the latter part of the nineteenth and early twentieth century. Between 1869–70 and 1909–10, the proportion of bachelor's degrees earned by women rose from 15 percent to 23 percent. During the teens and the twenties, the proportion received by women grew more rapidly, reaching 40 percent in 1929–30. The proportion remained about the same during the 1930s, but rose dramatically during the early 1940s as large numbers of men left home to fight in World War II.[54]

Another estimate places even more women in college: in 1870, 21 percent of U.S. college students were women, but by 1920, the proportion had risen to 47 percent.[55]

This increase in the number of women attending college does not mean that all of them were then embarking on careers. In 1895, Charles F. Thwing, president of the university that later became Case Western, heralded the role of educated women as wives, mothers, and homemakers:

> The fact is that about fifty-five per cent of the woman-graduates of our colleges marry. The fact is a happy one—happy for the wives and the husbands, and happy also for the homes. . . . The fact that most women prefer to marry is also a happy one for life itself. The home is the center of life; it is the source of life's best influences. No contribution for its enrichment is too costly. All that learning and culture can offer, all that the virtues can achieve, all that the graces can contribute, all that which the college represents and embodies, is none too rich for the betterment of the home. The college woman, therefore, as embodying the best type of womanhood, is bringing the best offering of herself to the worthiest shrine.[56]

Although it may seem counterintuitive, the dormitory itself was a training ground for future domestic hospitality. Some colleges operated so that the social spaces in the women's dormitories welcomed male students, too. As discussed in chapter 2, parties hosted by female students in genteel parlors were supposed to civilize brutish young men.

As historian John Thelin notes, between 1890 and 1910, "college enrollments represented less than 5 percent of the American population of eighteen- to twenty-two-year-olds."[57] Within this narrow band of American society there was a hierarchy: "Even though going to college conferred elite status on an individual, not every undergraduate enjoyed first-class citizenship in the campus community."[58] Given that first-class citizenship entailed belonging to a fraternity, deans in the early twentieth century sought to level the playing field by building dorms, so that those students who did not gain acceptance to fraternities or who chose not to join would at least be able to live on campus. A deep gulf separated the outsiders (mocked with names like "grinds," "barbs," and "fish") from the fraternity men, who were self-styled as happy-go-lucky, clubby, and physically fit. (To quote Homer Simpson: "Marge, try to understand, there are two kinds of college students, jocks and nerds!") For the wealthy, college was a chance to make connections. For middle-class students and those who were the children of immigrants, college was a more serious affair: it was the only way to leave manual labor behind, the only route to a profession.[59]

Around 1900, the adolescent—that sexual, angst-ridden, and impetuous being—erupted onto the collegiate scene. It was during the first decade of the twentieth century that psychiatrists began to see adolescence as a natural developmental stage between the onset of puberty and full adult maturation. Doctors described it as a turbulent time, but predictably so. Although G. Stanley Hall did not coin the term, he was the first to use it as a category in psychological analysis. While channeling widespread cultural influences on the emotional struggles and generational conflicts of adolescents, Hall was also responding to late nineteenth-century fears of emasculation and degeneration.[60] Indeed, boys, not girls, were central to his vision.[61] College was still seen as a way station between childhood and adulthood, and now there was a new name for the psychological condition of that in-between time. Hall believed adolescence should be prolonged. Young men needed activities that would enhance their vigor and "primitive strength" in addition to traditional study, which had the unfortunate side effect of causing weakness or even neurasthenia.[62] Youths should "be protected from premature adulthood," and "adolescents needed to be separated from the world of adults, except for those who would guide and nurture them."[63]

Young men, more so than young women, saw college as a kind of glorified playground.[64] They attended football games wearing bowler hats, wingtip shoes, and full-length raccoon coats. The fad was such a sensation that the band George Olsen and His Music recorded a dance tune called "Doin' the Raccoon," which celebrated (and teased) the "college men, knowledge men" who blindly followed convention. Crooners sang: "Rough guys, tough guys, men of dignity / Join the raccoon coat fraternity!" As the lyrics made clear, the collegiate man was a figure of fun in popular culture, not a serious political force as he would be decades later. Did this mean that he was out of touch with the realities of daily life? Perhaps. But Hall had said that "freedom is the native air and vital breath of student life," and that "the student must have freedom to be lazy, make his own minor morals," and "go to extremes at the age when excesses teach wisdom."[65] In the context of a scientific understanding of the needs of adolescents, these boys were healthfully delaying adult responsibility.

Many scholars of higher education have explored the period before World War II as the phase when elite universities contrived to keep out Jewish students. Universities that used standard college-specific entrance exams found that their percentages of Jewish students increased year after year. Harvard, Yale, and Princeton looked with horror at Columbia and Penn. At Harvard, rich students dwelled in private apartments, while the poorer and less-well-connected young men lived in older buildings in the Yard and elsewhere on campus, one of which was called "Little Jerusalem."[66] Admissions officials (themselves constituting a new profession) needed to develop ways of preserving slots for Old Stock Protestants, and so

Figure I.12. College men in raccoon coats singing a fight song. *Saturday Evening Post*, November 16, 1929. Illustration by Alan Foster. Collection of the author.

they invented desirable traits such as "well-roundedness," the lack of which effectively kept out young men who had high entrance exam scores but no extracurricular activities in high school. Admissions officials also gave preference to legacy students, those applicants whose fathers had attended the same colleges. Catholic students were affected by this systematic discrimination, but to a lesser degree than Jews, because Catholics had their own parallel world of higher education that relied on the teaching expertise of a variety of religious orders. African Americans attended college in such small numbers that while the admissions regulations did discriminate against them, the regulations were not aimed at them.

In the 1920s, male and female students began to date openly, in contrast to earlier forms of courting, which involved sanctioned social events such as dances and sleigh rides. Even one-on-one meetings between men and women were chaperoned. (It is not that college men were not having sex before this time—obviously, they were. College men sought out prostitutes or pursued women who lived in the town, who were considered more suitable for sexual liaisons than female students.)[67] Students who were dating in the 1920s often visited relatively new kinds of commercial establishments, such as amusement parks, ice cream parlors, and cinemas. Some adults saw these locales as benign, whereas others saw them as ripe with the possibility of delinquency, especially the dark, emotional hothouse of the movie theater.[68]

College officials tried their best to monitor the relationships between male and female students. At one university, the rules for dating were set out in a pamphlet that showed a cartoon hen pointing an accusatory wing at a beleaguered rooster. Her instructions included "Dress sharp and be sharp and you won't have a problem with the women." And, setting the bar a bit lower: "You are responsible for returning your date to the proper hall."[69] Students and administrators reached an impasse, as students asked for more freedom at the same time deans were seeking to protect female students from scandal, unwanted pregnancy, and ruined marriage prospects. At state-funded universities, especially, it was expected that on-campus students would be managed and controlled; state legislators insisted on it.[70]

Dating was one of many social changes that rocked female adolescents; riding in cars, smoking, cutting their hair, shortening their skirts, swing dancing, and petting became part of college girls' lives.[71] The automobile offered students privacy and mobility. Before the car, college officials never had to worry about any of their female charges being entirely alone with a man. A ride in a horseless carriage could be deadly for a young lady's reputation (not to mention just plain deadly). There was a general uptick in smoking across the entire American population in the

1920s; not surprisingly, this trend extended to college students. Smoking on campus was another vexed issue; tobacco was a substance common to men and prostitutes, neither association particularly advantageous for the so-called coed.[72]

During the 1920s and 1930s, student deans became more visible on college campuses. They valued their role as guardians, and they served in loco parentis. Their increased role did not necessarily lead to their having any influence on architectural projects, but they did weigh in on programming decisions. Gregory Blimling refers to this stage as "holism," when student affairs experts asserted that the residence hall was an integral part of the educational pathway.[73] Indeed, the term *dormitory* still makes many deans cringe. They much prefer *residence hall,* because the literal meaning of *dormitory* is a place to sleep. (Having buckled to colloquial usage, I continue to use both *dormitory* and *residence hall.*) A pervasive doctrine among student affairs professionals is that students must live on campus to enjoy the fullest benefit of the collegiate experience. Deans of students typically argue that it is not enough for the university to train the student's mind; rather, a person of strong moral fiber, a good citizen, a self-actualized individual, an authentic human being—a whole person—must emerge from the university. This principle was in effect before student affairs deans found themselves meeting the challenge that redefined their profession: the influx of students after World War II.

According to Thomas Hine, the word *teenager* was first used in *Popular Science* magazine in 1941 and came into wide usage during the war.[74] Hine elucidates: "What was new about the idea of the teenager at the time the word first appeared during World War II was the assumption that all young people, regardless of their class, location, or ethnicity, should have essentially the same experience, spent with people exactly the same age, in an environment defined by high school and pop culture."[75] By the mid-1950s, the stereotypical teenager represented fun: hand-holding couples danced the jitterbug on the pages of every magazine and on *American Bandstand.* Chuck Berry wrote and recorded "Maybellene" in 1955; Elvis Presley's first hit record, "Heartbreak Hotel," came out in 1956. Girls wore bobby socks and poodle skirts; boys sported narrow ties and suede shoes. That said, even very young returning veterans saw themselves not as carefree teens but rather as men (some hardened by war) who needed college degrees to climb up a rung or two on the social ladder.

In contrast to the 1950s, the 1960s was a time of overt radicalism on college campuses. Students rejected in loco parentis; they did not need caretaking. They were adults who wanted to be treated as such. In 1968, student protests were international. The French educational system broke apart, as did others. Protests against the Vietnam War, demonstrations supporting civil rights, freely available birth

Figure I.13. At Rutgers, students protested the Nixon administration's policy in Cambodia on May 4, 1970. They registered their disdain by occupying Old Queens, the first purpose-built home of the college, constructed between 1809 and 1826, which was then serving as the president's office and the administrative headquarters for the university. R-photo, student life, Special Collections and University Archives, Rutgers University Libraries.

control pills, and recreational drug use completely transformed the identity of the college student, even if not all students tuned in and dropped out. At Rutgers University and many others, protesters arranged takeovers of the main administration buildings. Occupying physical space was a means of demonstrating their considerable power. College students wanted to be seen as human beings, not raw material for the university–industrial–military complex. At the height of the Free Speech Movement protests at Berkeley in 1964, Mario Savio, a graduate student and movement leader, shouted from the top of a police car:

> And you've got to put your bodies upon the gears and upon the wheels, upon the levers, upon all the apparatus—and you've got to make it stop. And you've got to

> indicate to the people who run it, to the people who own it—that unless you're free, the machine will be prevented from working at all![76]

These were serious adults, albeit young, who wanted to turn the world upside down. How different from the lighthearted Jazz Age boys: those kids had no interest in throwing themselves on the machine, lest their raccoon coats get caught in the gears. One of the most peculiar aspects of the history of dormitories is that the building type itself has, by and large, persisted for centuries, even though the character of students has changed dramatically. Only a sliver of the population, almost all privileged, attended college in the colonial period. In contrast, in 2014, 52 percent of U.S. high school graduates from low-income families, 66 percent from middle-income families, and 82 percent from high-income families attended college.[77]

WHY STUDY RESIDENCE HALLS NOW?

Residence halls are just as important today as they have ever been, even though one might think that distance learning would make them obsolete. It is my hope that *Living on Campus* will serve as a resource for any curious person who has worked or lived in a dormitory, and for prospective students and their families, college administrators, architects, and designers. Fifty years have passed since the progressive Kresge College built its dormitories in the woods; much has changed in higher education. Everyone who has lived in a dorm is a self-proclaimed expert, even without the historical knowledge that experts ordinarily require. I hope this book goes a long way toward answering questions and encouraging people to ask new ones.

The Epilogue to this book explores current trends in student housing. A convergence of disparate forces in recent years (the corporatization of the university, growing inequality in society at large, the rise of online learning) might have doomed the residence hall, and yet a survey of current practices in higher education suggests an opposite trend: colleges are building ever more elaborate residence halls, some of which resemble five-star hotels. The question is not only "Why have residence halls survived?" but also "Why are collegiate officials building more of them?" They build residence halls because student affairs is now an established, entrenched profession; deans of students produce social science scholarship that demonstrates that living on campus improves graduation rates, produces happier students, and contributes to leadership skills. University vice presidents build residence halls because Americans are nostalgic, although we prefer that our nostalgia come with a lot of bandwidth. On the one hand, some parents remember their college days fondly; they want their children to have the same experience they had. On the other hand, there are parents who are stunned by the country-club ambience of the newest residence halls, like Osprey Fountains at the University of North Florida, where lightly clad students de-stress in curving swimming pools and bake in the sun within an arm's length of their splendid rooms. As universities compete to build the most elaborate residence halls, colleges that fall behind in the amenities "arms race," as it is frequently called, are unable to recruit the best students. Some parents see their children (and some students see themselves) as consumers: they demand parking spaces, Starbucks, and fast Wi-Fi for streaming movies, sports, and gaming.

The cost of living in a dormitory (whether or not it has the most up-to-date amenities) is greater than the cost of living at home. Less affluent students commute and work part-time jobs. Others take their classes online and thus have almost no opportunity for meaningful networking. (For distance learning, colleges have no need to provide dorms—or any architecture at all.) Differing housing opportunities exacerbate the social disparities between the poorest students and the richest. Members of the latter group spend their college days enhancing potential professional connections. But this is nothing new: it is merely the present-day expression of Benjamin Franklin's idea that students should attend college to "zealously unite."

1

College Housing for Men

Fellowship and Exclusivity

Among the best-known college novels is Owen Johnson's *Stover at Yale,* in which the idealistic football-playing protagonist, Dink Stover, conquers the Ivy League without attending a class or reading a book. Upon arriving at the brick-and-stone campus, he whispers to himself:

> "And this is it—this is Yale," he said reverently, with a little tightening of the breath.
>
> They had begun at last—the happy, care-free years that every one proclaimed. Four glorious years, good times, good fellows, and a free and open fight to be among the leaders and leave a name on the roll of fame. . . . "Four years," he said softly. "The best, the happiest I'll ever know!"[1]

It is worth questioning why college was supposed to be the best four years of a young man's life, just as it is worth looking at the buildings in which collegians dwelled. Was it the best four years because they memorized Cicero or studied Euclidian geometry? Probably not. Then as now, book learning was one small part of the college boy's life; socializing was the key to the collegian's heart.

This chapter analyzes two building types, closely related but quite easily distinguished: the dormitory and the fraternity house. We begin in the middle of the seventeenth century and progress quickly toward 1900. Both building types crisscross the boundaries between home and institution, between domestic and public (see the Appendix). The long period covered by this chapter allows for an exploration of the beginnings of on-campus housing for men, the dorm's downward turn after passage of the Land Grant Act (also known as the Morrill Act) in 1862 and the rise of the research university, and the subsequent burst of fraternity building. After the Civil War, officials at research universities and the land-grant colleges turned their attention to laboratories and lost interest in constructing dormitories. But the dormitory made a decisive comeback in the early twentieth century, when campus leaders and deans convinced many people that living on campus promoted the good character of young men. In terms of architecture, dormitories tended to be large facilities that featured long institutional hallways or several entryways, while fraternities resembled large houses with interiors such as might be found in men's clubs. Although this book is primarily about the architecture of dormitories, that story makes little sense without some background on the arrival of the upstart fraternity.

The typical college student during the colonial and Federal periods was a white boy between the ages of fourteen and eighteen who sought higher education to gain prestige as well as knowledge.[2] Clearly some youths aimed for careers in various churches, but historian of education John Thelin disputes the long-held notion that the early American colleges existed primarily to train clergymen. As Thelin points out, most eighteenth-century colleges had no divinity schools, thus it is reasonable to conclude that these institutions had multifaceted missions to shape boys into men.[3] Although colonial colleges did not teach trades or provide instruction that led directly to a profession, they set young men up for entry into the upper class. While memorizing Greek might not seem useful on the surface, the ability to insert a quotation from Homer into a legal argument, for example, signified gentlemanly skill.[4] Professors, students' parents, and students themselves considered the subjects of the college curriculum to be universal; they encompassed the basic knowledge that enabled a young man to enter public life. Although all college students were elite, in the sense that most men did not go to college at all, class stratification endured within the ranks. The less wealthy, who were destined to become teachers and ministers, and often studied hard, stood in opposition to the affluent, who would enter into the family business or take their place as landed gentry, a status afforded in the colonies by wealth rather than birth alone.[5] Helen L. Horowitz's outstanding scholarship on undergraduate life makes clear that class disparities were part of the social experience of collegians from the start. The wealthiest boys were the insiders, the consummate "college men."[6] They ridiculed the outsiders, seeing them as sanctimonious bumpkins.[7] The emerging affluent class treated college more casually than did their poorer classmates.

In 1636, Congregationalists in Cambridge founded Harvard, the first college in English-speaking North America. Harvard's earliest building, completed in 1642, was a three-story wooden structure that contained all the purposes of the new institution.[8] As one historian of Harvard has written, Harvard was meant to be "a society of scholars where teachers and students lived in the same building under common discipline, associating not only in lecture rooms but at meals, in chambers, at prayers, and in recreation."[9] In contrast to such lofty goals, the second building at Harvard—which was, in fact, the second academic building in the entirety of what would later become the United States—was a dormitory built especially to discriminate. The Indian College, completed in the 1650s, was a residence for Native American students. The Society for the Propagation of the Gospel in New England, a group that saw bringing Christianity to the New World's residents as the major purpose of the outpost colony, paid for the small structure. Almost no white person would dwell with an Indian, thus the British charity provided funds for the structure so that about twenty Native Americans would have somewhere to live in the vicinity of the college. In addition to spaces for sleeping, it included a kitchen, a dining area, and a room for a printing press, therefore it was not exclusively a living space. While the earlier college building was made of wood, the Indian College was of solid brick construction.[10] (In spite of its original sturdiness, it was decrepit by 1698, the year in which it was

Figure 1.1. Indian College, Harvard University, circa 1655, conjectural restoration by H. R. Shurtleff, in Samuel Eliot Morison, *Harvard College in the Seventeenth Century* (Cambridge, Mass.: Harvard University Press, 1936). The Indian College housed a small number of young Native American men, including Caleb Cheeshahteaumuck of the Wampanoag group. Cheeshahteaumuck was the only Indian graduate of Harvard during the colonial period. The Indian College was demolished in 1698.

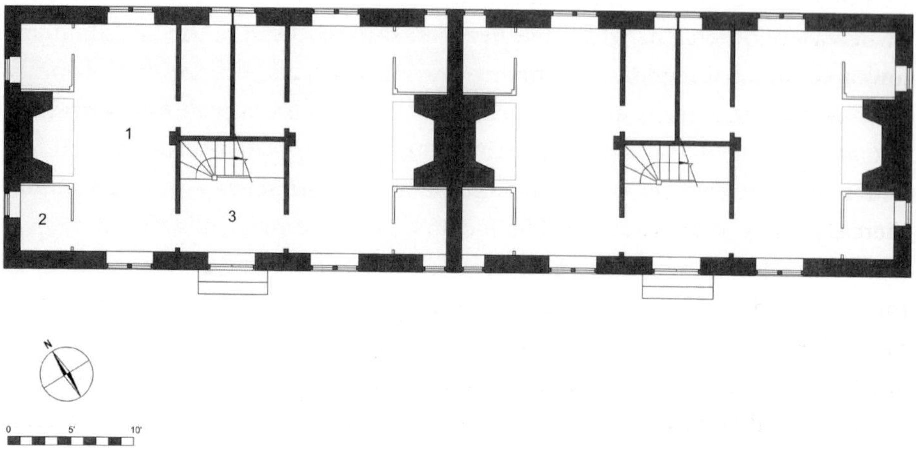

Figure 1.2. Indian College, Harvard University, circa 1655, plan. 1 = bedroom; 2 = study carrel; 3 = entryway and staircase. Drawing by John Giganti.

demolished.) From the very beginning of colleges in North America, student housing existed to establish hierarchies.

When Harvard students wanted to get together in small groups, they did so in their rooms or in their friends' rooms. Students' rooms did not contain much more than they needed to sleep and study. Some evidence of what students kept in their rooms is found in inventories submitted to the provincial government of the Massachusetts Bay Colony requesting remuneration after the fire that destroyed Harvard Hall in 1764. Ebenezer and Samuel Barnard, brothers, compiled a particularly detailed list, and their request was indeed granted. About fifty books (listed by title) and a set of maps went up in flames. The brothers also lost hats, jackets, a belt buckle, a stone jug, handkerchiefs, andirons, and a fishing rod. As most colonial-era college students did, they furnished the room themselves, and thus in the fire they lost not only the bedstead but also two tables and six chairs. If the Barnards had a bedroom with a small study attached, then they might have put two chairs in the study and the other four in the bedroom, although this is speculative. Their inventory listed each article of clothing and each individual book. They must have enjoyed tea in their rooms, because they had a kettle, three black teapots, "6 Silver Spoons," and "7 China Tea Cups."[11] (Their honesty is impressive: the whole building burned to the ground, so why not claim to have lost a full set of twelve teacups?) Several other students submitted inventories as well, and all seem to have had tea-making supplies in their rooms.

The Barnard brothers included bedding in their summary, noting that they had owned a "Very good Bed quilt," "2 blankitts," "2 Pr. of sheets," and "2 Pr. of pillowcases," but one "bedsted."[12] This indicates that they shared a bed, which would have been typical for that time. Stephen Peabody, a student at Harvard in the 1760s, observed in his diary that in addition to his chambermate, he shared his bed with so many unwanted "inhabitants" (bedbugs) that he had to "get it scalt by Mrs. Pierce."[13] (Mrs. Pierce was one of two women who maintained the residences.) Not coincidentally, Peabody's diary includes frequent mentions of itchiness, doctor visits, and the procurement of ointment. The day after Peabody discovered bedbugs, he found out his roommate was moving; this caused him some concern, and he quickly petitioned to have an acquaintance from home take the open spot. Since he would be living in such close quarters with his new partner, he did not want to take chances on a random assignment.[14]

Overall, documents from the period suggest that dormitory rooms were well furnished, but in terms of the daily life of the student and his comforts compared to a private house, the bedroom-plus-study was probably smaller than the several rooms (parlor, hall, bedroom) that a young man occupied at home. Early dorms purposely lacked spaces for socializing; professors wanted to keep collegians from congregating in large groups, because when they did, they frequently got into trouble by drinking, betting, and fighting.

The first Stoughton Hall, also at Harvard, was probably the first freestanding, fully specialized dormitory in the colonies. Built in 1698, Stoughton Hall had no purpose other than housing. It did not have an internal corridor. Instead, it employed a plan with bedrooms off of staircases. The structure was long and narrow, with a plan somewhat like that of the Indian College. In fact, the builders used bricks from the defunct Indian College to construct this new dormitory. In one early print, we see that the dormitory was longer than it was wide. Indeed, it was ninety-seven feet long and less than twenty-three feet in breadth. This Stoughton Hall was one room wide, with a wall that divided the long rectangle into two parts. On each side of this central wall, there were two chambers separated by a passageway. The plan may be deduced from the building's facade, and further hints survive in the form of a drawing made by Harvard president Edward Holyoke.[15] The Holyoke plan, made for the laying of a drain, allows us to conclude that there must have been stairs in the two passageways, even though they are not shown.[16] According to architectural historian Bainbridge Bunting, the structure, the first example of a gift from an individual to Harvard, was "four stories high and 23 by 100 feet in area, [and] it could house forty students."[17] The half-width windows corresponded to the locations of the studies inside the structure, and the larger windows admitted light into the sleeping chambers. Dormers punched through the roof, an arched ornament in the center on the second floor displayed the Stoughton coat of arms, the doors were flanked by pilasters, and the corners were bolstered by quoins.[18] Outdoor privies were located near the president's orchard. Students paid porters to bring water from the nearby well.[19] Built without a basement, Old Stoughton (as it was sometimes called) was not watertight, and thus Bunting praises it for its outward appearance, if not for its structural soundness:

> The orderly fenestration, the use of a clearly defined main cornice and . . . the presence of pedimented door frames, quoins, string courses, and an inscription panel topped by a small pediment mark this clearly as a Georgian design. Here at the very end of the seventeenth century Harvard finally put the Medieval tradition behind.[20]

Figure 1.3. "A Prospect of the Colleges in Cambridge in New England," print by William Burgis, 1743. Stoughton Hall, in the center of this image, was a purpose-built dormitory constructed in 1698; it was located between Harvard Hall (left, with the cupola) and Massachusetts Hall (right). Stoughton Hall was likely the first structure built exclusively to house college students in the English-speaking colonies. I. N. Phelps Collection of American Historical Prints, The Miriam and Ira D. Wallach Division of Art, Prints and Photographs, New York Public Library.

The building was demolished shortly after the Revolutionary War, partly because of damage caused by soldiers quartered there.

From 1695 to 1700, when Harvard had been in existence for six decades, the College of William and Mary erected its first building. It was not fully complete when it burned in 1705. The replacement, today considered to be the oldest continuously occupied academic building in the United States, is the so-called Wren Building of 1705. (Harvard and Yale can boast of having had earlier structures, but they are no longer standing.) The history of the Wren Building is complex, as several buildings were constructed on the same site, and the current structure was largely reconstructed in the 1930s.[21] However, its basic functions are known and were typical in their time: the multipurpose structure contained student housing, professors' offices, a chapel, a library, and classrooms.[22] In plan, the U shape contained smaller rooms on one range, with a chapel and great hall forming the

Figure 1.4. Wren Building, College of William and Mary, second building, 1705. Like many early collegiate structures, the Wren Building contained all the functions of the young school, including housing students. Daguerreotype, circa 1850. Special Collections Research Center, Swem Library, College of William and Mary.

sides of the U. Bedrooms were upstairs.[23] This is an example of a three-sided quadrangle, although the original intention was to construct a completely enclosed donut. A closed quadrangle can appear to be less public because it creates a decidedly private outdoor space. The U shape is more public and open, welcoming its audience. In the Wren Building, the second story of the front range had a central corridor with bedrooms on both sides.

The College of William and Mary was closely tied to the Anglican Church. Architectural historian Paul V. Turner has discerned ideological differences among

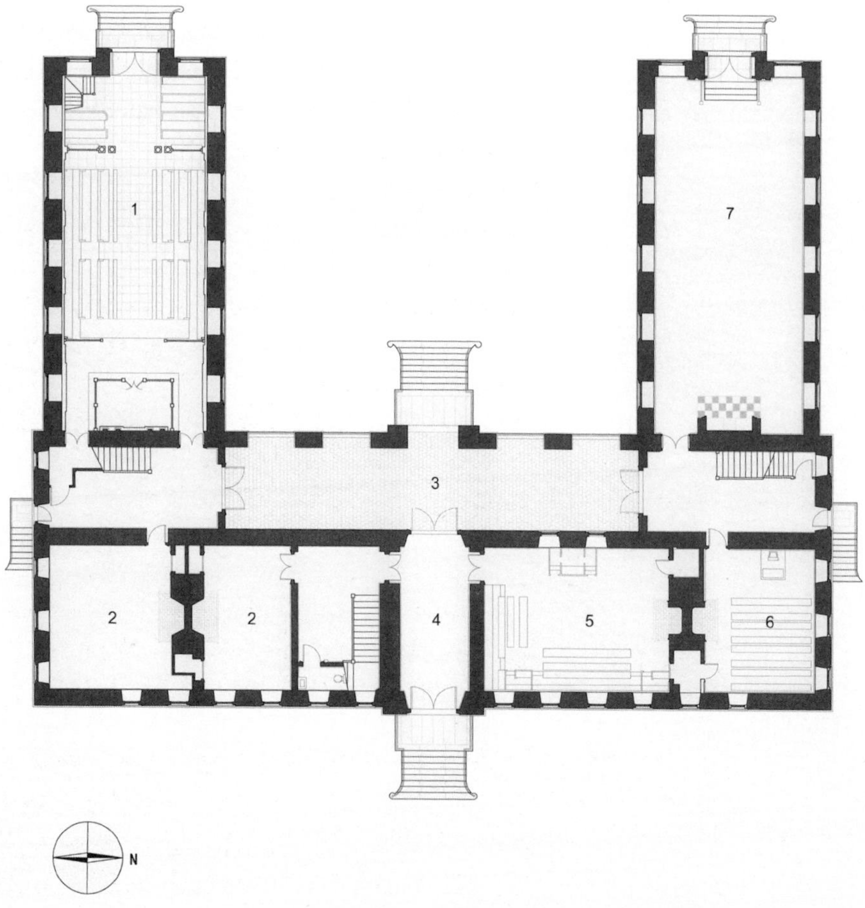

Figure 1.5. Wren Building, College of William and Mary, 1705, plan, first floor. The chapel was in the southern wing and was double height. The northern wing held the great hall. 1 = chapel; 2 = classroom; 3 = porch (piazza); 4 = lobby; 5 = grammar school; 6 = lecture room; 7 = great hall. Drawing by John Giganti based on a drawing from 1976 by E. Leroy Phillips for HABS/HAER, Library of Congress.

three architectural types associated with college campuses: the closed quadrangle (with roots in Catholic monasteries), the three-sided quadrangle, and the detached college building (associated with Puritans).[24] But as Douglas Shand-Tucci observes, in the case of Harvard, the association of detached buildings with Congregationalism is "a bit of a stretch."[25] The religious categorizations do not hold up in relation to the Wren Building, either. As noted above, and as Turner himself explains, the Wren Building was originally planned to be a closed quadrangle, but the fourth side was never added. It is hard to believe, therefore, that the three-sided

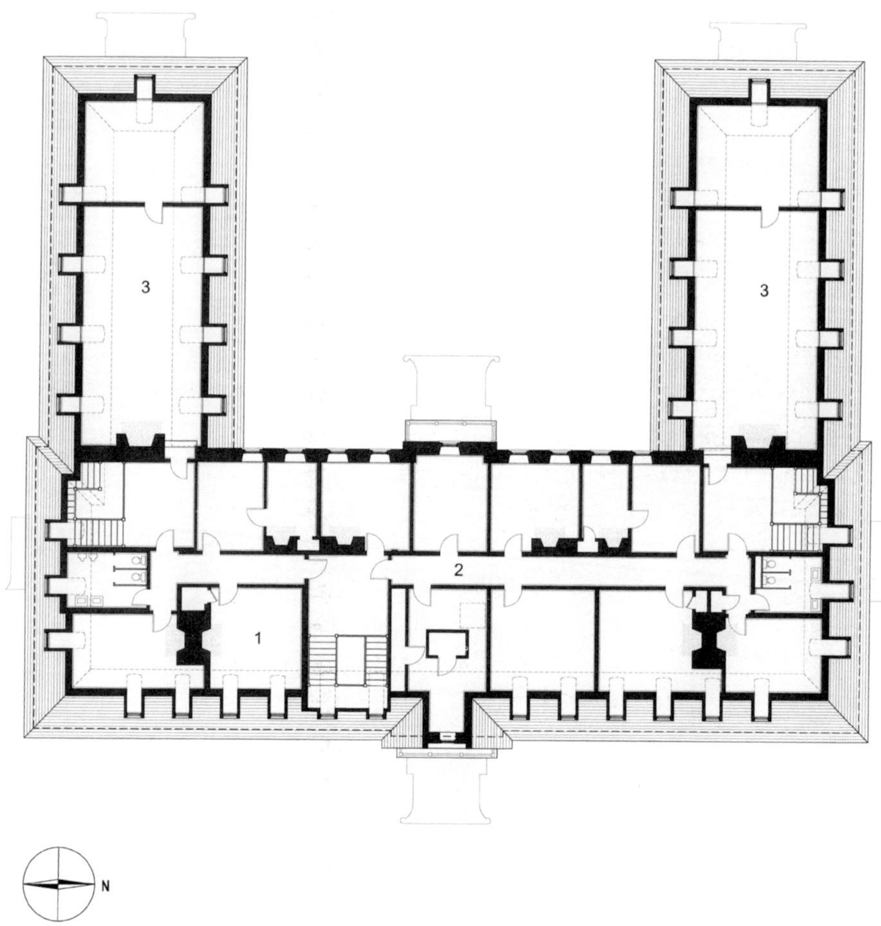

Figure 1.6. Wren Building, College of William and Mary, 1705, plan, third floor. Student rooms were on a double-loaded corridor in the front range. The two back wings served as storage. 1 = bedroom; 2 = corridor; 3 = attic storage. Drawing by John Giganti based on a drawing from 1976 by E. Leroy Phillips for HABS/HAER, Library of Congress.

structure was a meaningful anti-Catholic decision. Given that Thomas Jefferson, who held no great love for medieval Catholicism, planned to add the fourth range to the Wren Building, the link between the enclosed quadrangle and religion seems even less reliable.[26] Even so, Turner is surely right to emphasize that a U-shaped building addressed the street in a way that the closed quadrangle did not: the three-sided quad was more welcoming (albeit still formal), while the four-sided quad shut itself off from the city.

In 1804, Harvard replaced Old Stoughton with a similar building on the same site named after the same person; this structure also had no parlors or areas for assembly. Completed a full century later than the Wren Building, the new Stoughton Hall was the twin to an earlier structure, Hollis Hall. Both of these freestanding dormitories maintained the monumental character of the Yard. In some ways they

Figure 1.7. Stoughton Hall, Harvard University (then Harvard College), 1804, attributed to Charles Bulfinch. This building replaced the 1698 Stoughton Hall, seen in Figure 1.3. Both the original Stoughton Hall and this one employed the entryway plan. Courtesy of the Cambridge Historical Society, Cambridge Historical Society Image Collection, 5.3.96 CHS, Cambridge, Massachusetts.

resembled the original Stoughton Hall, except that they were wider and included pediments on the long side. Each floor had eight bedrooms.[27] Each bedroom was probably occupied by two or three male students, who shared a large fireplace and alcoves for study. The carrels were intended to prevent the scholars in training from bothering each other as they labored for hours, often speaking out loud, while memorizing lessons. Although Stoughton's plan can be viewed as a staircase or entryway plan, it can also be seen as a set of vertically stacked suites, albeit without bathrooms. (In today's parlance, a suite in a dormitory is a set of rooms for multiple people, usually two to four, who share bedrooms, a common room, and a bathroom. In the early years at Harvard, there were no indoor bathrooms, therefore we might think of the Stoughton suite as consisting of two bedrooms with studies.) The benefit of a suite, as opposed to a room that opens onto a corridor, was that a small social group could form within its confines.

Nassau Hall at Princeton, then the College of New Jersey, marked a milestone in collegiate construction before the Revolutionary War. According to Turner, Nassau Hall "struck a chord with many Americans of the period as the perfect collegiate building."[28] When completed in 1756, it dominated a rural site in central

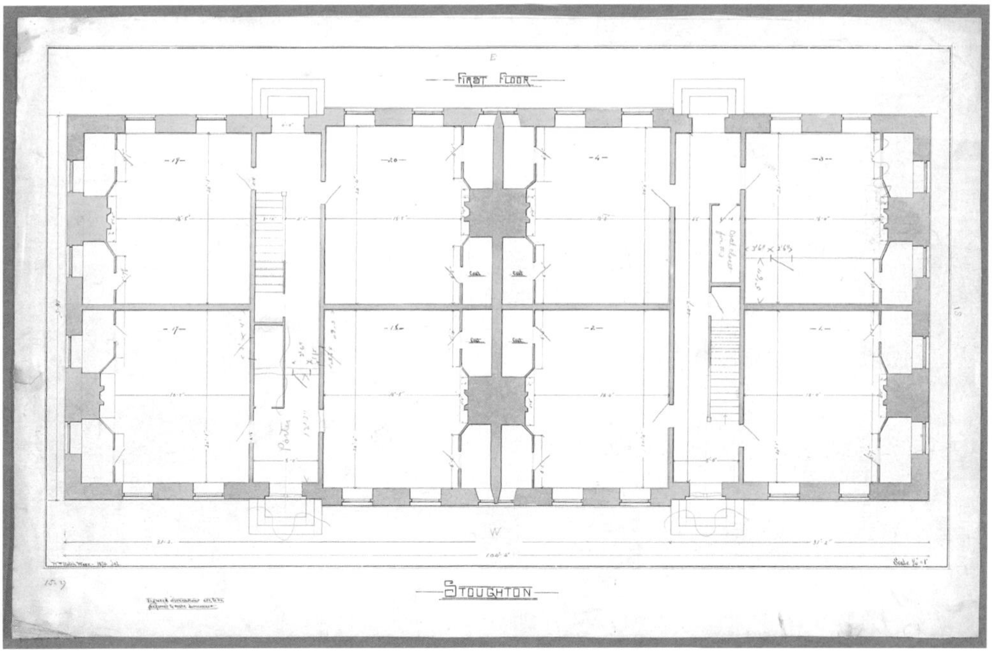

Figure 1.8. Stoughton Hall, Harvard University (then Harvard College), 1804, attributed to Charles Bulfinch, plan, first floor (drawn in 1874). Small study alcoves were tucked into the corners of each room. UA15.10.5, box 2, folder 31, Harvard University Archives.

New Jersey as the largest and most distinguished structure in the colony. The philosophy of many colonial and early American thinkers leaned toward the healing qualities of nature; cities were disparaged. Surrounded by farms and separated from the street by an ample lawn, Nassau Hall rested on an elegant greensward. Princeton president John Witherspoon, a signer of the Declaration of Independence, first used the term *campus* to describe the college and its environs, a term that remains with us today.[29] Robert Smith of Philadelphia designed Nassau Hall, which included a double-loaded corridor in the center of the structure, three entry doors on the north side, and two entries on the south. The doors gave access to staircases that led to student bedrooms on the upper floors. The first floor originally contained a prayer room on the south side.

Although there is no surviving architectural plan of the original Nassau Hall, Yale president Ezra Stiles visited New Jersey in 1754 and casually sketched the layout in his journal.[30] Stiles showed a long, thin, rectangular building with a central corridor crossed by two short hallways. Although he did not draw the steps on the outside leading to the short halls, we know they were there from many

Figure 1.9. Nassau Hall, Princeton University (then the College of New Jersey), 1754–56, Robert Smith, architect. The upper-left corner of this print shows the sun shining on various fields of academic endeavor. *New American Magazine* 27 (March 1860), opposite p. 104. Rare Book Division, Department of Rare Books and Special Collections, Princeton University Archives, folder "Nassau Hall Iconography." Courtesy of Princeton University Library.

surviving engravings. About the interior, historian W. Barksdale Maynard has explained: "Every student room (all doubles) had three windows, one lighting the sleeping chamber and the others for two closet-like alcoves or 'lobbies' that contained a chair and table, ultimately derived from the study cubicles of medieval Oxford."[31] Although it is an oft-repeated story, there is no evidence that Princeton students commonly lived on campus with their slaves.[32] A student named Samuel Blair described the little carrels as "large closets, with a window in each, for retirement."[33] (He meant *retirement* in the sense of withdrawing to a quiet place.) A comparison of Nassau Hall to the original Stoughton Hall reveals that Smith provided Nassau Hall with a double circulation system, which would have been good for surveillance (a professor could look down the hall) while also maintaining the traditional link to Oxbridge (because of the staircases). It would have been expensive, however, given that there was a generous amount of unassigned space compared

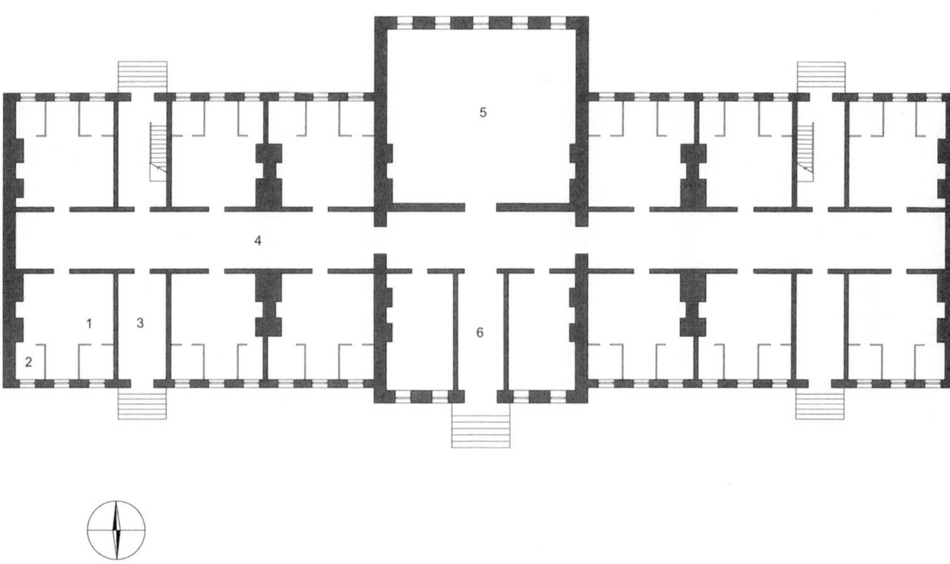

Figure 1.10. Nassau Hall, Princeton University (then the College of New Jersey), 1754–56, Robert Smith, architect, plan, first floor. Nassau Hall included three entrances on the north, two entrances on the south, and a central corridor. The rooms were doubles; each included two study alcoves. 1 = bedroom; 2 = study alcove; 3 = entry; 4 = corridor; 5 = chapel; 6 = main entry. Princeton University Archives. Drawing by John Giganti based on Henry Lyttleton Savage, *Nassau Hall, 1756–1956* (Princeton, N.J.: Princeton University Press, 1956), 17; and Kenneth Hafertepe, "Princeton and the Presbyterian Plain Style" (unpublished manuscript, 1993), 8.

to the amount of space set aside for bedrooms and other specific purposes. None of these early colleges would have had indoor plumbing, and thus students would have relied on chamber pots (emptied by servants or slaves) and outdoor privies.

The dormitory was a bastion of maleness and would have been a comfort to those who worried that weakness might creep into the republic's young men.[34] Witherspoon maintained that young men should be removed from the home to pursue higher education, because he believed they could best become hearty citizens within the confines of the purpose-built college and in the company of other men.[35] In his *Letters on the Education of Children and on Marriage,* Witherspoon explained that women and children should submit to the authority of the husband and father, and, in particular, that women should not sympathize with ("condole with") children when their fathers were reprimanding them.[36] Witherspoon's lessons about the negative influence of coddling mothers may be extended to a gendered interpretation of the dormitory itself. Some leaders considered it essential to remove boys from the home and separate them from their mothers; college was where boys became men.[37] This was an important, albeit nonacademic, purpose of the dormitory. Historian Margaret Sumner has written extensively about the colonial- and Federal-era faculty family. In particular, she has explored how such families were expected to set an example for students, modeling life after college.[38] Other than a handful of wives, daughters, servants, and slaves, almost everyone around the college campus was male. There was widespread fear among Protestant elites that the colonies and the early republic could not sustain a socially coherent nation. A related concern was that the youths would decline into soft and timid caricatures of manhood.[39]

Nassau Hall had many admirers (Plate 1). Other colleges copied the massing of Old Nassau in multipurpose, roughly oblong buildings with central towers. Some of these, all completed before 1835, may be found at Williams, Dartmouth, Dickinson, Brown, Georgetown, the University of North Carolina, the University of Georgia, and Wesleyan. (There were only 23 colleges in operation in the United States in 1820; by 1860 there were 217.)[40] Often these structures were nicknamed "Old Main" within a few decades of their construction. Pennsylvania State University, Arizona State University in Tempe, the University of Arizona in Tucson, Ohio State University, and Knox College, among others, have buildings known as Old Main. Oddly, neither Oxford nor Cambridge has an Old Main, although there is the Old Schools building at Cambridge. An Old Main was typically three or four stories and included housing for the university president and his family, apartments for the faculty, a chapel, a dining hall, a kitchen, several classrooms, and dormitory rooms.

Some collegiate buildings looked like the other Old Mains but never carried the moniker. One example is West College at Williams. In 1836, a freshman, Francis Henshaw Dewey, wrote a letter to his family in which he nicely outlined his first few days at school.[41] He described his dorm room as "nasty horrid dirty looking." He and his roommate hired someone to clean the room, but the hired hand did a poor job and left the floor so wet that Dewey had to sleep in another young man's room, because he had an extra cot. Dewey provided his own furniture, as was typical, purchasing most of it used in town. He lived in West College, a Federal-era multipurpose building and the first structure at Williams College, completed in 1791. Originally the rectangular building had two doors leading to the outside, centrally located, one on each of the structure's long sides, its east and west facades. West College contained both the Free School (a boarding grammar school) and the college. Under its roof, students worshipped in chapel, recited their lessons in classrooms, and slept (or tried to sleep) in bedrooms. Cooks prepared meals in a kitchen, inhabitants ate together in a dining room, and tutors dwelled among this lively group. Dewey gave a good idea of the close physical relationship of undergraduates and teachers when he complained that he had to memorize a reading to recite for Tutor Tatlock, who "rooms nearly opposite." "Rooms nearly opposite" suggests the tutor lived on the same floor but farther down the hall. Dewey objected to learning this passage from Livy, because the assignment came to him in the evening, and the recitation was to occur at 6:00 a.m.

Dewey took the opportunity of this first letter home to tease his little sister; he wrote that she would probably want to hear about his roommate, or chum: "Perchance little Katy will like to know who Chum is." (*Chum,* derived from the term *chambermate,* referred to a roommate, or someone with whom a student shared rooms.) He described his roommate, a former teacher and therefore a little older than the usual college boy, as a "good looking man from Framingham Massachusetts." The fact that he thought immediately of his sister's potential interest in his roommate reinforces Benjamin Franklin's view of college as a path toward making good marriages.

Franklin and Benjamin Rush, a businessman, philanthropist, and doctor, sought to improve the educational offerings of rural Pennsylvania and also to develop the backcountry economically. Although initially prejudiced against the Germans who lived in that region of the state, Franklin came to believe that they were educable. And, as Craig Steven Wilder has pointed out, Franklin and Rush agreed that if Pennsylvania could increase its population of Europeans (even lesser ones), that would assist them in their goal of pushing Native Americans farther west.[42] An evocative watercolor of Dickinson College, founded by Rush, emphasized the

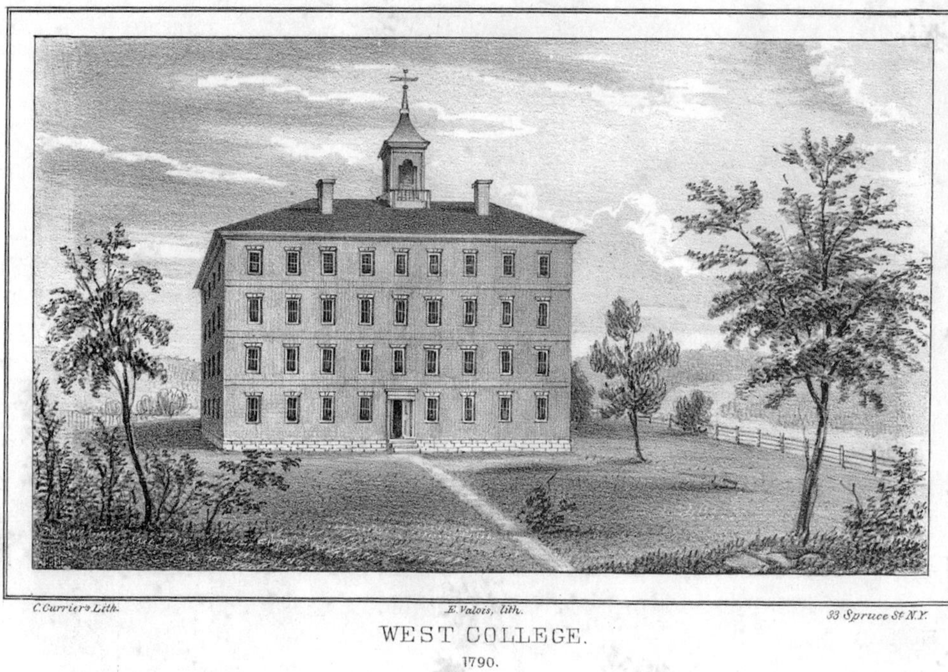

Figure 1.11. West College, Williams College, 1790–91. This single building contained every function of the college; the original plan employed an internal corridor. Special Collections, Williams College.

remoteness of the young college (Plate 2). It is no wonder the school needed to house its boys: there were simply not enough boardinghouses in the underpopulated part of the state where it was founded. Ulysses Hobbs, who studied at Dickinson in the 1840s, described his first trip to the college, a forty-five-mile journey he and his father made from Taneytown, Maryland, to Carlyle, Pennsylvania, which included rumbling along rough roads, staying in a barnlike hotel, traversing mountains, and fording a creek with "fresh courage"—a maneuver he compared to Caesar crossing the Rubicon.[43]

At the very center of a program to civilize the inner core of Pennsylvania, Dickinson exemplified architectural sophistication. Nationally renowned architect Benjamin Henry Latrobe designed the first building in 1803 as a modified and enhanced version of the much-admired Nassau Hall at Princeton. Given that Latrobe renovated Nassau Hall the previous year, he knew its plan well. Latrobe disliked the plan of Princeton's beloved building, noting that it "has many disadvantages, the chief of which are the noise, & the necessary darkness, of the passage,

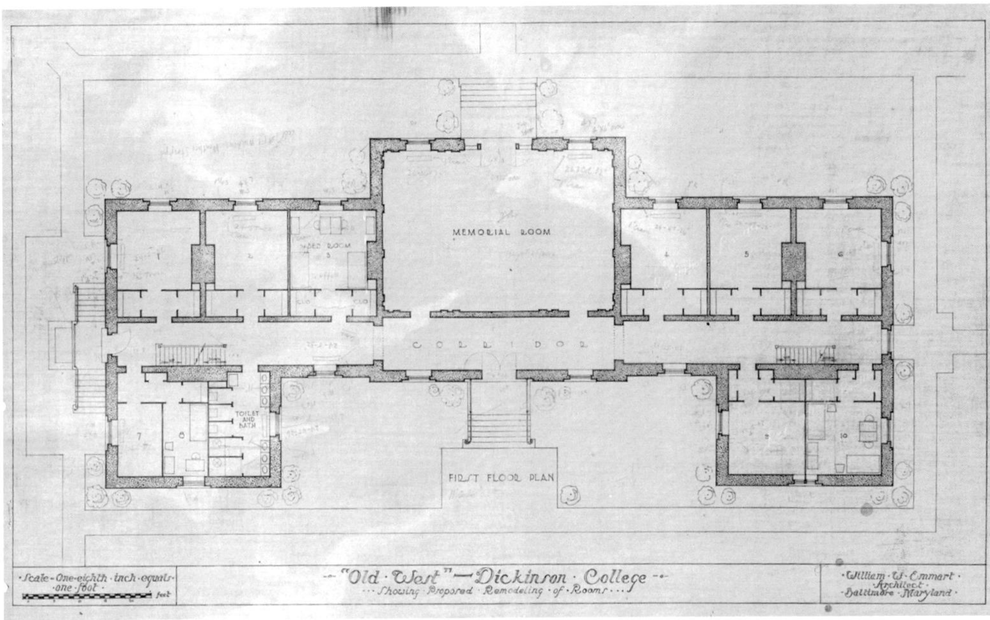

Figure 1.12. Old West, Dickinson College, 1803–5, Benjamin Henry Latrobe, architect, plan. Latrobe's innovative U-shaped plan included a corridor on the edge of the building instead of in the center. Archives and Special Collections, Dickinson College.

and the bad aspect of one half of the rooms."[44] Latrobe employed a shallow U in his plan, rather than a simple oblong shape. Above the first floor, he placed four double rooms and two triples on every floor, for a total of fourteen persons per floor. The double-height main hall was also used as a chapel.[45]

Latrobe relied on a creative reinterpretation of Princeton's main building. One of his major improvements was to move the long corridor from the center of the structure (as at Princeton) to the northern side. This shift counteracted the darkness he objected to in the Nassau Hall design, since the corridor now had windows. The rooms on the southern side of the hallway would have had a "good aspect," because the southern exposure offered light, warmth, and a pleasing view. Similarly, doctors recommended the single-loaded corridor for lunatic asylums, but it was infrequently employed because it was expensive.[46] When budgeting for a new building, an asylum or college had to account for the common area, which included corridors, stairs, and lobbies. If a building had only one range of rooms off the corridor, the cost of the common area relative to the occupiable space was high; it was more economical to construct two ranges of rooms off one corridor, since the corridor had to be built anyway. Federal-era colleges frequently ran out of

Figure 1.13. Old West, Dickinson College, 1803–5, Benjamin Henry Latrobe, architect. Archives and Special Collections, Dickinson College.

money and had to resort to fund-raising schemes. Few early schools had the funds to construct buildings with ample, single-loaded corridors.

Indeed, even at Dickinson, where officials were operating out of arguably the best-designed version of an Old Main in the young United States, single-loaded corridors were not included in the college's second building. The construction of East College was completed in November 1836 under the direction of the builder Henry Myers. East College was a purpose-built dormitory with space set aside for the president's house. A surviving cache of drawings from the planning of East College makes it clear that at no time was an internal corridor considered. In one early iteration, a rectilinear building had doors at grade level leading to student rooms; in another, curved metal staircases led to the *piano nobile.* Another drawing shows the final form of the building, a twelve-bay structure in which the three bays to the east formed the president's house. In all of these schemes, the building resembles a set of row houses more than a single institution. Presumably the

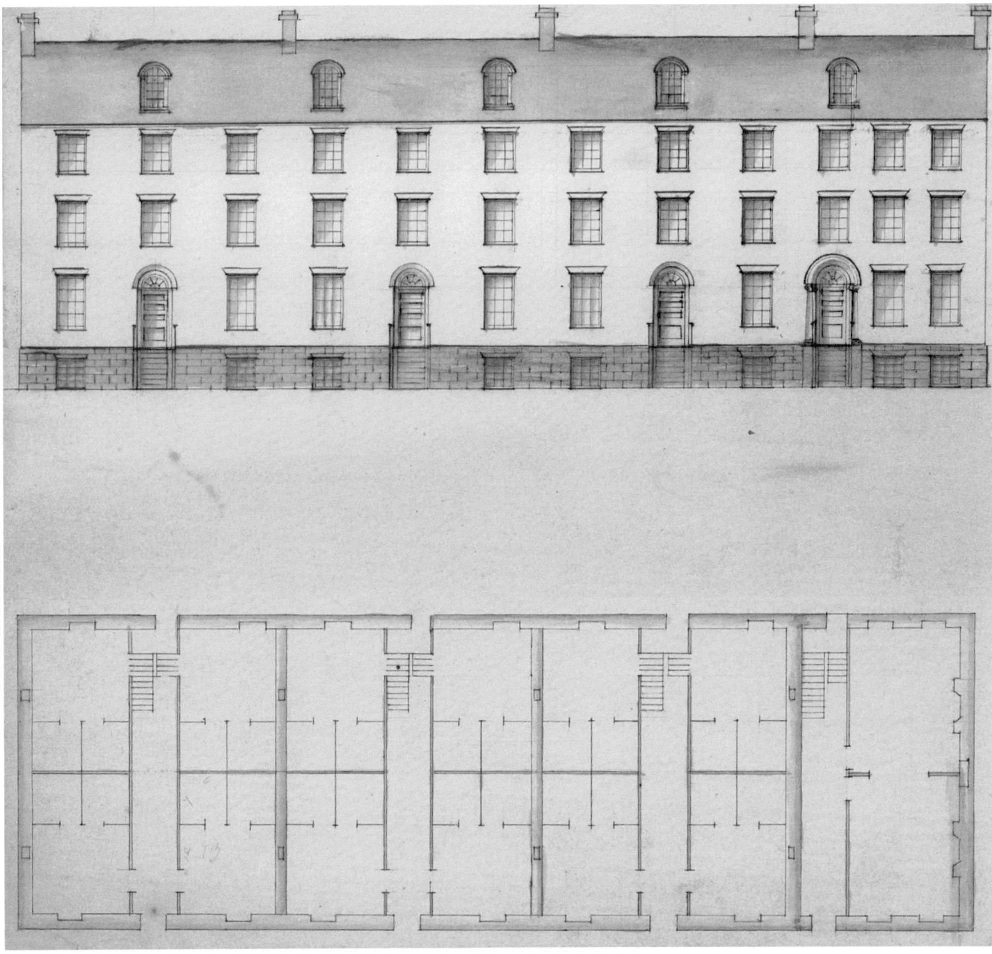

Figure 1.14. East College, Dickinson College, 1836, Henry Myers, architect, elevation and plan. The president's house occupied the three bays on the right side of this twelve-bay structure. Archives and Special Collections, Dickinson College.

ground floor was used for servants' quarters and services, such as heating equipment and trunk storage. The outdoor steps served as a gathering place, as reported by a Dickinson student in his diary from mid-November 1849:

> But the nights were far more beautiful than the days. I may here mention that just about half past Six oclock on those evenings the students all assembled on the steps in front of East College and united together in singing their favorite songs—but as I have said that the nights were so beautiful I must here mention what constituted their loveliness—about Seven the moon came forth in all her solemn

> grandeur—the stars the porters of the heavens and the glimmering planets shone forth like so many twinkling fires alighted up in the azure canopy and the stillness of the scene all combined to add beauty and loveliness to the scenes.[47]

Apparently the boys found ways of interacting in groups, even if the architecture did not provide common rooms or lounges.

Sumner's research on academic families in the antebellum era has demonstrated that professors and their wives and children felt they needed to live in houses that reflected the genteel world of the typical private family. This was sometimes difficult, as their dwellings were incorporated into existing larger structures, many of which were crowded and run-down. At Dickinson College one professor complained that his assigned rooms were very much out of repair, and after consulting the trustees, he added closets, partitions to create more bedrooms, and wallpaper.[48] These were some of the additions that families made to create domestic spaces within congregate structures. Students who lived in boardinghouses

Figure 1.15. East College, Dickinson College, 1836, Henry Myers, architect. This dormitory employed a variant of the staircase plan. Archives and Special Collections, Dickinson College.

faced the opposite challenge: while the buildings were actually houses, the interpersonal relationships within them were not familial.

BOARDINGHOUSES

Not all colonial- and Federal-era collegiate officials felt obliged to house their charges. During this period at Queens College (later Rutgers), students lodged in the town of New Brunswick, a busy river city with plenty of boardinghouses. Additionally, many of the young men attending the college were local, and they commuted from home. Rutgers was perpetually short of funds, and it went out of business twice before 1826. The college president traveled from farm to farm in rural New Jersey selling lottery tickets to raise money to complete the Old Main, which sat unfinished on the crest of a hill for almost seventeen years. Furthermore, the founders of Rutgers modeled it on Utrecht University, which did not have dormitories, so they might have assumed that housing was an unnecessary expense. In any case, they held no romantic regard for the English residential college system. The alma mater, written in 1873, portrayed the school as a place where boys became men by living in town: "My father sent me to old Rutgers, / And resolv'd that I should be a man, / And so I settled down, / In that noisy college town, / On the banks of the old Raritan." Rutgers did not build a dormitory until 1890, and even then the members of the board of governors were reluctant—they agreed only because the donor specified that the funds were exclusively for a dormitory.[49]

Boardinghouses, where students slept and ate, were technically distinct from rooming houses, where the proprietors served no food, but frequently these terms were used interchangeably. Boardinghouses came in a range from down-at-the-heels to well appointed, but as a type of lodging, regardless of comfort, the boardinghouse was threatening to middle-class values.[50] Architect Calvert Vaux asserted that families should never reside in boardinghouses, because such living arrangements lacked privacy and stability. Vaux and other Victorian observers noted that boardinghouse residents, who were often immigrants, moved in and out frequently, causing a haphazard and changeable environment. Families could not put their personal imprints on their living spaces. Boardinghouse life was more socially acceptable for undergraduates than for whole families, and in many cases, young scholars alone in the city had no other option.

Writing to his sister in 1861, Preston H. Sessoms, who was enrolled in the University of North Carolina and lived in a boardinghouse, gave an excellent account of a typical day: "I got my room and board at a widow woman's house, she is very good and nice, I like her very well, my room is up the stairs of her house." Based on his description, his boardinghouse was close enough for him to hear the bell in the Old Main:

> At every morning sunrise the college bell rings for you to get up and dress, the bell is a large one about 1½ foot through hung in the top of one of the college buildings [South Building], it is rung by a long rope and when it rings you can hear it about a mile off. The first time it rings in the morning is for you to get up and dress and about ¼ of an hour afterwards it rings again for to go to prayers, there is prayers up the college every morning and evening and preaching every sunday the professors preach in returns, and the students are bound to go to church every sunday and every sunday evening bound to say a bible lesson, each class.

The bell ruled his actions:

> We go to prayers in the morning before breakfast and soon after prayers we have to recite a lesson all the whole college recites the same time, but they recite in diferent [*sic*] rooms and there are four diferent classes, before breakfast recite one hour, the bell rings then we go from recitation right on to breakfast, after breakfast the bell rings for to go studying, study 3 hours then the bell rings at eleven o'clock to recite again, the whole college recite until twelve, being one hour at recitation . . . the college bell rings for dinner [the midday meal], after dinner we study again 3 hours, then the bell rings to recite again at four o'clock, recite 1 hour, soon after recitation is prayers in the evening, after prayers is supper.[51]

At Dickinson, Ulysses Hobbs recorded his elation one day when the bell's sound was muffled by ice clinging to its surface: fellow collegians had dumped water on it the night before.[52] Timeliness was a key aspect of the training of a future citizen, and the regimen of the student's day was intended to create a disciplined and responsible adult. There was nothing new about the use of bells to control populations—church chimes announced the time for weddings as well as funerals throughout Western Europe. Medieval monasteries used clanging sounds to announce the offices. In early nineteenth-century America, the college bell's powerful ringing might have connected students to slaves and factory workers, because all three groups were held in check by overseers who controlled their movements by manipulating time. Thus living in a boardinghouse did not mean one could escape the rigors of the clock.

Alfred B. McCalmont, a boardinghouse dweller at Dickinson, recorded in his diary in 1842 that he spent most of his time when he was not in class either in his room or in the rooms of other men in his own boardinghouse. He also spent time at other boardinghouses and the two dormitories on campus, where he enjoyed sharing in the contents of packages other students had received from home, practiced his recitations, read the Bible, studied phrenology, talked about pretty girls, sang temperance songs, and drew with india ink. He did not write about attending many large-scale gatherings, except for required chapel services and sermons at a variety of local churches.[53]

One measure of the gloominess of boardinghouse life may be found in how much students enjoyed the occasional meal in the setting of a traditional family home. McCalmont waxed poetic about a luncheon at a local gentleman's house:

> On entering the parlor the comfortable appearance of every thing, the lively conversation of the girls, the occasional rich odors of a fine dinner wafted from the kitchen and dining room as ever and anon the door opened affording a slight glance at the good things on the sumptuous board, and the merry sound of sleigh bells, as every moment they jingled past all conspired to afford comfortable sensations and call to mind the sweet pleasures of a winter *at home.*[54]

The boardinghouse where this young man lived probably took the form of a typical house, but he perceived it as not homelike. It is interesting to speculate about how different a large institution was from the boys' family homes. Whether they came from urban row houses or rural farmhouses, a dormitory would have been the largest edifice they had lived in or maybe even been inside (see Appendix).

Students perceived college rules and schedules as hardships. They survived morning prayers, endured nonstop classes, recited long passages of Greek and Latin, and prayed (again) in the evening religious service, all before a 9:00 p.m. curfew. Boys protested that the curriculum was dry. The pedagogy—drilling, repetition, and memorization—was mind-numbing.[55] The only accepted courses were theology, classics, mathematics, church history, and natural history. Teachers of science did not conduct experiments, but instead taught by rote. One exception was chemistry, which was taught in a laboratory. When a new subject was introduced, as astronomy was in the 1850s, it was an elective. Students could not get class credit for studying contemporary literature or politics, and many found the classical curriculum to be hopelessly detached from their daily lives.

Professors took responsibility for the moral development of their students in addition to encouraging their intellectual advancement. As we have seen, colleges built dormitories to promote an ideal world where faculty lived with students while molding their character. Such idealism, however, could not withstand the force of the wily student charges, who made the dormitories into hotbeds of prank pulling, drinking, gambling, and fighting. For a time, students favored a caper in which they herded a cow onto the upper floor of an administration building. A chronicler of Williams College noted in 1904 that "more than once did some disgruntled owner . . . find his cow with her head protruding from the Hall window, perhaps even from the third or fourth story of the college, and hear . . . a reiterated bellow that sounded both domestic and forlorn."[56] Troublemakers commonly captured the bellman and prevented him from sounding the call that summoned the community to class and chapel.[57] These irksome activities were supposed to be kept in check by the mere fact that a professor lived in the hall, but few professors were up to the challenge of keeping the boys in line. Teachers were inept at this part of their job, and most hated it.

As Horowitz has explained, the students' disregard for the faculty's authority reflected much more than casual boredom or mild dissatisfaction. Rather, it was the starting point for the formation of student life.[58] When youthful subjects agitated for change and actively worked against the faculty's control, they formed bonds *as* students. This resistance had a spatial dimension. The astute historian might observe that the poor cows ended up in the administration building.

The popular youths mocked industrious boys by calling them grinds, brownnoses, fish, and bootlickers, but there certainly were some intellectually adventurous students in the antebellum college. Such academically ambitious students founded the early literary societies.[59] At Williams, these societies met in well-appointed rooms, where the boys read fiction, talked about the news, and discussed politics.[60] It was a democratic and rational way for undergraduates to learn content that they felt was lacking in the old-fashioned curriculum.[61] At Williams, the Adelphic Society met on the fourth floor of West College, opposite the society's own library. The literary societies served as sites for socializing, but they did not require dwelling together. Unlike secret societies and fraternities, explicitly banned by colleges, most literary societies accepted anyone who wished to join. Some were selective without being surreptitious, as was the case with the Union Philosophical Society at Dickinson. Of his experience of being accepted in that society, Hobbs wrote, "When I considered that I had been admited into so honorable a league and when I looked about me and saw so many noble young men bound together . . . I considered myself honored if not in a great degree elevated—it made me also feel that I although ignorant and simple that I yet had a place."[62] Secret clubs, such as Yale's Skull and Bones and Wesleyan's Mystical Seven, did not have a housing component, unless the members chose to live together in a dorm or boardinghouse. (No one outside one of these clubs would know if members were living together, because the membership roster was confidential.) Students gradually transformed these secret societies and literary clubs into fraternities, changing their missions dramatically.[63]

The arrival of land-grant universities after 1862 marked a shift in higher education that had a complicated and multifaceted effect on student housing. As Thelin makes clear, the Land Grant Act was a response to changes already taking place in higher education, and although the act infused a great deal of federal money into colleges, the federal government offered little oversight.[64] Each state's land-grant history is unique, but across states the broad strokes are the same and well known to historians. In 1862, the government gave each state some federal land to sell, and the state was required to use the funds from the sale to build a university or add on to an existing university. (The state did not have to establish the new college on the land itself, as is sometimes erroneously assumed.) Of course, some institutions subsisted on state funding before 1862, but that was not the same as federal funding. Examples of state-funded institutions include the Universities of Virginia, Delaware, North Carolina, and Georgia. In the case of preexisting liberal arts colleges, such as Rutgers, the main outcome of the Land Grant Act was that federal funding nudged the institutions, many of which held fast to the classical curriculum, to broaden the range of subjects taught and the types of students served.

At Columbus, Ohio, the new venture was at first called the Ohio Agricultural and Mechanical College. The original structure, completed in 1873, was known as University Hall; it was intended "for instruction only," but, due to a housing shortage, bedrooms were included in the basement as an afterthought.[65] The second building at what became the Ohio State University was North Dorm, built in 1874 explicitly for student housing; it served as home for between sixty and eighty young men. North Dorm was three stories above a tall ground floor, with a porch on one corner and a central tower. The structure must have contained internal corridors, since there was only one main entrance. South Dorm, also known as the Little Dorm, was built in 1874 as well; it housed twenty men in rougher conditions, as it lacked stoves and plumbing.[66] The two dorms were on the far side of the agricultural fields, about half a mile from what later came to be known as the Oval, but at least the students could take the streetcar between the dorms and their classes.[67] The footpath from the dorms to the Old Main was so muddy that in 1877 the trustees recommended building a wooden sidewalk.[68] North Dorm and South Dorm were the only residence halls built for men on the OSU campus for thirty years—any additional housing for men that was added during the interim was provided by fraternities. Although OSU was coeducational from the time it opened, the university did not provide a women's dorm until 1908, and there were no residential sororities. As will be explored in chapter 2, OSU pursued a course different from that taken at Oberlin, Cornell, and Michigan, where purpose-built women's dorms preceded men's dorms.

An early graduate of OSU, James Ellsworth Boyd, class of 1891, later recalled a housing shortage in the early 1880s. The college was surrounded by cornfields. Only one fraternity had its own house, and the other fraternities operated out of North Dorm, where Boyd lived. In writing about his experiences in the dorm almost twenty years later, he proudly noted that there was almost no hazing in the dormitory and that close friendships were formed; the undergraduate-run association was strict and even wielded the power to evict someone who was caught stealing. Quiet boys were able to study in the evenings. "After supper many of the fellows collected in the front office and practiced dancing until seven o'clock. At this time the piano had to stop and each student was supposed to go to his room and study," recounted Boyd. In describing what was special about OSU, he wrote: "Most dormitories [at other colleges] are governed by some member of the faculty who attempts the impossible task of matching his eye and wit against the schemes of half a hundred students."[69] No faculty member could control the students anyway, so (in Boyd's estimation) they policed themselves, and more effectively. His favorable mention of the studious habits and limited hazing in the dorm was almost certainly a dig at later residential fraternities.

FRATERNITY HOUSES

The histories of dormitories for men and fraternity houses are interwoven. Fraternities created an elaborate world of ritual and exclusivity for the wealthiest young men. These societies, with undisclosed standards for acceptance, allowed men to choose their friends, feel part of a single-sex kinship unit, and resist the general social control that the college imposed on their lives. The clubs reflected a general American fascination with secret societies like the Masons; they invited class-based and religious self-selection as they continued the culture of rebellion, revolt, and indignation. They also offered mutual protection. Fraternity brothers mocked the religious tone that professors tried to establish. Pious, hardworking students did not typically join fraternities, either because they disavowed the values of the fraternity boys or because the brothers disavowed them.[70] Members of fraternities were overrepresented on athletic teams, in student government, and as editors of publications.[71] Fraternities set the tone for the social life on almost every campus, partly because they had the nicest rooms for parties and dances. This was especially true at schools that did not yet have dorms for men, like the University of Michigan, the University of Wisconsin, and Cornell.

As Horowitz flatly states: "Undergraduates under the spell of college life believed what you knew did not matter much. Whom you knew, however, mattered a great deal."[72] Fraternities intensified a desire for intimate bonding that was already present on campuses. The first building used exclusively for the purposes of a student fraternal society was a shack in the woods outside Ann Arbor, Michigan; this was in 1846. But it was not a dwelling. For the next thirty years, fraternities bought, rented, and sometimes built meeting halls near campuses.[73] Fraternities existed as social clubs for three decades before they built large houses in which brothers could live. General dissatisfaction with ramshackle boardinghouses, coupled with the lack of fellowship they offered, made joining a fraternity a very attractive alternative. According to historian Nicholas Syrett, the University of California at Berkeley can claim the first live-in house for a fraternity: there, in 1876, the brothers of Zeta Psi began living together in a purpose-built home.[74] Alumni donations footed the bill. No one looking at the exterior would have known that it was specifically for a fraternity. Zeta Psi was a two-story house with a lofty mansard roof, a front porch, and a central entrance, a housing type that was common in its time.

Despite their novel purpose, almost none of these early fraternity houses would have been recognizable as a new building type. At OSU in 1893, two fraternities owned their own houses. One of them was Sigma Alpha Epsilon, a group with roots in Alabama. The house differed from a typical boardinghouse only in that it had a generous porch and a tennis court. Otherwise, it fit the pattern of vernacular domestic architecture of the town, including the architecture of faculty homes.[75] At OSU, the university leased a house that had been used by a professor to the fraternity Beta Theta Pi for the brothers' residence. Beta Theta Pi paid rent, and the university president and faculty set the terms of the fraternity's occupation.[76] These three building types—faculty home, fraternity, and boardinghouse—were not that different from one another at this stage. But that was soon to change, with the fraternity house emerging as a distinctive type.[77]

From the point of view of the fraternity brother, the self-contained house had overwhelming appeal when compared to a dorm. To reside in one's very own house meant there was no professor or other collegiate authority to intervene in one's activities or interrupt secret rituals. Some fraternities had housemothers, but many did not. They might have cooks, housekeepers, and servants, but these adults were employees of the brothers and would have been beholden to them. Not surprisingly, fraternity houses surged in popularity. There may have been but

Figure 1.16. Zeta Psi House, University of California, Berkeley, 1876. This structure (on the site of the current Wurster Hall) was among the first fraternity houses in the United States. Although college fraternities had earlier built clubhouses and lodges for rituals, this was among the first purpose-built dwellings for brothers. Photograph by Edwin Rushmore Jackson. View of Campus Events, UARC PIC 04:142, brk00008409_24a.tif, Bancroft Library, University of California, Berkeley.

Figure 1.17. Sigma Alpha Epsilon House, Ohio State University, 1896, interior of a brother's room. The kinds of cards, concert posters, clocks, and photographs seen here were common decorations in both fraternity and dormitory rooms in the nineteenth century. Ohio State University Archives.

Figure 1.18. Sigma Alpha Epsilon House, Ohio State University, photograph circa 1889. The house had its own tennis court, seen at right; the tennis court was a shared resource, which might explain the coed group outside the fraternity house. Ohio State University Archives.

Figure 1.19. Boardinghouse, Ann Arbor, Michigan, date unknown. On the back of this photograph, the words "Co-ed's Ranch" were written, indicating that this was a boardinghouse for female students. Bentley Historical Library, University of Michigan.

one fraternity house in the United States in 1876, but, according to Syrett, "by 1920, 774 chapters of fraternities owned and resided in their own houses."[78]

Once the trend toward purpose-built houses took off, fraternities on every campus competed to construct the finest dwelling. Each group wanted its younger brothers to occupy a house that was an "architectural ornament"—a sign of the fraternity's wealth and a demonstration of the brothers' contribution to the college and the town in which they lived.[79] Soon, size began to distinguish chapter houses from their neighbors. Psi Upsilon House at the University of Michigan, designed by William Le Baron Jenney, resembled a private mansion more than an institution, and it loomed over its neighbors. The site was a potato field before the large house was built. A description of Psi U written in 1906 by a triumphant brother detailed the house's many attributes:

> The material is brick, the foundation being of blue field stone with water-table of light sandstone; the trimmings are of terra cotta with bands of black brick. The roof is of slate . . . in the gable facing South University Avenue, a shield bearing the

Figure 1.20. Panorama of fraternities at the University of Michigan, 1910. This photograph of men in front of Phi Sigma Kappa gives a sense of the larger streetscape. Bentley Historical Library, University of Michigan.

> fraternity symbols and surmounted by the owl and fasces rests upon an ornamented surface of terra cotta. The interior is finished in unpainted woods. A large dining-hall, kitchen, janitor's room, furnace-room, etc., are in the basement. Upon the first floor are the reception-room, smoking-room, two other rooms for guests and for general purposes, and several smaller compartments. Seven rooms for students are on the second floor; and on the third floor are three more of the same, besides the Chapter Lodge. The tower is eighty feet in height.[80]

The lodge, or ritual space, was on the third floor when the house was built in 1879, but this did not satisfy the brothers, who wanted a "closed Lodge on our grounds."[81] The lodge was necessary because "no well-informed brother can fail to recognize the vital connection between secrecy and success, between the properly conducted meeting and the reverential affection that is the main foundation of a secret order's permanent prosperity."[82] In 1892, the brothers expanded the house, moving the dining hall to the first floor and making the bedroom into suites with bathrooms, but no freestanding lodge was built.[83]

Figure 1.21. Psi Upsilon House, University of Michigan, 1879–80, William Le Baron Jenney, architect, tower extension, 1892. The house dwarfs the nearby dwellings. Bentley Historical Library, University of Michigan.

Fraternity men had already established themselves as a class (athletic, rich, and jaunty) by the time several midwestern colleges began admitting women. Initially, the fraternity boys avoided romantic pursuit of the female students, who were considered dour and humorless. (As Dorothy Parker said, "Men seldom make passes at girls who wear glasses.")[84] According to Syrett, when women began to study and live on campus, fraternity men (in reaction) heightened the public demonstrations of their own masculinity. Similarly, fraternities did not need to define themselves as Protestant bastions, because a common Protestant religion was assumed, but when Jews started to attend colleges in large numbers between 1880 and 1920, Protestant fraternities went out of their way to exclude them.[85] Jews then founded their own fraternities, as did African Americans.

Figure 1.22. Psi Upsilon House, University of Michigan, 1879–80, William Le Baron Jenney, architect, library. Antlers figured prominently in fraternity decor. Scrapbook of Stebbins Stowell, 1910. Bentley Historical Library, University of Michigan.

Figure 1.23. Psi Upsilon House, University of Michigan, 1879–80, William Le Baron Jenney, architect, reception room. A marginal note next to this photograph says, "Where Good Fellows Get Together." Scrapbook of Stebbins Stowell, 1910. Bentley Historical Library, University of Michigan.

One of the best examples of the power and influence of fraternities may be seen at Cornell, which was founded as an ambitious research university using private funds and also received the federal land grant for the state of New York. When Cornell was founded in 1868, its leaders were vigorously pro-Greek. To President Andrew Dickson White, it seemed as if fraternities solved several problems. First, each individual fraternity had the advantage of making the fast-growing university (resented by many people as anonymous) seem small. Second, if Greek organizations provided student housing, the university could spend its capital budget on laboratories and classrooms to serve the new and far-reaching curriculum. And third, fraternities ideally would create intimate groups of men, and such groups, according to White, would serve students as "the best substitute for the family."[86] Cornell did not build a dormitory for men until 1914.

Some fraternities, such as the affluent ones at Cornell, acquired the mansions of local industrialists to use as dwellings. In 1911, the alumni of Delta Phi bought the younger brothers a house—the fact that it happened to have been Ezra Cornell's own home may be taken as evidence of the social and monetary might of the fraternity. In a novel set in Ithaca as late as the 1950s, the naive protagonist recalls seeing the imposing fraternity houses on his first day on campus, where the gap

Figure 1.24. Llenroc, also known as Delta Phi House, Cornell University, 1865–75, Nichols & Brown, architects. Before it was purchased for the fraternity, this mansion was the home of Ezra Cornell. Henry Ware Jones Photograph Albums, 37-5-3864, Division of Rare Books and Manuscript Collections, Cornell University Library.

between the rich and poor was ever on display. The fraternities' porches, where the boys hosted parties, made an impression on him: there were "girls in skirts and cashmere sweaters, [boys] in light flannels and white bucks, and they looked like something out of the Philip Yacht Club."[87]

The brothers of Alpha Delta Phi at Cornell did not live in a renovated house.[88] In fact, they wore their fraternal status boldly, with a compelling sixteen-sided, star-shaped building, known as the Goat House, sitting near the road for all to see. Designed by the architecture firm Dean & Dean of Chicago, the fraternity's main house was a purpose-built Arts and Crafts–style dwelling. In the location of what would normally be that house's front yard, the domed, doorless, and windowless Goat House stood on the top of a hill, apart from the main house.[89] Given that we know the brothers at Psi U at Michigan wished for a freestanding building for their rites, it is clear that such a structure was a highly desired architectural amenity. The Goat House was connected to the main house by an underground tunnel that could be accessed from the basement, near the boiler and trunk room. Pledges were called goats; thus the name of the house was probably a reference to initiation rites performed there.[90] Material culture scholar William Moore, who has conducted fascinating (and difficult) research on secret societies in the nineteenth century, including the Masons and Odd Fellows, explains that the common Victorian expression "riding the goat," rather than being merely metaphorical, was a reference to pranks in which blindfolded riders were hoodwinked into mounting goats. Both real and mechanical beasts were pressed into service.[91] In the particular case of Alpha Delta Phi's Goat House, until the 1980s the brothers used the building almost as a sanctuary; the interior was probably too serious and lugubrious for playful goat riding.[92]

According to the members, the Goat House was "frequently used for meetings of the brotherhood and play[ed] an important role in our initiation ceremonies."[93] An inwardly focused structure with lithic surfaces and a somber presence, the Goat House resembles a mausoleum. Indeed, Bascom Little provided the funds for the building as a memorial to his brother Hiram Little, who was also a member of Alpha Delta Phi, and who died of typhus in 1903.[94] Just below the eaves, there is a strip of green tile with the Alpha Delta Phi symbol (a star above a crescent moon) on the corner. Medieval monastic chapter houses were often centralized structures, where brothers sat in a circle for their meetings, which might explain the round shape of the Goat House. It is not easy to know precisely how the meetings were conducted, but another fraternity, Sigma Chi, organized the seating for its meetings in this way: "Seating should be circular according to seniority and *not in rows.* The surroundings of the room should be pleasant so as to create an

Figure 1.25. Goat House, Alpha Delta Phi House, Cornell University, 1900–1903, Dean & Dean, architects. Given the value that fraternities placed on secrecy, there are no interior photographs of the Goat House. Photograph by author.

Figure 1.26. Alpha Delta Phi House, Cornell University, 1900–1903, Dean & Dean, architects, view from side. This main house burned in 1919 and was replaced by a Gothic Revival house on the same plan; the Goat House still stands. James C. Plant et al., *Cyclopedia of Architecture, Carpentry and Building*, vol. 3 (Chicago: American School of Correspondence, 1907), after p. 298.

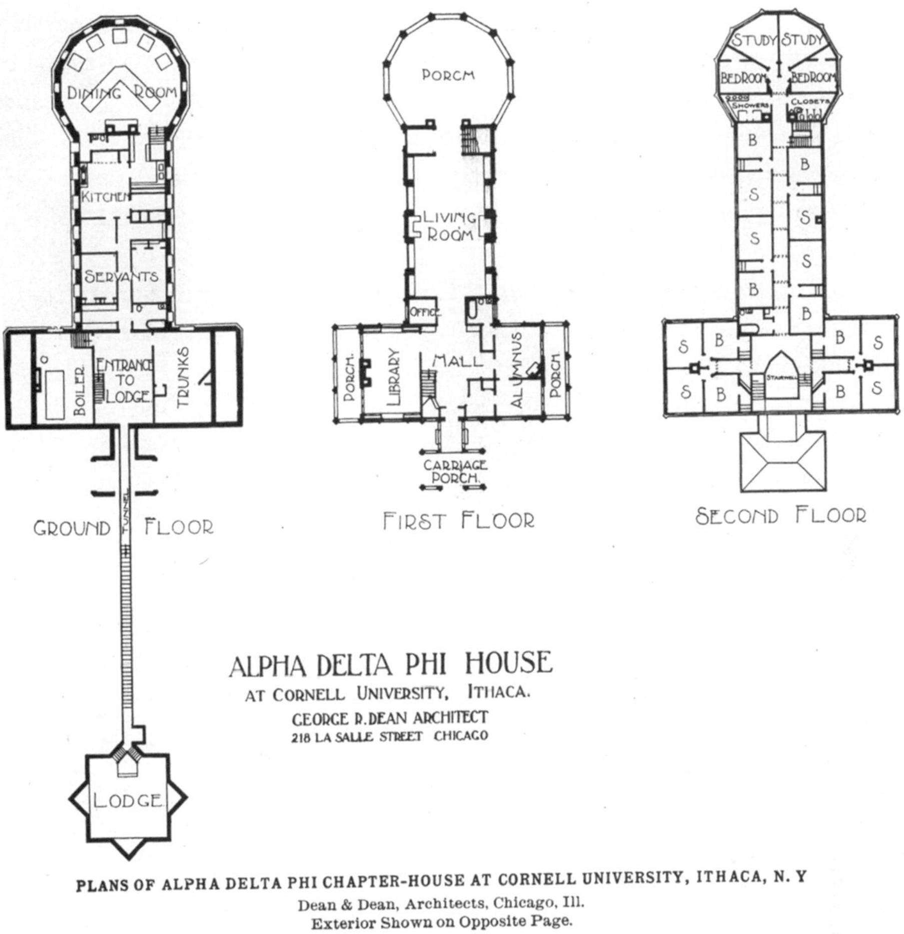

Figure 1.27. Alpha Delta Phi House, Cornell University, 1900–1903, Dean & Dean, architects, plans. James C. Plant et al., *Cyclopedia of Architecture, Carpentry and Building*, vol. 3 (Chicago: American School of Correspondence, 1907), after p. 298.

atmosphere conducive to a congenial chapter meeting."[95] The meeting places of other collegiate secret societies—the ones not associated with fraternities, such as the Skull and Serpent at Wesleyan—are small, closed-off, foreboding structures without windows and thus resemble funerary architecture. At Yale, the secret society buildings are called tombs, although not by their members. The Goat House is a building that advertises morbidity, elitism, secrecy, mystery, and exclusion.[96]

In the half basement at the back of the Alpha Delta Phi main house, there was a semicircular dining hall, where Mackintosh-influenced high-back chairs surrounded an L-shaped table. Above the tunnel to the Goat House, at grade level, the driveway to the main house curved in front of the door under the porte cochere. On the first floor, directly above the dining hall, was an ample glassed-in porch with nine large windows.[97] The rooms were finished in stylish Arts and Crafts details and unpainted wood. Taken as an architectural ensemble, Alpha Delta Phi House was remarkable for the craftsmanship and tastefulness of its elegant public rooms, juxtaposed with the presumably dreary subterranean tunnel that led to the Goat House.

Looking at the plan, it is difficult not to see an architecturally modified phallus. Architectural historians will be reminded of Claude-Nicolas Ledoux's proposal for the Oikéma, or House for Sexual Instruction, which is sometimes referred to as a brothel. As Paulette Singley has wryly observed, "The Oikéma functions as an educational element only for men, and it offers no redeeming rituals for women."[98] The same might be said of a turn-of-the-century American fraternity. Singley and others have noted that the phallic shape of Ledoux's temple would not have been

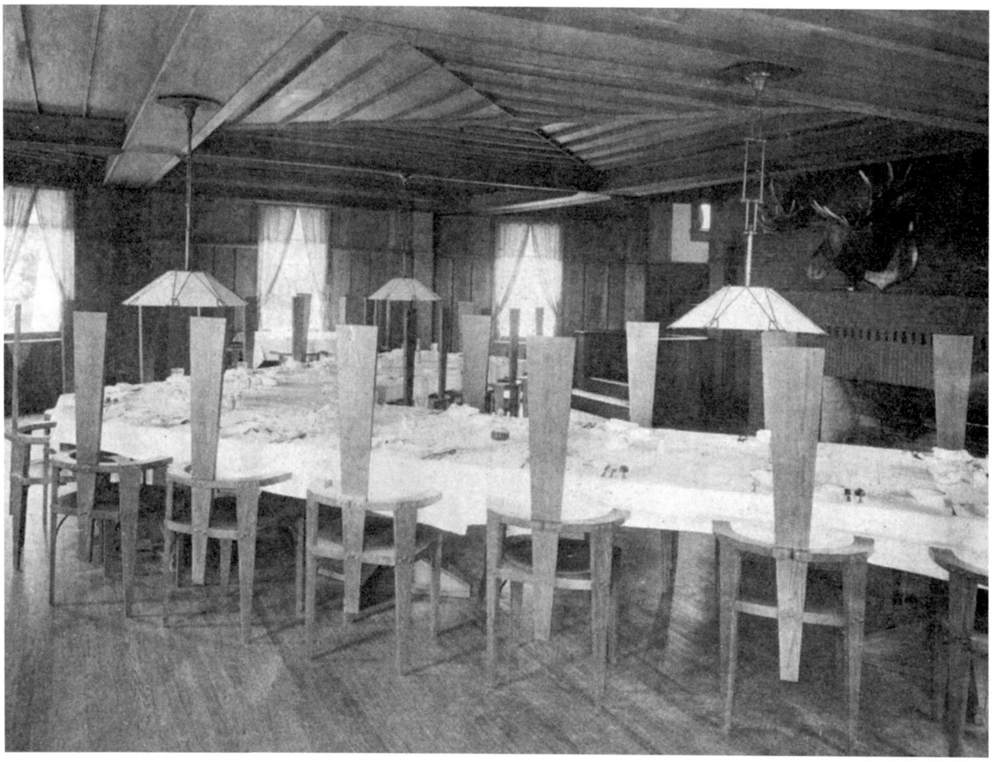

Figure 1.28. Alpha Delta Phi House, Cornell University, 1900–1903, Dean & Dean, architects, dining room. James C. Plant et al., *Cyclopedia of Architecture, Carpentry and Building*, vol. 4 (Chicago: American School of Correspondence, 1907), after p. 298.

readily visible to a passerby: the joke exists in the plan, which would also have been true of Alpha Delta Phi. (On the other hand, the fraternity's plan nearly jumps off the official Cornell campus map.) Ledoux was not well known in the United States around 1900, but George R. Dean, the lead architect for the Alpha Delta Phi House, studied at the École des Beaux-Arts from 1891 to 1893.[99] Perhaps he saw Ledoux's book and the Oikéma in that venerable school's library, and it gave him an idea for a fraternity plan that would speak of clubby humor, sexual prowess, and masculine privilege.

The phallic and star-shaped plans for Alpha Delta Phi were not typical by any means. A much more ordinary example of a fraternity house may be found in the home Albert Kahn designed for Sigma Phi at the University of Michigan, around the same time Alpha Delta Phi House was built at Cornell. The red-brick and white-trimmed Dutch Colonial house was three stories tall, with a welcoming temple front. Two verandas joined the porch, offering casual outdoor spaces. The

Figure 1.29. Alpha Delta Phi House, Cornell University, 1900–1903, Dean & Dean, architects, library. James C. Plant et al., *Cyclopedia of Architecture, Carpentry and Building*, vol. 4 (Chicago: American School of Correspondence, 1907), after p. 298.

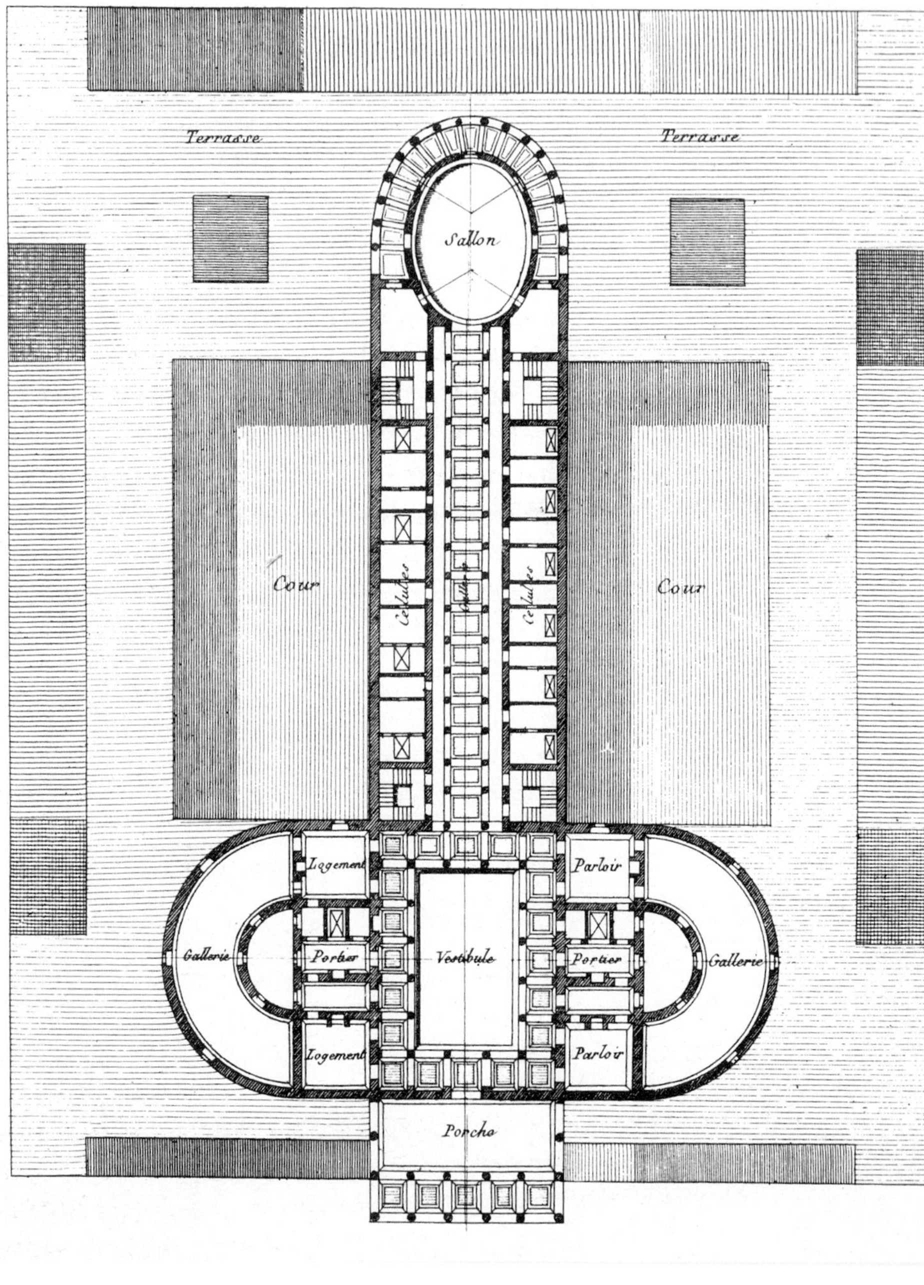

Figure 1.30. Oikéma, or House for Sexual Instruction, Ideal Town of Chaux, project, 1802–4, Claude-Nicolas Ledoux, architect. Originally published in Claude-Nicolas Ledoux, *L'Architecture considérée sous le rapport de l'art, des mœurs et de la legislation* (Paris: C. F. Patris, 1802–4). The illustration also appeared in *Architecture de C. N. Ledoux*, edited by Daniel Ramée (Paris: Lenoir, 1847), plate 240.

ground floor was devoted to public functions, emphasizing the importance of sociability. It included a library, reception room, main hall, and lounge. The main hall and lounge flowed into each other, occupying the whole space from front to rear facade. A sliding set of doors allowed these already large rooms to be combined to form even bigger spaces for parties.[100] The second floor was made up of studies and chambers (bedrooms), with one shared bathroom. The below-grade dining room was half round, and the basement also included a vault and an anteroom with an ironclad door. Most of the lower level was taken up with the Lodge Room, used for meetings and rites, which had an elliptical alcove enclosing a semicircular stage at one end. Since the interiors of fraternity houses were secret places, interior photographs do not usually exist, but this set of plans offers rich historical information.

While fraternities today are known for rushing and hazing, they cannot be held liable for inventing either of those activities; sophomores tormented freshmen before fraternities formed, and fraternity rush practices were an extension and amplification of class-year bonding. The Rutgers alma mater referred to class-year hazing by name: "And then, as Soph, my turn began, / And I hazed the poor Fresh

Figure 1.31. Sigma Phi House, University of Michigan, 1900, Albert Kahn, architect. Postcard. Collection of the author.

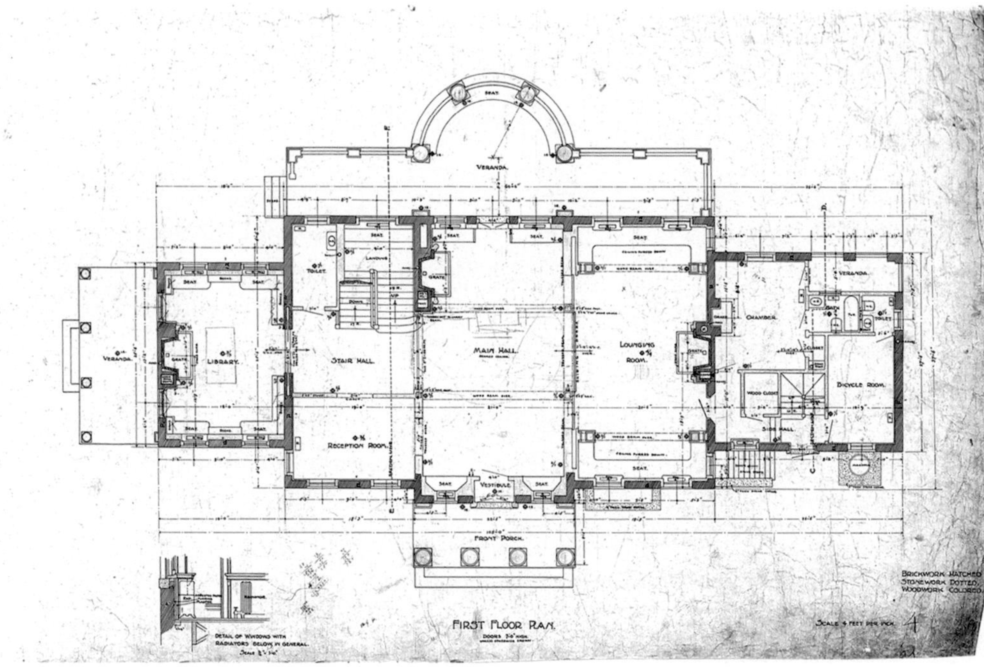

Figure 1.32. Sigma Phi House, University of Michigan, 1900, Albert Kahn, architect, plan, first floor. The main floor featured large rooms that could be reconfigured for parties and recreation. Albert Kahn Associates, Bentley Historical Library, University of Michigan.

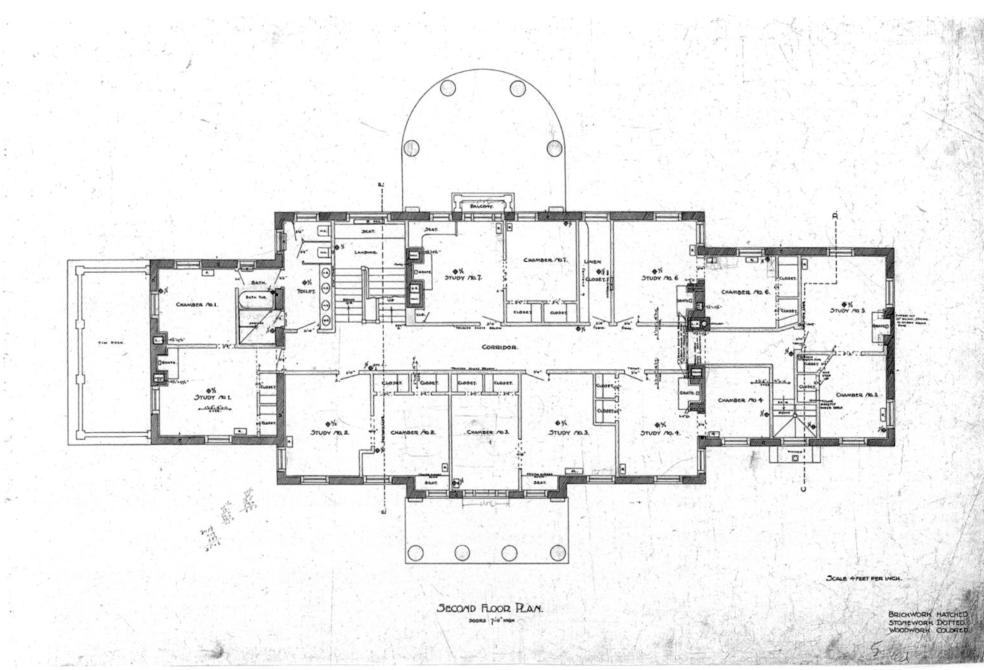

Figure 1.33. Sigma Phi House, University of Michigan, 1900, Albert Kahn, architect, plan, second floor. This floor was the main sleeping area for the brothers; it included studies and chambers (bedrooms) and a shared bathroom. Albert Kahn Associates, Bentley Historical Library, University of Michigan.

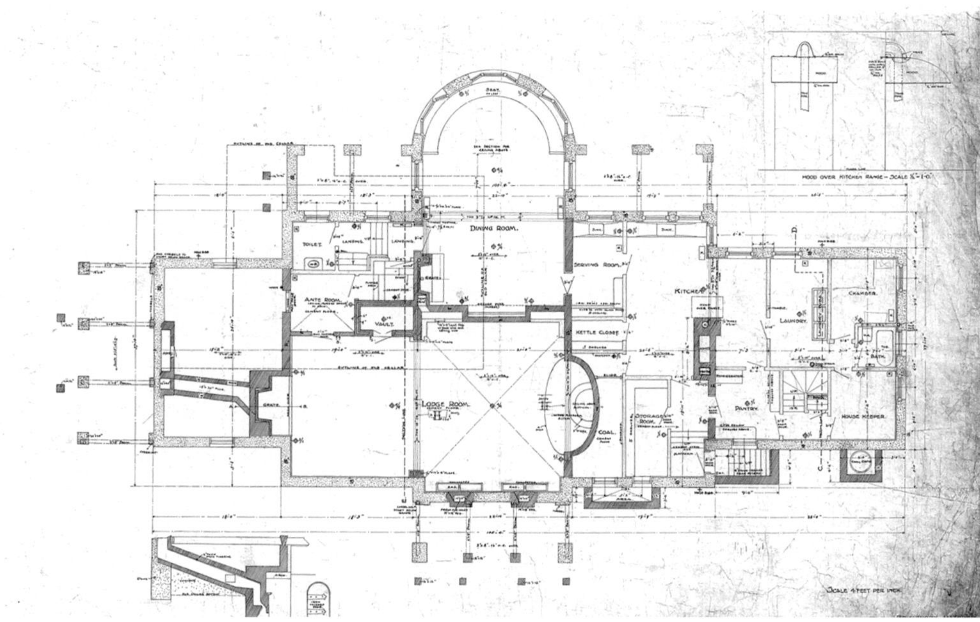

Figure 1.34. Sigma Phi House, University of Michigan, 1900, Albert Kahn, architect, plan, basement. This level housed the fraternity's private spaces, including a vault, an anteroom with an ironclad door, and the Lodge Room, which had an elliptical alcove with a semicircular stage at one end. The dining room was also located on this level. Albert Kahn Associates, Bentley Historical Library, University of Michigan.

so, / That they longed for Heaven, I know." Although it is hard to know what happened in purposely secretive places, historians are on firm ground in concluding that woods and other natural environs were sites of hazing. In 1872, Mortimer Leggitt, who was pledging Kappa Alpha fraternity at Cornell University, fell to his death in an Ithaca gorge. He was wearing a blindfold.[101] This is the first known case of death by fraternity hazing in the United States, but there were almost certainly others before it. Hazing belongs to a large category of initiation rites that mark the transition from outsider to insider, and from boyhood to manhood. Most such rituals of crossing into manhood are founded on violence enacted on a boy's body and include actions that are both homoerotic and homophobic. The bodily humiliations associated with the practice were intended to make the youths cast aside their childhoods as they entered manhood and also shed their individuality as they joined the brotherhood. In the nineteenth century, hazing included forcing pledges to ingest disgusting food (often raw liver), drink alcohol excessively, smoke tobacco until nauseated, remove clothing, withstand freezing temperatures, jump off bridges, fight under water, find their way home from distant rural locations, and (most infamously) submit to paddling. The purposeful degrading of pledges supposedly tested their courage and loyalty. By the end of the experience, the pledges were meant to feel grateful to the older members and therefore accepted into a substitute family. The question of consent was (and remains) a difficult one—these were young adults who agreed to participate in what they knew would be a painful, humiliating, and possibly life-threatening process.

As fraternities developed, they spurned the intellectual promise of the literary societies and instead became highly efficient instruments for the networking side of higher education. Acceptance into a fraternity lasted beyond college; it was a bond that paved the way for later membership in urban men's clubs; it was a launching pad for any number of careers.[102] The social bonds extended beyond individual institutions: by attending annual conferences with chapters at other schools, fraternity men created associations of elite brothers all across the nation. Unlike the choir or the lacrosse team, a fraternity was a club that offered lifelong membership.

Once fraternities started building lavish houses, they increased their annual dues, which reinforced the class hierarchy that was endemic to intrafraternity competition. The need to pay fees was an obvious and definitive way to separate the rich from the poor.[103] Whichever fraternity charged the highest dues was the one that attracted the wealthiest and most powerful men. Fees perpetuated a hierarchy among the Greeks and the non-Greeks.

No single architectural style dominated fraternity house design, in spite of the fact that all such houses served the same purpose. This was a period of eclecticism in American domestic architecture, and fraternities were no different on that score. In 1907, the yearbook of the University of Michigan included photographs of the exteriors of most of the fraternity houses; one could illustrate the entire history of American domestic architecture from 1870 through the first decade of the twentieth century using these houses alone. Based on the pictures, the styles of fraternity houses in Ann Arbor in 1907 included Queen Anne Revival (Phi Kappa Sigma, Delta Chi), Richardsonian Romanesque (Delta Kappa Epsilon), Dutch Colonial Revival (Sigma Phi), Gothic cottage in the style of A. J. Downing (Phi Kappa Psi), neo-Colonial (Acacia, Phi Delta Theta), Tudor Revival with half timbering (Phi Gamma Delta), Greek Revival (Alpha Phi), French with a mansard roof (Kappa Alpha Theta), and Arts and Crafts (Delta Sigma Delta).[104] At Cornell, there was a similarly wide range, as shown in the 1909 yearbook: Tudor Revival (Chi Phi, Phi Delta Theta, and Beta Theta Pi), Richardsonian Romanesque (Kappa Alpha), Colonial Revival (Phi Sigma Kappa and Theta Delta Chi), Shingle Style (Delta Upsilon), and Arts and Crafts (Alpha Delta Phi).[105]

The nineteenth-century dormitory was more democratic than the fraternity, because Greek life was by its nature exclusive (tension between Greeks and non-Greeks, or independents, is a theme of chapter 3). As long as students were randomly assigned to dormitories, no stigma could be associated with one dormitory or another. And if residence halls were small, or divided into small units, independents could also enjoy the enviable esprit de corps associated with the Greeks.

Dormitories started out serving two primary functions. First, they were intended to emulate the colleges of Oxford and Cambridge by providing physical structures that would make possible the idealized life of the student, who would live in close contact with faculty, under the same roof as a chapel, library, and dining hall. Second, because early American colleges were often built in rural locations, reflecting their missionary origins and an antiurban bias that governed much elite thinking during the colonial and Federal eras, they needed to provide housing to stay in business. Even so, during the antebellum period, most colleges had only one or two dormitories. After the Civil War, largely because of the Morrill Act, the student population expanded rapidly, but colleges did not immediately add more beds. With the rise of the research university based on the German model, many university presidents, like Michigan's Henry Tappan, looked at their financial accounts and concluded that dormitories were an unnecessary expense. In his inaugural lecture in 1852, Tappan outlined the necessities for running a great state university. He asked his listeners a provocative question: "Are buildings required?" He answered: "Buildings of course are required. But in our country we have ever begun at the wrong end. We have erected vast dormitories for the night's sleep, instead of creating libraries and laboratories for the day's work."[106] Universities needed revenue for libraries, classrooms, and laboratories to serve the research faculty and burgeoning graduate programs. The rise of the research university marked the temporary demise of the dormitory, and the research university marched in lockstep with the ascent of science. As Julie Reuben has noted, by the end of the nineteenth century, "attention to morality shifted away from the course of study to . . . extracurricular influences. In this change, morality became associated with behavior rather than belief."[107] Pastoral care exited the classroom. Professors now concentrated on the production of new knowledge and jockeying for status among their peers. They were happy to leave character building, discipline, and cow removal to other collegiate officials.

2

The Coed's Predicament

Women's Dormitories at Coeducational Colleges

Olive San Louie Anderson enrolled at the University of Michigan in 1871. Shortly after she graduated, in 1875, she wrote a novel, *An American Girl, and Her Four Years in a Boys' College,* which offers a blunt yet optimistic portrayal of a pioneering coed, Wilhelmine "Will" Elliott. Will has trouble finding a place to live in thinly disguised Ann Arbor, where one boardinghouse owner finds the mere idea of a "lady-student" "odd."[1] The college steward soon directs her to one of his cousins for lodging; Will then manages to take the placement tests and starts her classes. Unfortunately, she finds herself caught in a hazing battle between the sophomores and the freshmen, which she describes in a letter to her younger sister: "The missiles . . . consisted of hymn-books, sticks, anything movable; a great apple-core struck me right in eye, which caused me to see a whole solar system of stars; but I bore it bravely, feeling something of that rapture that the old martyrs must have felt—for, was I not suffering in the cause of coeducation?"[2]

The word *coed* was originally used as an adjective, a shortened form of *coeducational*—as it still is today. It then began being used to refer to individuals, a use that is jarring to modern ears. *Coed* in reference to a female student suggests second-class status, and indeed women *were* second-class citizens in the educational landscape of the late nineteenth and early twentieth centuries. During that period, *coed* was regularly used as a noun, meaning a female student at a mixed-gender college. Nobody needed the word *male* to modify *student.* Coeds were women. Students were men.[3]

Where did coeds live? Some in boardinghouses, and others in purpose-built dorms. As we have seen in chapter 1, the dormitory was a communal dwelling, and thus was different from a library, a chapel, or a classroom building. It necessitated the sharing of intimate spaces by people of the same gender, which in turn heightened fears about homosexuality. In the nineteenth century, and for much of the twentieth, it was taken for granted that the sexes would be separated in dormitories. Precedents for women's dormitories may be traced to the convents of the Middle Ages, just as men's dormitories harked back to monasteries. A closer precedent in terms of function may be found in the workers' housing of mill towns such as Lowell, Massachusetts, although the forms were quite different.[4] The dormitories examined in this chapter range from large houses to purpose-built cottages to congregate structures. The official language surrounding residence halls claimed that they were homelike, but even at the time people knew this was a fiction. In general, a women's dormitory benefited from a plan that facilitated genteel surveillance: wardens or housemothers needed to monitor the girls, and strangers needed to be kept out, but the overall appearance could not be prison-like. Indeed, these buildings had to envelop parents and students with comforting quasi-domestic imagery.

Midwestern universities experimented with educating men and women together long before East Coast colleges like the Ivies. Even so, the arrival of women on coeducational campuses was gradual and uneven. Although sources differ slightly on the statistics, it is clear that the numbers of female college students rose steadily over the period from 1870 to 1915. According to a report published by the National Center for Education Statistics, the proportion of bachelor's degrees earned by women increased from 15 percent in 1869–79 to 40 percent in 1929–30.[5] Another estimate places even more women in college: in 1870, 21 percent of college students were women, but by 1920, the proportion had risen to 47 percent.[6]

Just as the word *coed* connoted a meager subset of the group designated by the word *student,* women's places on college campuses were often bracketed-off subterrains of the campuses as a whole. All the spaces of a college campus were assumed to be for men, unless they were specifically carved out for women. Helen L. Horowitz's study of the all-female Seven Sisters colleges demonstrates the paradox that educators faced when designing women's colleges. On the one hand, single-sex education kept women away from men during vulnerable early adulthood, enabling the women to maintain their good reputations and marriageability. On the other hand, some educators, like the founders of Smith College, argued that women could become unfit for real-world domesticity—for lives as wives and mothers—if they were locked away from society in the company of other bookish females. This led to the development of a system of housing for female students that replicated family-like groups.[7]

Horowitz's findings also pertain to coed schools. In fact, most of the issues she discusses were amplified at coeducational schools, where women's spaces were in tension with spaces for men, both male professors and students. As historian Margaret Lowe has shown, female students on coed campuses "developed their collegiate identity before a watchful and often critical male audience."[8] Lowe's study of college women and body image has had a fundamental impact on this chapter, as has Nicholas Syrett's book on white fraternities.[9] Both Lowe and Syrett studied the lives of students through close readings of archival documents, including diaries, and thus revealed much about collegiate life from the student's point of view. Unlike Horowitz, neither Lowe nor Syrett specialized in the study of the built environment, and therefore their research lacks spatial analysis. Both Lowe and Syrett emphasize that differences in class and race rose to the surface of nearly every social encounter they examined, whether in their analyses of a student's clothes, hobbies, or place of residence. By looking at the built environment, we can better understand the lived experience of young men and women; we can look closely at where men and women were separated and where they were allowed (and sometimes encouraged) to be together. Coeducation required college officials to rethink the spatial configurations of their campuses.

COEDUCATION AND WOMEN'S HEALTH

Coeducation did not arrive without struggle, and the fight over educating women alongside men had vocal critics on both sides. Those opposed to higher education for women used a medical argument, claiming that the weight of intellectual study would wreak havoc on women's bodily cycles. Edward H. Clarke, a physician, wrote in 1875, "Girls lose health, strength, blood and nerve by a regimen that ignores the periodic tides and reproductive apparatus of their organization."[10] Clarke asserted that women and men could not be educated together because they were constitutionally too different. If young women strained their bodies while using their brains, they would become barren, an argument that tapped into larger dominant-culture fears about the decline of the white race.[11]

In spite of opponents like Clarke, public universities acquiesced to pressure from legislators to provide education to young women because public elementary and secondary schools were in urgent need of teachers. Many educators believed in the efficacy of teaching women and men together; it was cheaper than creating entirely separate colleges, given that it did not require duplication of administrative structures, extra faculty, or more buildings. But even supporters of mixed-gender higher education believed that women needed special attention if they were to survive in the rough-and-tumble environment of college. The administrators who were in charge of female students, called "lady principals" and, later, "deans of women," pressed for safe, secure, and attractive housing, and through their efforts, women's needs rose in the hierarchy of college concerns. At some coed schools, dormitories for women preceded those for men, just as the position known as dean of women preceded that of dean of men in many college administrations.[12] These women leaders professionalized their own practice, protected their charges, and emphasized architecture as an agent of reform.

Eliza Mosher, the first such dean at the University of Michigan and a medical doctor, wrote extensively on women's health, including an article on correct posture for women and its effects on the reproductive system, published in 1893. Supporters of coeducation such as Mosher pushed back against Clarke's medical argument by professionalizing the care of girls' bodies *and* minds. In fact, female educators and other defenders of higher education for women claimed that college life made young women healthier and stronger.[13] The job of the dean of women was to give academic advice and ensure that young women attended classes, got regular exercise, made friends, participated in extracurricular activities, ate healthy food, and stood up straight. Women's bodies were always a matter of concern for administrators: as they saw it, if a girl was too flirtatious or "lively," she risked making her body too available, and if she was shy or industrious, she was seen as overly serious.[14]

OBERLIN: A COEDUCATIONAL AND INTEGRATED COLLEGE

Historians typically recognize Oberlin College, founded in 1833, as the first coeducational institution of higher learning in the United States. A Presbyterian clergyman (John Jay Shipherd) and a missionary (Philo P. Stewart) who believed that labor and faith would lead to an egalitarian society together founded the town of Oberlin and the college. Oberlin's early presidents were abolitionists, and thus the town emerged as a significant stop on the Underground Railroad. Women were educated with men from the time the pioneering college opened, although initially the women's curriculum was somewhat less rigorous than the men's, and women and men followed different academic tracks. Starting in 1835, Oberlin also taught African American men and women alongside whites. In classrooms, students sat wherever they chose, and whites and blacks shared the same work spaces.[15]

Classes initially met in a two-story wooden building, Oberlin Hall, which contained both instruction space and living quarters.[16] Surprisingly, Oberlin Hall housed both men and women. As reported by the *Oberlin News* in 1896:

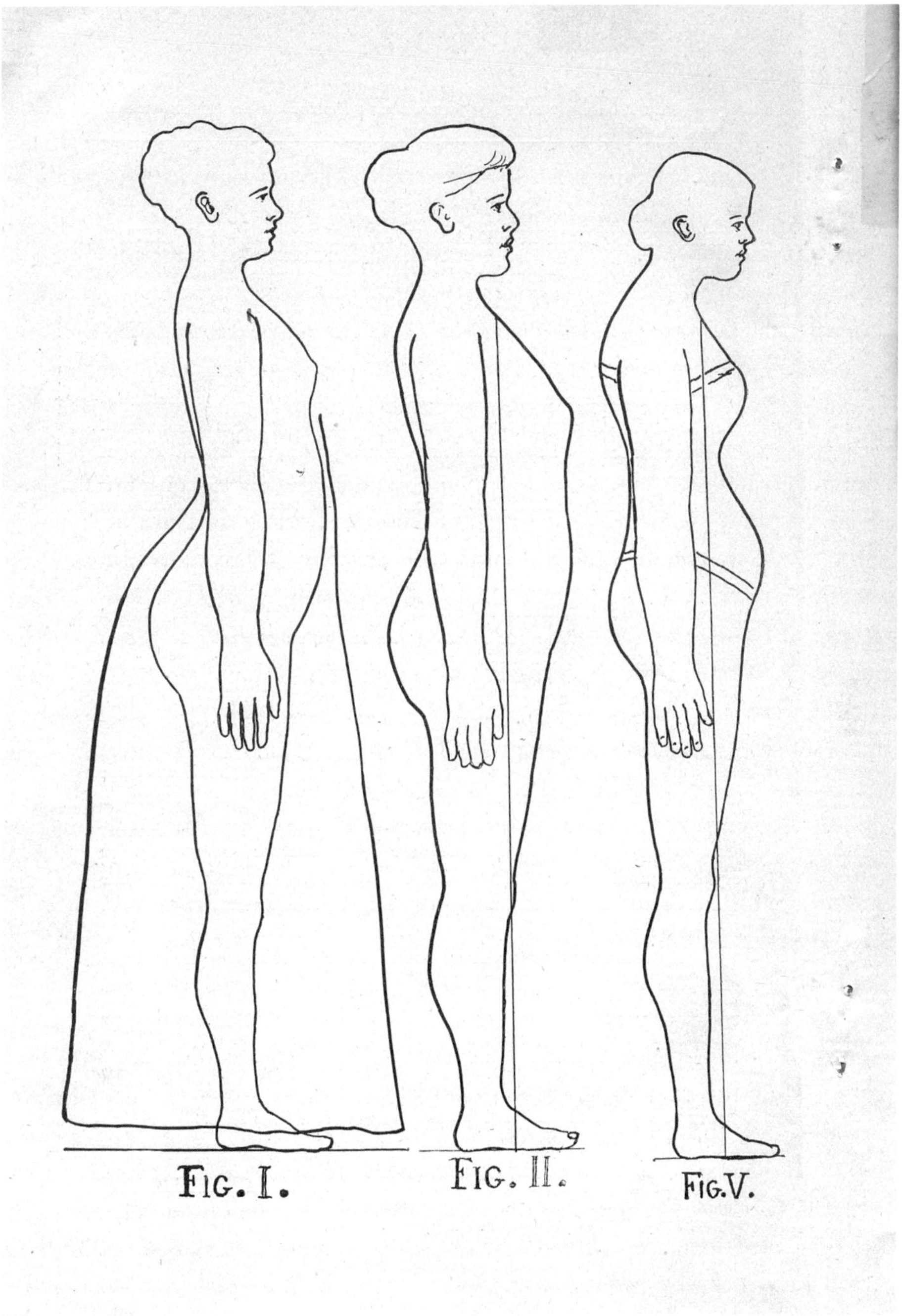

Figure 2.1. Correct posture for women according to Eliza Mosher, M.D., dean of women at the University of Michigan, 1893. Mosher explained that good posture was essential for women's reproductive health. The figure on the left has too much sway in her lower back; the one in the middle has proper posture, or "equilibrium"; and the one on the right is standing in a way that makes her upper back curve over her corset. Mosher believed that physical education, including advice about posture, could lead to fewer pelvic diseases in women. Eliza Mosher, "Habits of Posture a Cause of Deformity and Displacement of the Uterus," *New York Journal of Gynæcology and Obstetrics* 3, pt. 2 (November 1893): 963.

> When President Fairchild and his brother came here as students, sixty two years ago [in 1834], the college was housed in one building [Oberlin Hall], thirty feet wide by forty long. The young women of the college roomed in the second story, next to the chapel, while the young men occupied spacious apartments, eight feet square [eight feet on each side], in the attic. These rooms were furnished with the necessary furniture of a room, including a bed that would turn up against the wall each morning, leaving all the floor space available.[17]

The college sold Oberlin Hall in 1854, but it remained standing until the 1880s.

The fact that men and women lived in Oberlin Hall together, although on different floors, was highly unusual, and—probably for that reason—the arrangement did not last long. Beginning in 1835, the women moved to First Ladies' Hall, a house with two wings on the back. (Around the same time, male students relocated to a new brick building, Tappan Hall, which included living space for men in addition to recitation rooms; also, many male students lived in town.)[18] The monumental Second Ladies' Hall, completed in 1865 and made of brick and stone, housed one hundred women. The dining room served both men and women. Although no plan of Second Ladies' Hall survives, the footprint of the building was likely L-shaped.[19] The three-story building had round-headed windows set within round-arched niches.[20] Educators considered Second Ladies' Hall a benchmark in women's housing; Berea College copied the structure closely.[21]

Two leading figures in coeducation, Andrew Dickson White and Henry Sage, visited Second Ladies' Hall when seeking ideas for housing women at Cornell, which was founded in 1868 and accepted its first women in 1870. They were impressed by the orderly and polite conversation that took place in the mixed-gender dining hall, and they observed that women conducted themselves with aplomb in the classrooms. Sage donated the funds for a women's residence at Cornell in 1872, and Sage Hall opened its doors in 1875. The finely detailed structure employed a square donut–shaped plan. Female students had access to their own library and swimming pool.[22] Given that Second Ladies' Hall was far less elaborate than Sage Hall and did not share its plan, it does not seem likely that its architecture influenced Sage's designers, even though its size and prominence on the campus may have.

When Oberlin's Second Ladies' Hall burned in 1886, the hundred women residents escaped unharmed, but the building was completely destroyed.[23] Two smaller structures, referred to at the time as "cottages," replaced the large dormitory. In the parlance common to nineteenth-century institutions, a cottage was a freestanding residence that housed anywhere from twenty to eighty people.

LADIES' HALL.

Figure 2.2. Ladies' Hall, (first) Oberlin College, begun in 1835, occupied until 1865. The first building specifically for female students at Oberlin was this frame house with two wings on the back. Photograph courtesy of Oberlin College Archives.

Reformers at both colleges and lunatic asylums promoted cottages as homelike, and thus more like residences in the world outside the institution.

CONGREGATE AND COTTAGE DORMITORIES

This pattern of development—a massive multipurpose building replaced by cottages—is outlined by Horowitz, who describes the range of attitudes that leaders of women's colleges took toward congregate and cottage plans.[24] She argues for a three-stage history, in which the congregate-to-cottage shift represents the transition between the first two stages. First, Vassar was founded as one large building

Figure 2.3. Second Ladies' Hall, Oberlin College, 1861–65. This building, which housed approximately one hundred female students, was destroyed by fire in 1886. Photograph courtesy of Oberlin College Archives.

Figure 2.4. Second Ladies' Hall, Oberlin College, 1861–65, dining hall, photograph from 1870s. Men and women dined together in this women's dormitory. Original caption: "The Common Dining Room of the New Ladies' Hall." 30/24, source 1, box 21, folder 2. Photograph courtesy of Oberlin College Archives.

with a varied program to shelter women from society. Second, university officials, like those at Smith in the 1870s, turned against monolithic structures for fear that women would develop unduly close, homosocial friendships in all-female settings.[25] Horowitz leans heavily on a quotation from the editor of *Scribner's,* J. G. Holland, who wrote that keeping girls cooped up in a big building under one roof was an "unnatural" system that led to "diseases of body and diseases of imagination," as well as "vices of the body and imagination."[26] Taking Holland's fretful language to be evidence of a widespread fear of lesbianism, she concludes that cottages, which were soothingly domestic in appearance, were an architectural response to the massive college building. Cottages were intended to create homelike spaces that would prepare girls for their lives as wives and mothers. "The cottage separated residence from instruction. This freed the academic side from the moral and religious constructions, focusing the spiritual mission of the college on the domestic environment."[27] The third stage was the full embrace of English congregate buildings such as those at Bryn Mawr College.

Individual, dispersed cottages were more difficult to supervise than one large building, and therefore officials had to accept a trade-off: practical surveillance gave way to imagined domesticity. Horowitz notes that the pattern of congregate structures superseded by cottages was seen also in the development of Victorian insane asylums. Given that some late nineteenth-century cottages were quite large, one might reasonably ask why these buildings were assumed to be more domestic than a congregate dormitory. Cottages, even large ones, were designed without double-loaded corridors, and such corridors were strongly associated with institutional forms. Internally, cottages often had semipublic rooms on the ground floor with bedrooms above. Cottages possessed a domestic air: "Like the home in the same period, the cottage served as the repository of values, a feminine refuge from the challenges of contemporary life."[28] One problem with this analysis is that at asylums and orphanages, males as well as females were housed in single-sex cottages, which undermines the claim that the cottage was a "feminine refuge." On the other hand, there were no cottages for men at coed or all-male colleges. One possibility is that most colleges attended by men (although not Oberlin) had fraternities that filled the same niche in the housing market that cottages would fill. Both types were freestanding, single-sex residences, with semipublic rooms on the first floor and bedrooms above. Both types were more substantial than middle-class houses, yet vaguely domestic in shape. The cottage, therefore, might have been a way for college leaders to reinvent the fraternity house as a space for women.

Baldwin Cottage and Talcott Hall at Oberlin, designed by the firm Weary and Kramer and completed in 1887, were richly colored Richardsonian Romanesque buildings that were attuned to the street and sidewalk. They were larger than the nearby houses, but their masses were irregular and staggered so as not to appear bulky. Talcott housed seventy women, and Baldwin housed thirty-one.[29] The semipublic rooms in Talcott operated as the center of student life, as they had previously in Second Ladies' Hall. At the beginning of the twentieth century, social life at Oberlin revolved around the women's dormitories. Male students were scattered around the town.[30] Given that Oberlin refused to allow fraternities (because such clubs reinstated societal hierarchies) and had no student center, the women's residences were the heart of the campus.

Architecture was one way to manage student circulation; enlisting staff members was a more obvious method. Lady principals, deans, and matrons enforced a wide range of parietal rules. In 1901, Oberlin produced a set of guidelines for three houses, including Baldwin and Talcott. The houses needed to be quiet from 7:00 p.m. to 10:00 p.m., girls were not allowed to "walk noisily in halls," and every light had to be out by 10:00 p.m. In a possibly vain attempt to control interactions between girls and their suitors, the rule book noted: "Clapping shall be the only response to serenades."[31]

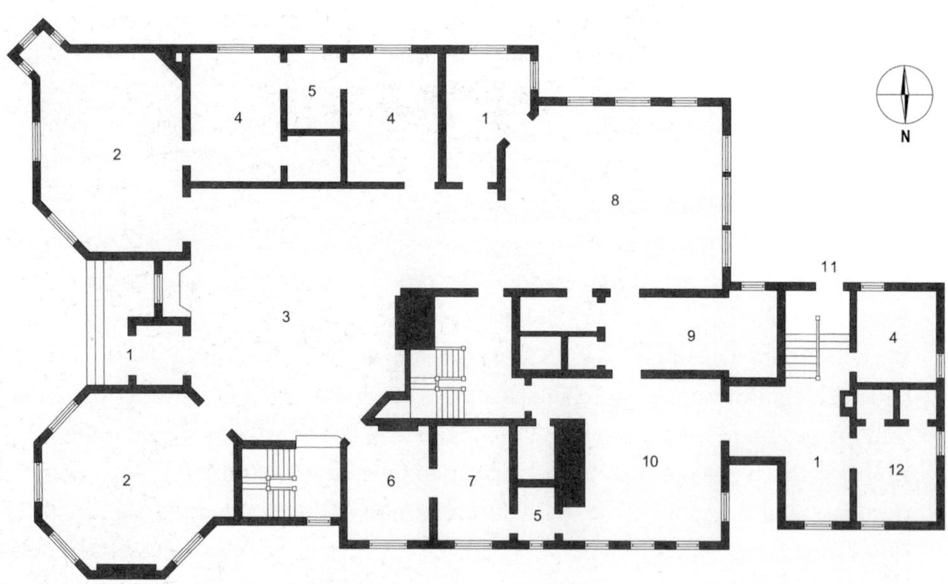

Figure 2.5. Baldwin Cottage, Oberlin College, 1886–87, Weary and Kramer, architects, plan. The front door is on the left in this plan. 1 = entry; 2 = parlor; 3 = reception hall; 4 = bedroom; 5 = bathroom; 6 = matron's parlor; 7 = matron's bedroom; 8 = dining hall; 9 = china closet; 10 = kitchen; 11 = service entrance and exit; 12 = store room. Drawing by John Giganti.

Figure 2.6. Baldwin Cottage, Oberlin College, 1886–87, Weary and Kramer, architects. This was one of two structures that replaced the congregate Second Ladies' Hall. Photograph by author.

Figure 2.7. Talcott Hall, Oberlin College, 1886–87, Weary and Kramer, architects, interior of the main reception hall in 1903. Photograph courtesy of Oberlin College Archives.

Figure 2.8. Talcott Hall, Oberlin College, 1886–87, Weary and Kramer, architects. Photograph by author.

Male students responded swiftly to these two new cottages at Oberlin. They were openly envious of the good accommodations afforded their female classmates and rallied for a dormitory of their own. Their prayers were answered when an anonymous donor gave funds for the first men's dormitory in 1910. The 1911 edition of the Oberlin yearbook, the *Hi-O-Hi,* included an exuberant description of the new building, which was then still under construction. The author, presumably a student, reassured readers that the new building would not undermine Oberlin's dedication to coeducation:

> With perfect equality of opportunity for both sexes there should also be afforded opportunity for women to meet with women and men to meet with men. . . . The women have been afforded this opportunity in large part by the dormitory life of Talcott [and] Baldwin. . . . The men of Oberlin have never had the association and fellowship that the fraternity house and the college dormitory afford in many institutions.[32]

By their very nature, fraternities were exclusive, and Oberlin continued to forbid them—but this stance was unusual.

Sadly, in spite of Oberlin's dedication to social equality, racism at the college made national news in the 1880s. First, a professor objected to a black student rooming with a white student, even though the students were satisfied with the arrangement.[33] Around the same time, a group of white women students refused to eat at the same table as African American students, even though students had shared the same dining hall and tables for decades. The matron asked the black students to sit at a separate table, but President James H. Fairchild overrode her action. The dining room in Second Ladies' Hall was the site of this controversy. Distraught alumni, both men and women, expressed outrage and disappointment about the moral decline of their college in Oberlin and Cleveland newspapers. Historian Cally Waite concludes that Oberlin was "affected by the nationwide rise in discrimination against Blacks in the post-Reconstruction era."[34] While Fairchild forbade segregation anywhere on campus, including dorms, dining halls, classrooms, and church, his successor, Henry C. King, reversed this position in 1903.[35] President King segregated the dormitories, thus forcing black women to live off campus.[36] Furthermore, the segregation of the dorms (but not the classrooms) is evidence of the intimacy of the residence hall as a building type. One can speculate that the physical closeness of bodies, dressing and undressing, showering and bathing, heightened the prejudice of the white students, who tolerated mixed-race classrooms.

UNIVERSITY OF CHICAGO: DEANS OF WOMEN MAKE THE QUADRANGLE WORK

Like Oberlin, the University of Chicago was founded as a coed and integrated institution. An organization called the American Baptist Education Society seized the chance to establish a major university in Chicago to compete with the eastern Ivy League schools. John D. Rockefeller, a practicing Baptist, donated by far the largest amount of money to the burgeoning institution. Although its first president, William Rainey Harper, was also a dedicated Baptist, religious doctrine did not guide the university.[37] The first class included an African American woman, Cora Bell Jackson. As at Oberlin, controversies about gender and race played out in the social sphere and living quarters of the students.

In the 1890s, the most admired female college educator in the United States was Chicago's first dean of women, formerly Wellesley's president, Alice Freeman Palmer. Palmer, who was reluctant to leave her presidency, agreed only to a part-time position, and thus she brought along her colleague Marion Talbot (also from Wellesley) to help run the program. Talbot, like Palmer, was a national leader among women's deans and in the field of domestic reform. Her first major assignment was to organize the university's housing. Although almost all of the students who lived in the dormitories were undergraduates, a small number of female graduate students were allowed to live on campus. In fact, one reason Chicago attracted Palmer and Talbot was that it offered doctoral-level education to women. The university was a bold experiment, and women were in the game from the start.

The University of Chicago's major contribution to higher education in the United States was the combining of the Oxbridge-style residential college with the model of a German research university.[38] Looking back at the founding from a distance of eleven years, President Harper observed, "There was some question in the minds of the Trustees as to the merits of the so-called 'Dormitory System' of college life." He described these concerns as follows:

> Effort was made on the part of certain educators at the time of opening of the University to show that dormitory life was a survival of the Middle Ages, and that it was something entirely injurious to the development of proper manhood and womanhood. Our own experience has been exactly the opposite. With each recurring year, the demand for residence on the grounds is greater, and the results of such residence are more clearly apparent. This is especially true in the case of women.[39]

Harper did not spell out the precise benefits in the 1903 report quoted above, but an excellent enumeration of those benefits may be found in the records of female deans. At the 1903 meeting of the Conference of Deans of Women of the Middle West, the subject of dormitories was the first agenda item. Talbot attended, as did Myra Beach Jordan of the University of Michigan. A dean from Wisconsin applauded dormitory life for its role in the "democratization of students" and its influence in developing "social polish" and "enthusiasm in college matters," and another participant commented that dormitory life was "less trying on the nerves." Observing that students who lived on campus were more likely to eat healthy food, one dean reported that the hearty dormitory diet was necessary for "women doing brain work."[40]

Given that Palmer supported cottages at Wellesley, it is unlikely that she favored the large-scale quadrangular plan that was already locked in place by architect Henry Ives Cobb's master plan for the University of Chicago. The women's dorm was in the southeast corner of the site with a frontage on the Midway Plaisance.

Figure 2.9. University of Chicago, 1892–93, Henry Ives Cobb, architect, rendering of master plan. Kelly, Green, and Beecher Halls are located at the lower left in this image. *Inland Architect* 22 (August 1893): n.p.

Although the women's halls were not stylistically different from the rest of Cobb's Gothic Revival campus, their internal organization showed the influence of female leaders (Plate 3).[41]

Working as a team, the two deans of women, Palmer and Talbot, tackled the job of making the large building feel smaller. Architectural historian Edward Wolner celebrates Palmer and Talbot's contribution to fitting these new dorms into the collegiate environment while at the same time achieving a balance between independence and social cohesion.[42] The deans accomplished this by breaking the side of the quadrangle into vertical subdivisions. These houses (as they were called) were named Kelly Hall, Beecher Hall, and Green Hall.[43] Kelly and Beecher were built first, with a space between them that was later filled in by Green Hall. Main entrances were on the ground floor on the inside of the quad. Each house offered rooms for forty students, and a housemother or dean lived in each house. An early brochure reproduced the plans, not giving any indication that the houses were part of a quadrangle.[44]

A less typical feature was the provision of doors between the bedrooms, which allowed the girls to go back and forth from single room to single room without moving through the corridor.[45] Talbot felt very strongly about this part of the

Figure 2.10. Beecher and Green Halls, University of Chicago, 1893–98, Henry Ives Cobb, architect, view from the courtyard. Photograph by author.

design, and five years later, in 1898, she expressed irritation with the architects when they attempted to eliminate the communicating doors from Green Hall.[46] She was offended that the architects and administrators did not recognize her years of expertise on the "domestic and social side of women's halls." She returned the insult: "In fact, I have never known a building planned and constructed so completely from a counting room and with as little regard to special needs as this [Green Hall] was in my experience." Finally, she noted:

> I am sure you will see it is entirely improper to require women to sleep in isolated rooms on the first floor of such a building. There should be opportunity to communicate with an adjoining room in case of illness. The experience we had in all the halls with burglars also makes it desirable that each woman should be able to reach easily another woman, as will be possible from all the rooms in the upper stories.[47]

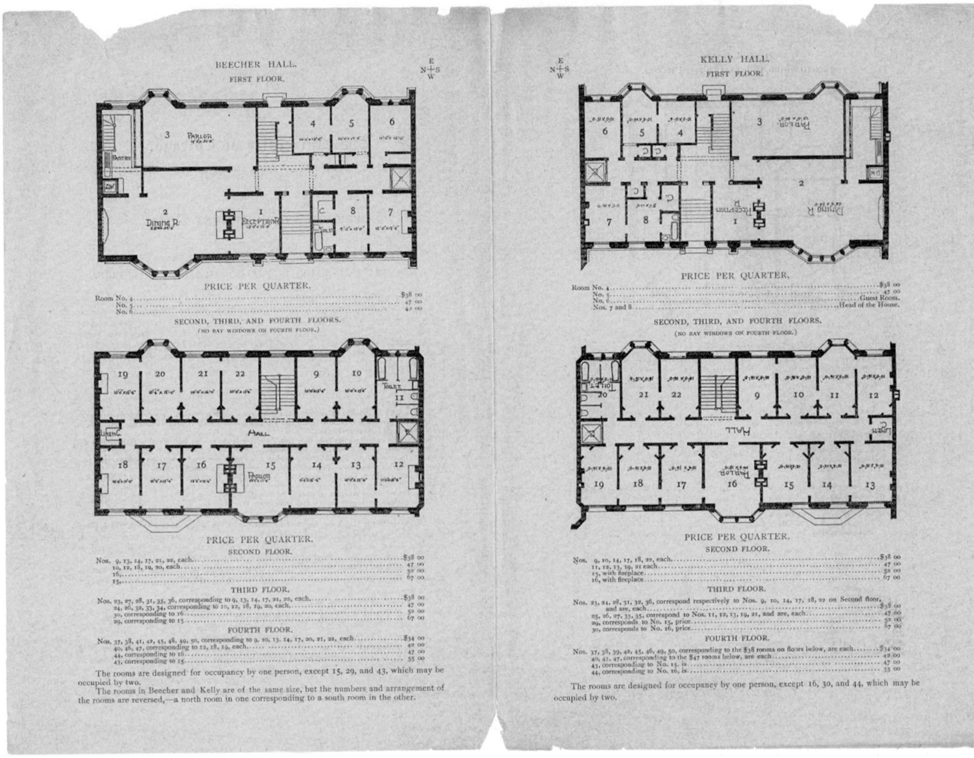

Figure 2.11. Beecher and Kelly Halls, University of Chicago, 1893–94, Henry Ives Cobb, architect, plans from a brochure sent to prospective students (no date). Beecher and Kelly flanked Green Hall, which was a later addition. From these two pages, it is not evident that the houses were not freestanding or that they formed one range of a quadrangle. Special Collections Research Center, University of Chicago Library.

Figure 2.12. Beecher, Green, and Kelly Halls, University of Chicago, 1893–98, Henry Ives Cobb, architect, plan, second floor. 1 = bedroom; 2 = corridor; 3 = additional door connecting bedrooms. The doors connecting bedrooms were intended as a safety feature: they allowed women to move from one bedroom to another without entering the corridor. Drawing by John Giganti.

Talbot eventually made the architects and university officials agree to include connecting doors on the upper floors as well as the lower ones. Clearly, protection and mutual care were among the special requirements for women's halls.

The women's dorms at Chicago contained more social and shared spaces than the men's dorms. Urban historian Robin Bachin points out that the men's dormitories lacked common rooms, whereas the women's dorms had "ample room for social gathering and communal assembly." Further, in women's dorms, "parlors and dining rooms provided suitable sites for sociability."[48] In contrast to the colonial- and Federal-era dorms described in chapter 1, which had no public spaces, these women's dormitories emphasized spaces for entertaining. Deans of women purposely engineered the social life of both male and female students so that it revolved around the women's dorms. Talbot believed that the women students should extend hospitality to the campus as a whole, because hospitality was part of the educational function of the dormitory: "An element of educational value is added to a college home when hospitality may be extended with freedom and ease, and in the new University the contribution of the Women's Halls to the general social life seemed of significance."[49] Talbot saw gracious entertaining as a worthwhile pursuit in itself. She was a fierce supporter of women's education, but she was not naive enough to think that all of her charges would achieve careers as doctors or lawyers. Since most female students were destined for lives as cultured middle- or upper-class housewives, she wanted the buildings to offer spacious common rooms that would bring gentlemen into a quasi-domestic sphere. This was an additional reason the women's dorms became the social heart of the whole university.

Another unusual planning feature was the inclusion of a "cooperative" kitchen in the basement that connected all three houses underground and was arranged to make the laborers' work more efficient.[50] Importantly, the students did not work in the kitchen. Nor was this the type of cooperative kitchen described by historian Elizabeth Cromley in relation to the collective apartment building; in that case, a communal kitchen managed by experts lifted the burden of preparing food from the shoulders of the single urban women living in the building.[51] For apartment-dwelling city spinsters, having food cooked and delivered was a liberating amenity, but for college women, it was de rigueur.[52]

A former classmate of Talbot, Ellen H. Swallow Richards, served as a faculty member in sanitary science at the Massachusetts Institute of Technology. Sparrow designed a cost-saving model kitchen for the 1893 Chicago World's Fair, and its up-to-date technology was moved from the fair to the University of Chicago.[53] Richards's kitchen, located below grade, provided food for the dining rooms in Kelly, Beecher, and Green Halls. In establishing the kitchen, these pioneering women—Talbot and Richards—had more on their minds than economy. The delivery of healthy food was directly related to the overall agenda of educating young women. As historian Margaret Lowe explains, maintaining the health of the female body was essential for convincing critics of coeducation that higher learning would not damage the girls.[54] Richards and Talbot even published a book based on research conducted in their first year at Chicago, in which they investigated the effects of diet on undergraduate women. They wryly observed that more effort had been made to study the diet of American cows than to study that of American citizens.[55] In *Food as a Factor in Student Life: A Contribution to the Study of Student Diet,* Richards and Talbot produced dozens of tables that compared different types of meat, amounts of protein, cost estimates, and the like, and made various conclusions about how to improve the health of female students. This preoccupation with the bodily vigor of female students can be traced back to Michigan dean Eliza Mosher's writings on proper female posture.

Richards and Talbot stated that they wanted their women's residence halls to have an atmosphere opposite of that found in typical boardinghouses.[56] They explained that the dormitory needed to be as decorous as possible, in addition to supporting the students physically. All types of boardinghouses were the subject of widespread moral concern in the nineteenth century, not just the ones that rented rooms to students. They lacked privacy and stable social structures, because tenants moved in and out all the time. The boardinghouse did not accord with middle- and upper-class values, which partly explains the disdain deans of women held for this building type. There were other reasons as well. For one thing, houses in town were difficult to supervise and thus undercut the deans' powers. Further, the houses were often decrepit and susceptible to fire. And trekking back and forth from boardinghouse to campus was tiring and time-consuming. At Cornell, the first woman to enroll dropped out partly because of the difficulty she faced daily as she climbed up and scampered down the steep hill between her boardinghouse and the campus in a long skirt and petticoat.[57]

In 1903, at the meeting of the Conference of Deans of Women of the Middle West (which was hosted by Talbot at Chicago), Myra Jordan of the University of Michigan reported that she and her staff inspected boardinghouses as well as they could, but there were always greedy landladies who "took lodgers solely for pecuniary profit."[58] At the same meeting, a dean from Ohio State University observed that sanitary conditions could not be controlled in boardinghouses. While it was not easy for a university to police properties owned by city residents, the deans of women successfully monitored the quality of the houses in which students resided by assessing the available houses and producing an official list of approved dwellings. To make the grade, a house had to let rooms to female students only, be in good condition, and have first-floor parlors.

Nonetheless, the boardinghouse haunted female educators for decades. In 1921, still concerned about living conditions in off-campus housing, the American Association of University Women conducted a survey of deans of women to collect data about housing conditions. The authors of the resulting report expressed regret that at most state universities, women's housing had been left up to private enterprise. A dean from an unnamed teachers' college was particularly vehement. She summarized the problems with rooming houses as follows: "scattered student body," "lack of college spirit," "impossibility of securing high social standards," "difficulty teaching morals," "inadequate heating," "incomplete and unattractive furnishings," "no provision for segregation in case of illness," and "no provision for quiet." She also commented on inadequate bathing facilities and inappropriate spaces for social interaction, as well as the difficulties of providing balanced meals and establishing fair prices.[59]

In contrast to Oberlin, where the students worked as part of their education, the female students at Chicago were relieved of such "duties as could be performed by others."[60] By not requiring women to work on campus, the deans allowed them to concentrate on their studies. The fact that the female students did not need to work is further evidence of the University of Chicago's embrace of the intellectual life of all students, including women. Oberlin certainly trained women's minds, but only at the undergraduate level, and the studies were balanced with physical work.

In 1907, a storm erupted over racially integrated housing when Georgiana Simpson, an African American PhD student in philology, moved into Green Hall.[61] Several white women protested. Talbot and her assistant, Sophonisba Breckinridge, defended Simpson's right to live in the dormitory and asked the complainers to move out. When President Harry Pratt Judson learned of the deans' actions, he reversed the decision, forced Simpson to move off campus, and put in place an informal policy that prohibited African Americans from living in university housing.[62] (Breckinridge later asserted herself as a major force in Chicago in the Progressive Era.)

Cobb's quadrangles were inward-facing. As Bachin notes, the names of the houses were posted on the inside of the buildings, facing the courtyard; thus the quadrangle plan, having no doors on the street, put up barriers to the neighborhood.[63] The square donut plan created a private, enclosed courtyard, but from the sidewalk, only off-putting stone walls were visible. Furthermore, as Bachin points out, President Ernest DeWitt Burton wanted to heighten the sense of enclosure by adding hedges to fill any gaps between the buildings.[64] The colleges at Oxford and Cambridge turned their backs on the small cities that housed them, and Chicago did the same. This ambitious new university was entirely separate from the City of the Big Shoulders. The life of the mind was incompatible with the grit of the mercantile city, especially when the safety of young women hung in the balance.

Judging from remarks made by the university's cashier (an administrative post similar to a bursar) in 1923, the dormitories were very popular with their target audience, white undergraduate women. The cashier complained to President Burton that only one-third of female students who wished to be housed on campus could be accommodated; given the limited number of dorm rooms available, he thought that preference should be given to the youngest girls: "It seems entirely logical to me that we ought to give the protection of the halls to the younger girls who need it most." He observed that the rooms off campus were "isolated and rather depressing."[65] He couched his concerns in the language of protection and made it seem as though the women's halls were *too* successful. The older students did not want to move out and make space for the incoming classes.

One University of Chicago student, Hedwig Loeb, composed a souvenir photograph album in 1899 that offers welcome glimpses into the inner workings of a women's dormitory.[66] In contrast to the "isolated and depressing" rooms at boardinghouses, Green Hall appears to have been a happy nest of communal cheerfulness. The photographs show girls spending time together in the hall and outside in the garden. They also document several of the young women's rooms. Hedwig decorated her room with textiles, porcelain busts and other knickknacks, and personal photographs, which she tacked to the wall. One photograph in the album showing some girls socializing is labeled "At a Spread." A spread was an informal party in a girl's room, occasioned by a package of special items from home, a school event, or a birthday.[67] It usually included treats like chocolate and cake. Spreads took place after curfew, and although they were technically against the rules, most deans tolerated them. Other photographs show girls playacting in corridors and bathrooms, offering rare glimpses of the well-built, unadorned, wood-trimmed service areas of these buildings. In one picture, we see a girl at a bathroom sink, and the caption in the album reads "Our Washer Lady," a joke that demarcated class difference. She was most certainly not a servant, even if she did occasionally do her own laundry.[68]

Figure 2.13. Hannah Loeb and three other students in Green Hall, University of Chicago, circa 1899. According to the 1900 census, Hedwig lived in Green Hall, and her sister, Hannah, lived in Beecher Hall. Hedwig Loeb's photo album, 1899–1900, Hedwig L. Loeb Papers, Special Collections Research Center, University of Chicago Library.

Figure 2.14. Hedwig Loeb's room in Green Hall, University of Chicago, circa 1899. Loeb decorated her room with patterned fabrics, sculptures, and photographs. Hedwig Loeb's photo album, 1899–1900, Hedwig L. Loeb Papers, Special Collections Research Center, University of Chicago Library.

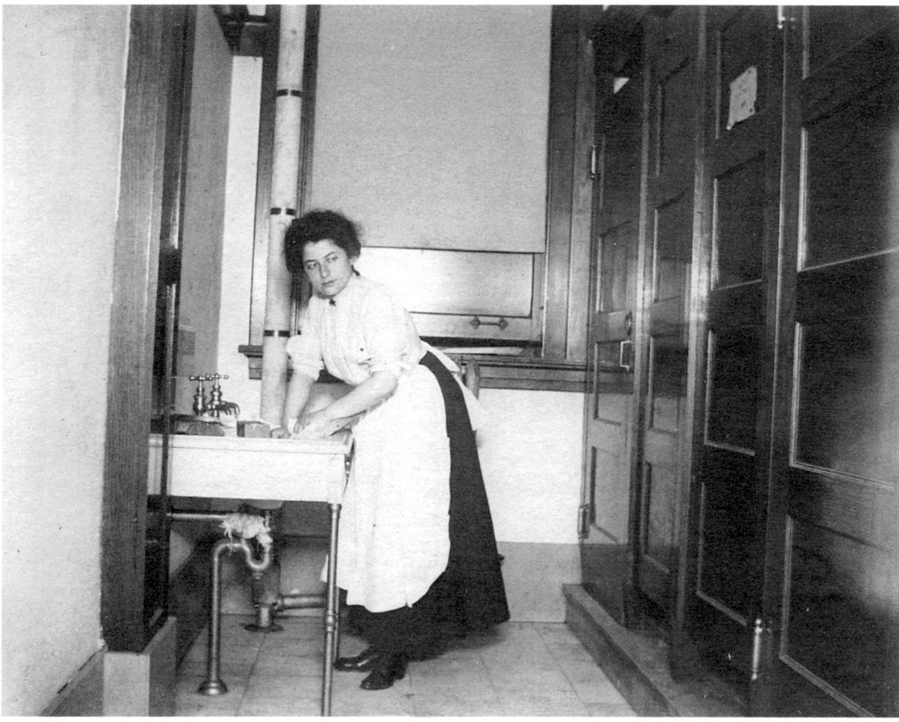

Figure 2.15. Student, probably Hannah Loeb, in the bathroom of Green Hall, University of Chicago, circa 1899. This photograph was jokingly labeled "Our Washer Lady." Hedwig Loeb's photo album, 1899–1900, Hedwig L. Loeb Papers, Special Collections Research Center, University of Chicago Library.

THE MARTHA COOK BUILDING AT THE UNIVERSITY OF MICHIGAN: A MODEL WOMEN'S DORMITORY

The University of Chicago's earliest women's dormitories left behind a cache of documents that offer rare insights into the lives of students. As we have seen, the male leaders of the university gave the deans of women room to maneuver, and the women adapted their ideas to preexisting architectural plans. As Deborah Miller has argued, the dormitory's "very emergence as a building type during the nineteenth century was predicated on women's struggle to gain access to higher education."[69] But in the particular case of the Martha Cook Building at the University of Michigan, there was no reform agenda. Instead, an opinionated male donor, William W. Cook, took charge of a very visible women's dorm. One might even reverse the argument in this case: Cook's conservativism may have been a response to the growing power of women.

Michigan's first president, Henry Tappan, advocated for the German system of higher education, thus emphasizing research and diminishing the residential college so beloved of Anglophiles. In his first annual report in 1853, Tappan called the dormitory "a mere remnant of the monkish cloisters of the middle ages, still retained in England . . . but banished from the Universities of Germany."[70] The anti-Catholic tone of Tappan's remarks is not surprising, given the period. Although Michigan was not officially affiliated with any particular religion, faculty and students were presumed to practice varieties of Protestantism. Tappan continued: "The Dormitory system is objectionable in itself. By withdrawing young men from domestic circles and forming them into a community, they are often led to contract evil habits, and are prone to fall into disorderly conduct. The difficulties of maintaining a proper discipline are thus greatly increased."[71] Tappan poured money into laboratories, libraries, and classrooms—spaces for the production of knowledge, not the lodging of bodies.

A chief difference between Oberlin and the University of Michigan, however, was that Michigan embraced fraternities (see chapter 1). Tappan did not foresee that fraternities were just as likely as dormitories to cause disciplinary problems—perhaps more so, given that secrecy was fundamental to their rites and that hazing often followed in the wake of secrecy.[72] Residences for Greek organizations, like Ann Arbor's large and elegant Psi Upsilon House, offered young men extracurricular activities and a sense of community within the larger university. "Like any society that includes some people and excludes others, fraternities gain prestige precisely through that exclusion," notes Syrett.[73] One can argue that fraternities did not introduce class distinctions to student life. Instead, they exacerbated socioeconomic disparities that were already there.

Fraternity men pushed the boundaries of acceptable student behavior. According to Syrett, "At some schools, men in fraternities, often under more lax supervision than those in dormitories, were able to bring women to the house for sexual entertainment."[74] At Michigan and other colleges, fraternity brothers made it known that so-called coeds were not allowed at their parties, and that local women were the preferred guests. The brothers saw lower-class women as sexually available and "ostracized those female classmates who threatened their hegemony on campus."[75]

From 1880 to 1900, groups of female University of Michigan students rented houses together in Ann Arbor. Attaching themselves to local sororities or national Greek letter organizations was a logical next step. The university had little control over the sororities, because it did not own their land or their houses.[76] The first charter for a sorority at UM was granted in 1879, but the organization did not have its own house at that time. Sororities offered strong friendship networks and some experience of self-governance, which were definite advantages, but they reached only a fraction of students. Clubs for privileged girls tended to be cliquish; for this reason, deans of women were wary of them. On the other hand, the deans found sororities to be better than boardinghouses, which they considered detrimental to young women's healthy development.

As a physician, Dean Mosher taught hygiene and managed the women's gymnasium.[77] When Mosher's successor, Myra Beach Jordan, took over the job of dean of women (which she held from 1902 to 1922), she asked to have her office in the gymnasium, even though the president offered her an office in Michigan's main administration building. The location of her office serves as further proof of the close association between establishing women in the university and strengthening their bodies.[78]

Jordan focused her work on improving the living conditions for women students. Under her leadership, the university built five new women's residence halls.[79] Jordan worked closely with the Women's League, a group of concerned alumnae who volunteered to assist female students, especially coeds who were isolated in boardinghouses.[80] The Women's League, formed in 1890, included both sorority sisters and independent students; it sponsored dances, teas, and other get-togethers, and members greeted new women students at the train station. League members raised money for a gymnasium and a playing field exclusively for women.[81] And they also fought hard for dormitories for women.

The energetic secretary of the Women's League was Myrtle White, who led an impressive fund-raising effort for a proposed new ladies' dormitory. White observed, "A great many parents will not send their daughters [to the University of Michigan], inasmuch as at eastern schools, better housing conditions are afforded."[82] She spent four months on a fund-raising trip on the East Coast, during which time she met wealthy lawyer William W. Cook, who agreed to speak to the university's president.[83] President Harry Burns Hutchins tracked White's activities, but she had a great deal of autonomy. She traveled with drawings for a potential new dorm prepared by Zachariah Rice of Detroit. The drawings showed a carefully composed Tudor Revival dormitory with pitched roofs and pointed arches along the facade on the ground floor.[84] There were two projections to either side of the porch, each of which contained a parlor. A dining room jutted out to the back. The second floor contained bedrooms and group bathrooms. Overall, the exterior had a decidedly domestic attitude, in spite of the building's large size.

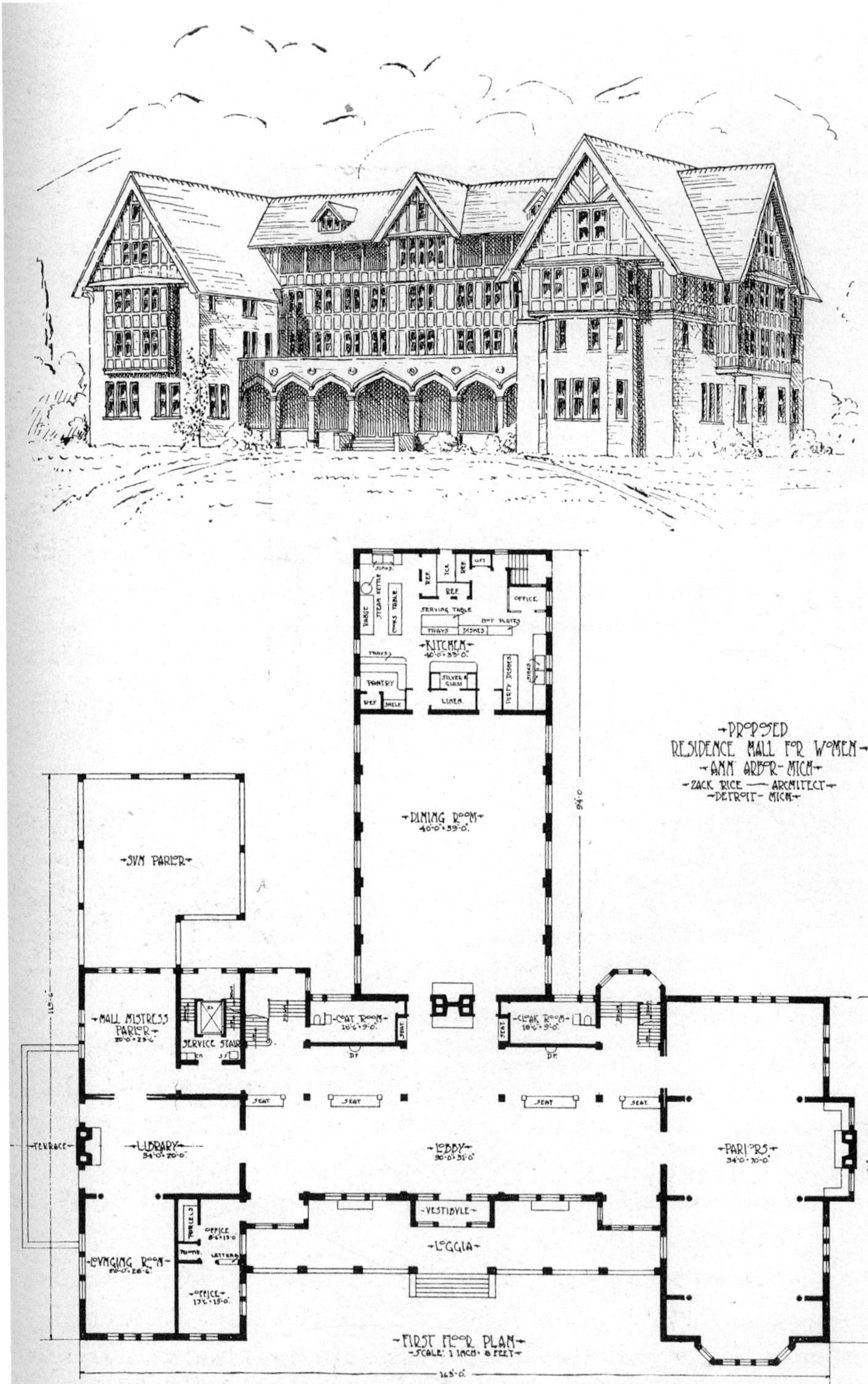

THE PROPOSED RESIDENCE HALL FOR WOMEN

Figure 2.16. Proposed residence hall for women, University of Michigan, 1910–11, Zachariah Rice, architect, view and plan, first floor (never built). *Michigan Alumnus* 17 (May 1911): 467. Bentley Historical Library, University of Michigan.

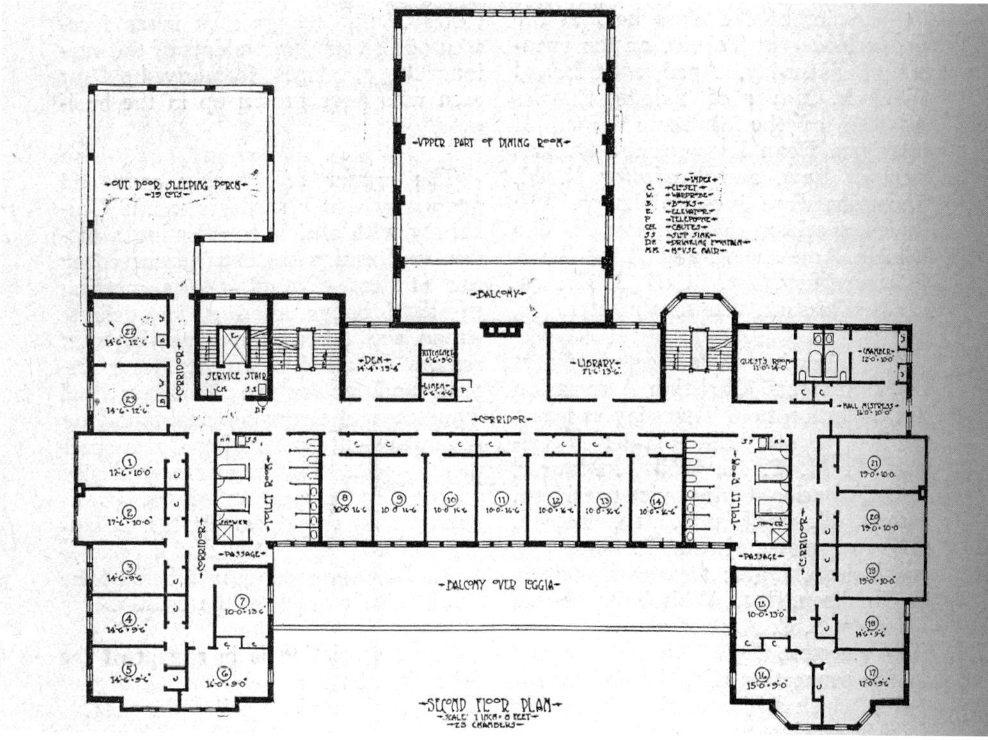

Figure 2.17. Proposed residence hall for women, University of Michigan, 1910–11, Zachariah Rice, architect, plan, second floor (never built). *Michigan Alumnus* 17 (May 1911): 466. Bentley Historical Library, University of Michigan.

Rice was generous with his time and effort and did not press the Women's League to pay him for his design work when it was short of funds.[85] In July 1911, he asked plaintively, "Are prospects for starting work growing any brighter?"[86] The answer was yes, but not for him. The Women's League garnered an enormous gift, and the University of Michigan built a splendid dorm, but Rice did not get the job.[87] Instead, Cook, the benefactor of this world-class women's dormitory, insisted on his own architects. Cook was a Michigan alumnus living in New York City, and he required that York & Sawyer, who had just built a house for him, design the model with its English references.

Cook's brother Chauncey was on the board of directors of the state asylum in Kalamazoo, so William Cook might have known something about purpose-built reformative communal dwellings. Perhaps William and Chauncey subscribed to the principle considered operative in the nineteenth century, that such buildings, if carefully and systematically designed, could transform their residents. Agnes

Parks, a leader of the Women's League, mentioned this affiliation jokingly in a letter to another alumna, noting that Chauncey Cook "has some decided opinions about buildings of this sort (having planned for crazy people)."[88] She hinted that Chauncey did not like Rice's plans, but she did not elaborate.

Cook was a lawyer, and the terms of his gift reflected his legal mind. He donated funds for the building, but the university had to agree to pay for the heat, light, and power in perpetuity.[89] The university also provided the land.[90] The dormitory would be managed by a board of directors made up of women appointed by the regents. Cook anticipated that the building might one day generate a surplus—if so, this profit was to be plowed back into the building in the form of furniture, works of art, and scholarships.[91] On February 10, 1914, he sent the official announcement of his gift. Eight days later, architect Edward P. York was in Michigan presenting plans to the regents. It seems reasonable to assume that Cook had engaged York & Sawyer in advance.

Cook had no interest in small plans.[92] In 1911, President Hutchins had asked him if he could spend Cook's initial $10,000 donation to buy the home of a retired professor in order to transform the house into a cottage for fewer than twenty girls. Cook shot down the request, writing, "The plan of purchasing a private residence for the accommodation of sixteen to twenty of your four hundred and fifty residents does not appeal to me from any point of view." Then, just as rudely, he continued: "A little later I may increase my subscription and help you to do something worth while."[93] From this exchange, it is clear that Cook thought cottages or retrofitted buildings were unsuitable. Perhaps he was impressed by contemporary dormitories at Bryn Mawr College, which were covered in *Architectural Record* in 1910.[94] Perhaps he wanted to make a larger impact. Or perhaps he strategized that a reused professor's house would not achieve one of his main goals, which was to create a refined space for the whole campus. Or maybe he had in mind a more generous gift that was befitting the memory of his mother, for whom the building was named. Based on Cook's dismissal of the small house and the subsequent form of the Martha Cook Building, we know that he preferred the large-scale building over the cottage plan (Plate 4).

The Martha Cook Building had one main entry, on the street, on the short end of the building. The matron's office was adjacent to the door, and all the main entertainment rooms were on the first floor, off a long groin-vaulted corridor. The gallery on the first floor was on the long side of the building, the east, and offered access to a terrace and views of the garden. The shared rooms on the west side included spacious parlors. It was helpful to have the formal, social rooms on the first floor, because they were used by other constituents, including family members and male visitors.

Figure 2.18. Martha Cook Building, University of Michigan, 1915, York & Sawyer, architects. Martha Cook Building Records, Bentley Historical Library, University of Michigan.

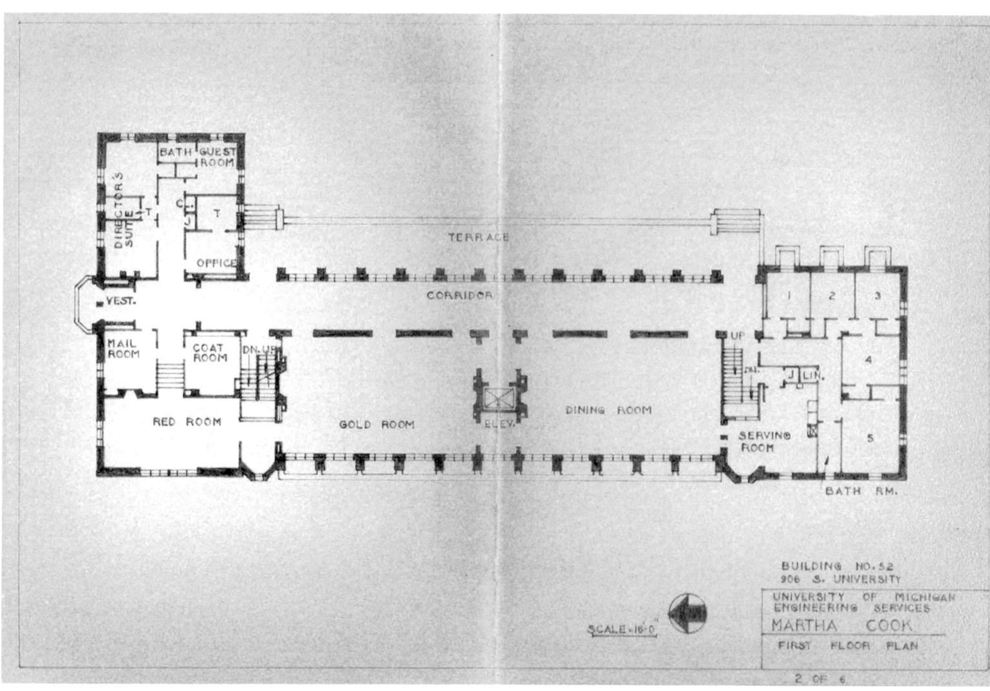

Figure 2.19. Martha Cook Building, University of Michigan, 1915, York & Sawyer, architects, plan, first floor. Martha Cook Building Records, Bentley Historical Library, University of Michigan.

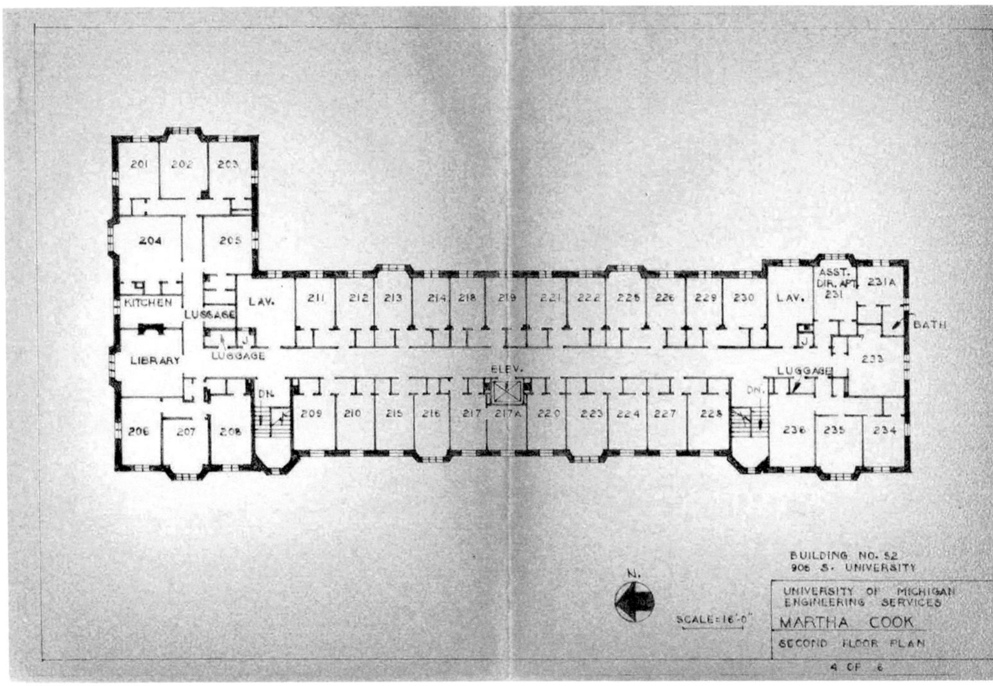

Figure 2.20. Martha Cook Building, University of Michigan, 1915, York & Sawyer, architects, plan, second floor. Martha Cook Building Records, Bentley Historical Library, University of Michigan.

Student bedrooms cascaded along double-loaded corridors on the second, third, and fourth floors. In each room, just inside the door that opened to the corridor, there was a transitional space that contained a sink and closet. The advantage of this arrangement was that girls did not need to go down the hall to the group bathroom to wash their faces or brush their teeth, and the group bathrooms did not require as many sinks. The group bathrooms included showers, bathtubs, and toilets. Most of the bedrooms were singles. As the development of the Martha Cook Building demonstrates, the architects and the patron worked to create an exemplary structure, deliberating every decision and carefully considering programming issues. In Cook's words, "The social life of the university should be dominated, led, moulded, and perfected by the charm of the Martha Cook Building."[95]

Soon after the building opened, Cook wrote to his brother Chauncey and argued for keeping the cost of room and board low so that "poor girls" could have some of the "luxuries of life" that others enjoyed, but his later comments contradicted his earlier sympathy for less affluent girls.[96] Nine years after the dormitory opened, he promoted the acceptance of "girls of a high social type" only. He wrote

Figure 2.21. Martha Cook Building, University of Michigan, 1915, York & Sawyer, architects, upstairs corridor. Photograph by author.

Figure 2.22. Martha Cook Building, University of Michigan, 1915, York & Sawyer, architects, typical student bedroom. Almost all of the rooms in this building were singles. Martha Cook Building Records, Bentley Historical Library, University of Michigan.

that recruiters should avoid "straight-A students," because they had a "blue stocking tang that is entirely out of place." (A bluestocking was a woman with a taste for literature and scholarship, and such women were assumed to be unattractively studious.) He hammered on this point: "How to act is as important to a woman as how to think."[97] Cook's ultimate motive was *not* to produce an egalitarian environment that would lead to equal opportunity for women and men.

Only white American girls of Anglo-Saxon descent were welcome. Cook bluntly rejected diversity. As he put it: "I don't see why the Orientals are there. That building is not the League of Nations."[98] In his quest to create young women of outstanding sophistication and savoir faire, Cook paid particular attention to the qualities of the housemistress. He wrote to the building's board of directors to ask them to fire the social director, Miss Clark, whom he had never met. He noted there was little for the social director to do, other than "cultivate in the occupants the social graces, [and] this Miss Clark cannot do, because she hasn't them herself."[99] Cook intended for his building to offer further refinement for the already well-heeled. Promoting intellectual equality was not on the agenda; instead, his goal was to use the dormitory as a charm school within the greater university.

The reception rooms on the ground floor were essential to the social engineering aspect of Cook's strategy, because events at the residence hall—receptions, concerts, and teas—were intended to have a civilizing influence on anyone who attended. The Gold Room and the Red Room were both elegantly appointed parlors, with soft upholstered furniture that mimicked what might be found in an upper-class home.[100] In contrast, the interiors of fraternities resembled urban men's clubs, which were quasi-public spaces.[101] A Steinway piano with an elaborately painted art case added gilt to the Gold Room's lily. As Annmarie Adams shows in her analysis of gendered interiors at the Royal Victoria Hospital, male medical students played billiards, whereas female nurses tickled the ivories.[102] Just off the

Figure 2.23. Martha Cook Building, University of Michigan, 1915, York & Sawyer, architects, Gold Room. Martha Cook Building Records, Bentley Historical Library, University of Michigan.

Gold Room, there was a space nicknamed "the sparking nook," a bench with enough room for one highly respectable society girl, one suitor, and one chaperone. Martha Cook coeds were groomed to be brides.

From Cook's perch in New York City, he might have witnessed various examples of the New Woman—women riding bicycles, wearing bloomers, and fighting for suffrage—but these were not the sorts of girls he sought for the Martha Cook Building, as the motto over the fireplace in the dining room, which he devised himself, made clear. The dining room was centrally located on the first floor, and it accommodated all the residents at once, about 110 women. Over the fireplace, the words "Home: The Nation's Safety" summarized Cook's intention that the university would "preserve the home and reconcile it with the public duties which woman is rapidly assuming."[103] He accepted that women were entering public life, but he believed that the primary role of a woman was to act as the virtuous center of the family and the caretaker of the home. Cook may have been nostalgic for earlier times, when women's sphere was more clearly defined as the home; after all, the name of the building memorialized his mother, whom he remembered as a dutiful, nurturing parent.[104]

Inscribed above the dining room fireplace and writ large in the whole building, Cook's moral lessons were aimed at men as well as women. He argued that the residence hall "should have a definite social purpose to improve the manners of the University, especially of the barbaric young men."[105] Fraternity men were probably the targets of this comment, given that their private houses were sites of alcohol consumption, illicit sex, and other controversial behaviors. Although there were non-Greek venues for parties and dances, such as gymnasiums and YMCAs, fraternities dominated social life on every campus that permitted them to exist, and since they excluded many people, many college officials perceived a need to have non-Greek spaces for social interaction.

For support of the idea of the dormitory as a shared social space, we can look back to the men's dormitories at Chicago, which had no common rooms, while the women's residence halls on Talbot's campus had spacious social rooms for parties.[106] In a related case, the Royal Victoria College, a women's residence hall at McGill University, held many public social events, including concerts, dances, and receptions. The hall had the nicest rooms on campus, and men from various departments of the university booked them so often that it became an annoyance for the warden.[107]

Ephemera in college archives offer glimpses into what these social activities entailed. There are invitations to dances and teas, dance cards, pictures of "baby day" (when the girls played with the small children of faculty families), playbills from talent shows and theater productions, and menus from formal dinners. Gracious entertaining was a worthwhile pursuit in itself. Students in the 1910s and 1920s had many more options than the previous generation, and although most women graduates married, they also pursued vocations for a short time after college. It was having children that prevented them from continuing to work.[108]

Cook was an unusually attentive patron who cared deeply about the interior decoration of the public spaces of his building. One of his pet projects was a copy of the Venus de Milo, carved from marble on a slightly smaller scale than the original. To this day, it occupies a place of honor in the Martha Cook Building as the focal point of the long first-floor corridor. It is the first thing a visitor sees upon entering the building. It also appears in numerous photographs, as a sort of mascot. Martha Cook residents, known as "Cookies," posed in the corridor

Figure 2.24. Martha Cook Building, University of Michigan, 1915, York & Sawyer, architects, group of women in the main downstairs corridor, photograph circa 1920. The copy of Venus de Milo is visible in the background. Martha Cook Building Records, Bentley Historical Library, University of Michigan.

wearing white dresses and holding musical instruments while the goddess of love looked over their shoulders.

York & Sawyer accepted the Venus with good humor, but they were not pleased with Cook's intention to furnish a Minerva sculpture for the niche above the outside door. The problem, as they saw it, was that a classical goddess could not be shoehorned into the Tudor Gothic exterior. The architects recommended a medieval figure and gave a rather drawn-out explanation:

> In placing the classic Venus in the place of chief importance in a building used by the modern woman, Mr. Spicer-Simson [the sculptor] suggested an historical sequence in which the Venus and the girl-students form the two extremes, and we wonder whether you would not find it appropriate to place over the entrance the mean of these extremes, the Medieval lady, a Figure representing the highest type of womanhood which exists midway between antiquity and the present.[109]

Cook dismissed the idea of "the Medieval lady" and further specified that saints and angels must be avoided. Instead, he told York & Sawyer to command the sculptor to "get busy" on a statue of "Shakespeare's greatest lawyer, who exposed 'quaint lies,' and brought to book the bloodthirsty Jew—a full-throated woman, of vivacity, poise and feminine charm."[110] Again, in his selection and characterization of Portia from the *Merchant of Venice,* Cook displayed anti-Semitic attitudes that were typical of his time, and his dislike of saints and angels probably reflected a distaste for popery and Catholic immigrants. His choice of a lawyer for the statue was also meaningful, given that he was a graduate of Michigan's law school, and his next donation to UM—a huge one indeed—was to build a state-of-the-art law school with an integrated men's residence hall, about three times the size of the Martha Cook Building and across the street from it. Portia can see it from her niche.

Significantly, when the Law Quadrangle was constructed in 1922–23, just a few years after the Martha Cook Building, it used the staircase (or entryway) plan, with doors that opened to an outside courtyard—not the single front door with internal double-loaded corridors. Men's dormitories had a long history of using the entryway plan.[111] This specific comparison at UM helps to isolate the gender issue, because the Law Quad was paid for by the same patron (Cook), designed by the same architects (York & Sawyer), and built within the same decade on the same college campus.[112] Although there were men's dorms that used the economic and space-saving double-loaded corridor, in this particular case, the university adopted the staircase plan, which allowed the men greater freedom of movement and placed the coeds under tighter control. Margaret Vickery describes a similar situation at the founding of Girton College for women at Cambridge. There the staircase system used for men's colleges was rejected and an interior corridor plan used instead. The corridor plan offered greater community than the staircase plan, because with "no connecting corridor, each student would be isolated in her own stairwell from the mistress and those students who did not share her stairwell."[113] One measure of the porosity of the staircase plan is that it was not used for prisons or asylums.

When completed, the Martha Cook Building was admired as far away as Australia. E. R. Holme praised it as the best of its kind. Holme lauded American universities generally for their emphasis on communal living, and he was pleased to observe that the residential impulse was moving from private colleges into

Figure 2.25. Law Quadrangle, University of Michigan, 1922–23, York & Sawyer, architects, view of the courtyard. The doors that opened to the courtyard led to student bedrooms. Bentley Historical Library, University of Michigan.

state-funded ones. He wrote that the best state universities were embarking on ambitious dormitory construction projects:

> Michigan already possesses, by the generosity of a private benefactor, perhaps the most beautiful dormitory for women in America—the Martha Cook Hall. It is a large and stately building of the collegiate type in a prominent position near the other University buildings. The architect had quite a free hand to make it a model of its kind. From entrance hall to kitchens it combines utility with comeliness and its two great purposes—to be a worthy memorial to a good woman, and to provide some of the women-students of Michigan a collegiate home fitted by its beauty and convenience for all the needs of individual study and common life.[114]

Holme zeroed in on the building's exceptional qualities: that it demonstrated a high level of architectural finesse, that it was a successful as a "collegiate home," and that within it the individual—as part of a community—could thrive.

From the colonial period until World War I, American higher education was intended for boys and dominated by men. Women were accommodated unevenly, in fits and starts, and with bumps along the way. At Oberlin, Cornell, and Michigan, the first women's dormitories preceded the first men's dormitories. While Oberlin shunned fraternities, Cornell and Michigan embraced them. Compared to Greek organizations, dormitories were more democratic, because they were open to any student. Deans of students celebrated the dormitory as an essential part of the educational experience, one that enhanced morality and character. Some students agreed. As the 1916 Michigan yearbook intoned: "Contact with his fellows affords the only means whereby the vulgarian or the prig can be rendered good company for intelligent men and women."[115] The physical space of the residence hall made such personal development much more likely to occur; living in a boardinghouse offered no such advantages.

Standing as they did on prominent sites in college towns, women's dormitories at coed colleges demonstrated that so-called coeds were there to stay. On the other hand, elegant residence halls advertised that women required special care. There is nothing particularly surprising about the fact that nineteenth-century reformers (even the most progressive) thought women needed surveillance and protection. It is, however, historically significant that women's dormitories served as on-campus social centers, albeit closely chaperoned ones. It was even hoped that these feminine spaces would tame unruly male students.

3

Quadrangles in the Early Twentieth Century

The dormitory declined in popularity during the last quarter of the nineteenth century, but it made a stunning comeback in the early twentieth century, when college leaders convinced many people that living on campus promoted the good character of students. More specifically, American educators sought to emulate aspects of the education offered by Oxford and Cambridge. Charles Van Hise, president of the University of Wisconsin, stated in 1903 that if one were to name the most fundamental characteristic of these English institutions, it would be "the system of halls of residence." He then went on to make an astonishing claim—that those residential colleges gave rise to the British Empire:

> The college system may seem absurd, but for some reason these universities have produced an astonishingly large proportion of great statesmen, writers and scientists. The men of Oxford and Cambridge have been largely instrumental in extending the empire of Britain over the earth; they have contributed liberally to the greatest literature of the world; they have furnished many fundamental ideas to science. In view of these stupendous results we need scarcely wonder that the Englishman is not eager to make over Oxford and Cambridge after the Yankee or German model.[1]

This rather extreme endorsement acts as a starting point for this chapter, which explores the ascent of student affairs, the quadrangle, and the residential college in the United States at the beginning of the twentieth century. By looking at a range of colleges, we can explore the intense affection for the dormitory as a space that shaped student character. University officials claimed that residence halls were essential contributors to higher education. The kind of social exchange that transformed inchoate children into responsible moral adults did not take place in the classroom; it took place *outside the classroom.* As Van Hise asserted: "Nothing a professor or a laboratory can do for the student can take the place of the daily close companionship with hundreds of his fellows."[2] Furthermore, we can see the quadrangle as an ideal form for networking and sociability.

WHAT IS A QUADRANGLE?

The term *quadrangle* has two primary meanings in collegiate architecture. In one use, it refers to a collection of boxy structures arranged around a rectangular open space. This whole ensemble is often called "the Quad," as is the case at the University of Alabama, the University of Missouri, the University of Rochester, the University of Illinois at Urbana–Champaign, and dozens of other colleges. The kind of quadrangle of interest here, however, is the single building in the shape of a square donut. This is the traditional shape of the cloister in a monastery or an Italian Renaissance palazzo. Sometimes, quadrangles of this type are linked to one another in series, as in the quintessential form seen in the medieval institutions of Oxford and Cambridge (see Figure I.11).[3] In addition to calling up visions of Oxbridge, the geometry of the quadrangle creates an enclosed, private outdoor space, which reinforces the smallness of a community within the larger university and sets a firm boundary that prevents the outside world's possible encroachment.

THE STUDENT PERSONNEL MOVEMENT: THE PROFESSIONALIZATION OF DEANS OF WOMEN AND DEANS OF MEN

In the early twentieth century, college professionals began to assert their concern for the "whole student" in every aspect of college management. They sought to reconnect the college's intellectual life to its social life. According to historians John Brubacher and Willis Rudy, "This is the development which has interested educational visitors from abroad more than any other aspect of American higher learning. In most other countries, students in institutions of higher education have been regarded as responsible adults, and the province of the university has been thought to be strictly that of training the mind. In the United States by way of contrast, college students have been thought of as immature adolescents, requiring guidance at every return."[4] Julie Reuben has explored how professors became increasingly focused on their own research agendas and grew weary of the pastoral care of students, a role shortly taken up by deans of men and women. As she explains: "In the 1920s renewed interest in the community life of students and expanding enrollments pushed dormitories into the forefront of university concerns. University presidents regularly discussed the beneficial influence of dormitories."[5] Deans of women and deans of men decisively took up the mantle of teaching democratic values to their charges, and the residence hall was the greatest tool in their tool kit.

The deans went through a self-conscious process of professionalization, which, although well known to historians of higher education, is mostly unfamiliar to architectural historians, thus I will briefly review it here. In previous chapters, I have noted the importance of deans of women at Oberlin, the University of Chicago, the University of Michigan, and other colleges. According to some accounts, Marianne Dascombe became the first student affairs officer when she took the position of principal of the Female Department at Oberlin College in 1834.[6] Historian of education Michael Hevel explains the overlapping causes that led to the rise of student affairs: college presidents and faculty members lost interest in monitoring students "at the same time that coeducation spread, generating public concern that such monitoring was never more important."[7] In chapter 2, we met Alice Freeman Palmer, the first person to hold the title dean of women, which she took when she left the presidency of Wellesley to move to the University of Chicago in 1892. She was followed in the job by Marion Talbot, who also loomed large in the growing profession. As Hevel notes: "The dean of women position spread fast and far. A survey of 55 institutions in 1911 revealed that 44 (80%) employed a dean of women."[8] Almost twenty years went by before Thomas Arkle Clark's post at the University of Illinois was assigned the title dean of men in 1909.[9] As noted in chapter 2, at some coed schools, like Oberlin and the University of Michigan, dormitories for women preceded those for men; in the same way, the office of the dean of women preceded the office of the dean of men. This did not necessarily bode well for female administrators. As Jana Nidiffer observes, "The beginning of the end of the position of dean of women was the creation of the position of dean of men."[10]

Both groups of university leaders (women and men) emphasized architecture as an agent of reform. The first meeting of deans of women of the Midwest was in 1903; it was followed in 1910 by the first national meeting of deans of women. Deans of women from both private and public colleges attended these conferences. The first meeting of deans of men was not held until 1919. The "student personnel movement" grew in esteem in the 1920s, taking as its model personnel management in the world of business and government, or what today would be called human resources. In a corporation, the idea was to match up workers with specific jobs to improve efficiency. In colleges, the goal was to help each individual student align his or her strengths with an appropriate major as well as activities, clubs, and housing options. Proponents of this view broadened the concept of education to include physical, social, emotional, and spiritual functioning—not just intellectual advancement. Furthermore, the student was assumed to be "a responsible participant in his own development and not . . . a passive recipient of an imprinted economic, political, or religious doctrine, or vocational skill."[11] In short, the student personnel point of view considered the student as a whole.

WHAT DID DEANS OF WOMEN DO?

As discussed in chapter 2, Palmer, Talbot, and other female leaders sought to assist women students in intellectual, physical, and social venues. The diverse concerns of deans of women included their charges' involvement with cars, mixed-gender houses, food, and sex. In 1903, the automobile posed a new threat. During that year's meeting of midwestern deans of women, Miss Mayhew, dean of women at the University of Wisconsin, said that if students went out in a car, they were required to return to their housing by 8:00 p.m. Dean Luce of Oberlin stated that a woman was not allowed to be in an automobile with a man unless there was a chaperone also present—which would seem to have eliminated two-seat vehicles. Dean Slowe at Howard forbade all motoring. Mixed-gender boardinghouses were another hot-button issue. Mrs. Jordan of the University of Michigan objected to men and women dwelling in the same house and forbade male students from visiting female students at any boardinghouse that did not have a first-floor parlor. Miss Evans from Northwestern reported (with a distinct tone of disdain) that in California, it was "customary for men and women to live in the same houses, and for men to be received in bed-rooms."[12] Food was a perennial agenda item. All the deans agreed in 1903 that healthy food was imperative, just as they concurred that nutritious fare was easier to provide in a dormitory than in hundreds of disparate boardinghouses run by different people with profit (rather than gastronomy) as their goal. The subject of sex caused lightheadedness. At the 1910 national meeting of deans of women, a dean from the University of California at Berkeley said that she found that "some women always faint in Freshman Hygiene when the subject of menstruation comes up," but when it came to general "sex questions," men keeled over even more readily than women.[13] Secret weddings were another heated topic. Mayhew objected strenuously to covert nuptials among students, noting that any student who married secretly should be forced to withdraw. Her rationale was that such marriages were likely to be against the wishes of the students' parents, or else they would not be secret. In addition, they led to scandalous

Plate 1. Nassau Hall, Princeton University, 1754–56, Robert Smith, architect; cupola added in 1855 by architect John Notman. This stately building, with its central tower, was a model for many later college buildings. Nassau Hall contained all the functions of the early college, including housing for students. Photograph by Elijah D. Reiss.

Plate 2. Old West, Dickinson College, 1803–5, Benjamin Henry Latrobe, architect, watercolor by Latrobe, 1802. The emptiness of the landscape illustrates the isolation of some colonial- and Federal-era colleges. At Dickinson, college leaders provided housing for students because there were not enough boardinghouses in that rural part of the state. Archives and Special Collections, Dickinson College.

Plate 3. Kelly, Green, and Beecher Halls, University of Chicago, 1893–98, Henry Ives Cobb, architect. This side of the quadrangle contained three housing units for female students. Photograph by author.

Plate 4. Martha Cook Building, University of Michigan, 1915, York & Sawyer, architects. This view of the exemplary women's dormitory shows a generous terrace and its private lawn on the long side of the thin rectangular structure; the main entrance was on the short end of the building facing the street. Postcard. Collection of the author.

Plate 5. Adams and Tripp Halls with refectory, University of Wisconsin–Madison, 1924–26, Arthur Peabody, architect. Adams and Tripp Halls were the first dormitories for men at the University of Wisconsin in two generations; the entirely enclosed quadrangles recalled medieval colleges but limited students' views of the lake. Postcard. Collection of the author.

Plate 6. Interior of a typical bedroom in one of the University of Wisconsin–Madison's first men's dormitories, from a brochure directed to potential residents published in 1926. The welcoming interior and small social groups in this dormitory complex were intended to recruit male students who would otherwise join fraternities. Courtesy of the University of Wisconsin–Madison Archives (2018s00144).

Plate 7. Harkness Memorial Quadrangle, Yale University, 1917, James Gamble Rogers, architect. This ample quadrangle set the keynote for the Gothic Revival at Yale and nostalgically employed gray stone over a steel frame, reminiscent of the residential colleges of Oxford and Cambridge. It predates the fully developed residential college system at Yale. Postcard. Collection of the author.

Plate 8. River Dorms, Rutgers University, 1955–56, Kelly and Gruzen, architects. This set of three modernist slabs along the Raritan River let everyone know that the state university was looking toward the future, not the past, and thus rejecting the elitism associated with collegiate Gothic, neo-Georgian, and other historicist styles. The dean of men argued against balconies on every room, which was the preference of the architects; they reached a compromise by placing balconies on lounges. Postcard. Collection of Elijah D. Reiss.

Plate 9. New York University Uptown, 1956–61, Marcel Breuer and Associates, architects. This building complex included a dormitory, a community hall (with dining), a combined laboratory–classroom building, and a lecture hall in distinctive rough-cast concrete. The underside of the sculptural lecture hall can be seen set against the smoother surface of the laboratory–classroom building (originally called the Hall of Technology), which was clad in beige brick to resemble nearby buildings in color if not in style. Photograph by author.

Plate 10. The lofty heights of Lincoln and Morrill Towers balanced the considerable heft of the football stadium at the Ohio State University. Constructing such tall dormitories left green space at ground level for playing fields. *The Makio* (yearbook), 1967. The Ohio State University Archives.

Plate 11. Morse and Stiles Colleges, Yale University, 1958–62, Eero Saarinen, architect. In rejecting the quadrangle in favor of the hill town, this building ensemble retained the private courtyard space of a traditional Yale college, but with a range of building heights, crooked paths, and rough-hewn walls. Library of Congress, Prints and Photographs Division, Balthazar Korab Archive at the Library of Congress.

Plate 12. Cowell College, University of California, Santa Cruz, 1963–66, Wurster, Bernardi and Emmons, architects. A Mediterranean feel permeated Cowell College, where outdoor spaces provided opportunities for casual meetings among the tall trees in the mild climate. Courtesy Special Collections, University Library, University of California, Santa Cruz.

Plate 13. Kresge College, University of California, Santa Cruz, 1967–73, MLTW, architects. An Italian hill town was the inspiration for this postmodern residential college, with street-like spaces painted bright white with colorful accents. Its main streets snaked through the redwoods, and it consisted of apartments rather than traditional dormitories. Photograph by Marc Treib.

Plate 14. The District on Apache, near Arizona State University, Tempe, 2015, Humphreys & Partners, architects. Today's residence halls (many of which, like this one, are privately managed rather than run by the colleges where they are located) feature amenities reminiscent of water parks to compete for student residents. Photograph by author.

rumors (when the students lived separately and yet maintained conjugal relations) and sent other parents an alarming message when they learned of the university's dereliction of duty.[14] An overarching goal for women deans was to protect female students' marriageability.

WHAT DID DEANS OF MEN DO?

The work of a dean of men was similar to that of a dean of women, but without the academic component. Deans of men paid more attention to solving issues related to drunkenness, dishonesty, and violence. Certainly deans of women had to handle cases of inebriation and cheating, too, but fisticuffs and brawling were less frequent among the coeds. In the records of the annual conferences of deans of men, beginning in 1919 and stretching to the mid-1930s, the frustration of the deans is palpable. They believed that other university officials held little respect for their expertise. Student discipline was the "most visible responsibility of deans of men," but the deans themselves did not see that as their true calling.[15] Deans of men hoped to serve as positive role models, not disciplinarians; in fact, the two roles (friendly adviser versus policeman) were at odds. Most deans of men were concerned with creating an atmosphere of mutual respect and fellowship. In contrast to deans of women, who were at the top of the hierarchy of female academics, and who reported directly to their institutions' presidents, deans of men were in a middling position, with many other men ahead of them on the organizational ladder. The dean of men at Purdue, Stanley Coulter, complained in 1934, "I discovered that every unpleasant task that the president or the faculty did not want to do was my task."[16] Knowing that most professors and students thought of deans of men as cruise directors and killjoys only made them crave respect more desperately. If you were a dean of men seeking respect, the residential colleges of Oxbridge were a handy vehicle—why not hitch your wagon to the medieval model, which was old, prestigious, not entirely academic, and required an adept administrator?

THE DORMITORY AS A RESPONSE TO FRATERNITIES

At universities with fraternities, the deans of men held a modicum of authority over the Greeks, but often in an ambiguous and symbolic way. A majority of deans found fraternities to be a threat to the democratic life of colleges. Once a campus had fraternities, the Greeks dominated social life, which meant that the richest boys ruled. The fraternity men also held most of the important extracurricular jobs on campus, from running the newspaper to leading the glee club. One of the best ways for a university to counteract the power of fraternities was to build dormitories. This is not to say that deans of men opposed fraternities—they merely wanted to add housing options for the non-Greeks as part of working toward a more level playing field for all students.

At the 1930 national meeting of deans of men, the participants tackled the fraternity problem head on. One dean noted that at some campuses, the fraternity men were well housed, but every other man was left to "fend for himself."[17] He went on to state:

> A comprehensive housing program is a necessary plank in any college or university's platform. And the strongest force behind seeing that such a policy is put into effect should be the Dean of Men. This merely emphasizes that we deans of men must acquaint ourselves thoroughly with dormitory and fraternity architecture.[18]

Also at the 1930 meeting, S. L. Rollins, dean of men at Northwestern, spoke plaintively: "[Another] undesirable result is the situation where the fraternity men are well housed while the independent men are not. This inequality in housing is the predominant cause for the feeling of inferiority and the feeling of animosity toward the fraternity system by the independents."[19] Today it might seem laughably naive that he thought animosity arose from poor housing, rather than from economic, racial, and religious discrimination. He went on to say that it was not the fault of fraternities that such animus existed, and that fraternity men could not be expected to solve a problem they had not created. It was the university's job to intervene and smooth the torn fabric of college life by constructing good dormitories.[20] He argued that a college needed a comprehensive housing policy that would cover all students, whether they dwelled in fraternities, dormitories, or boardinghouses. (By boardinghouses, he meant everything from tall brick apartment buildings to small frame cottages.)[21]

Deans also served as liaisons between students and the wider community. Dean Scott Goodnight at the University of Wisconsin caught the brunt of this on several occasions. Goodnight admired fraternity men for their school spirit and fun-loving ways, but when their antics got them into trouble, he was on the hook. Judge Ole A. Stolen, who handled the delinquency cases for the county in which Madison was situated, wrote to Goodnight to excoriate fraternities for corrupting young boys. Stolen said that juveniles (ages thirteen to sixteen) had appeared before him in court charged with breaking and entering: they had been stealing the fraternities' empty whisky bottles to sell to bootleggers.[22] These Prohibition-era fraternities were not only in trouble for consuming alcohol and consorting with lawbreakers, they were also complicit in the criminal downfall of boys. This is one of hundreds of examples that can be gleaned from student newspapers, archives, and other sources from the period. Thus deans of men emerged *because of* and *in reaction to* fraternities.

THE DORMITORY AS A RESPONSE TO BOARDINGHOUSES: "OUR WEAKEST POINT"

In 1925, Dean Robert Reinow of the University of Iowa complained that there was no supervision over students living in boardinghouses: "It is our weakest point and that is why we are going to spend money on dormitories immediately."[23] One of the curious aspects of the boardinghouse arrangement was that the landladies (and most were ladies) were in an odd relationship with the university. In a sense, they were unpaid, unsupervised employees—and the colleges could not have existed without them. During the 1920s phase of the development of student affairs, a primary role for deans was the inspection of private boardinghouses. At one university, the deans of men and women together inspected more than one thousand houses.[24] Such inspections were undertaken once a year, during the summer months. The rest of the time, it was difficult for the deans to know what was happening with students in the boardinghouses unless they received complaints from students or parents. Some grievances were about price gouging, as when a landlady in Madison increased a student's rent from sixty dollars per semester to ninety dollars; the parent blamed the dean, and the dean blamed the property owner.[25] A more scandalous example of boardinghouse trouble was reported in the *Washington Post* even though it occurred in Madison, Wisconsin. Judge Stolen, apparently a thorn in Dean Goodnight's side, gave a speech at a local church in which he assailed the morals of male college students. The judge said he knew that taxis were called to "the men's rooming houses," and "drunken girls wrapped in blankets" were taken in said taxis back to their rooms.[26] In addition to causing trauma to the women, these incidents served to demonstrate how unsafe living off campus could be. This made the construction of new dormitories seem all the more important.

UNIVERSITY OF WISCONSIN: ADAMS AND TRIPP HALLS

Fireworks over the lake: that is how the University of Wisconsin celebrated the dedication of its first men's dormitories, Adams and Tripp Halls.[27] This was a fitting celebration for a project that was more than two decades in the making. The housing of students at UW followed a twisted path. The first structure on campus was North Hall, from 1851; for four years, it served all the functions of the university, including housing for thirty students.[28] As was typical of the time, there was no running water; to make matters worse, the students (not particularly concerned with hygiene) regularly overturned the outhouses or set them on fire.[29] South Hall, completed in 1855, provided new spaces for the expanding university, and in 1863 it became a residence for women.[30] Paul Chadbourne, president of UW from 1867 to 1870, was opposed to the education of men and women together in the same classrooms, but he did believe women could be educated in a separate "female college." During his leadership, the Madison campus was awarded federal land-grant status, and in 1870, the state legislature approved the new Female College Building, which indeed was swiftly constructed. Women moved into it, allowing men to take over both North and South Halls.[31] The Female College Building was L shaped, accommodated eighty students, included bedrooms and classrooms, and had generous porches. John Bascom, president from 1874 to 1887, achieved a higher degree of gender integration when he abolished the concept of the female college, allowed men and women to study together, and gave the Female College Building a new name: Ladies' Hall. Bascom sought to increase the prestige of the faculty and meet the continuing pressures of the land grant, and he desperately needed classroom and laboratory space. So when the science hall, which included classrooms and housing, burned in 1884, he arranged for the removal of all the male students from that one building and repurposed it for instruction.[32] At this point, boys were cast out into the city, an urban area now dense enough to supply boardinghouses. In the interim, fraternities sprouted up along the campus's periphery.[33]

After Bascom moved men off campus, Wisconsin would not have dorms for them for four decades. Fraternities took up the slack. But at least one president tried to promote dorms for men: Charles Van Hise, president from 1903 to 1918, was deeply concerned about student development and tirelessly promoted the English residential system. His plea for teaching morals outside the classroom came with a call for new buildings. In Van Hise's inaugural address as university president, he announced: "The communal life of instructors and students in work, in play and in social relations is the very essence of the spirit of Oxford and Cambridge."[34] He noted that when the individual colleges at these venerated British schools became overcrowded, they built more quadrangles on the model of the earlier ones.[35] Van Hise's promotion of the idea of dormitories for men had a delayed impact. He conceded that some people might find the residential system to be old-fashioned, but what some observers found "absurd," Van Hise found laudable. The halls of residence, the playing fields, and various clubs made boys into men. The most important part of higher education lay in a young man's gaining the "capacity to deal with men, to see the other fellow's point of view, to have sympathetic appreciation with all that may be good in that point of view, but to return firmly to his own ideas."[36] Van Hise placed a lot of faith in the dormitory's influence on the student: "In the intimate, communal life of the dormitories he *must* adjust himself to others. He must be genial, fair, and likable or else his lot is rightly a hard one."[37]

As president, Van Hise, leading the university's board of trustees, commissioned a master plan in 1905 that, like Columbia University's splashy new campus design by McKim, Mead & White, was a grand scheme in the manner of the City Beautiful Movement. The architects, Paul Philippe Cret and Warren Laird, emphasized

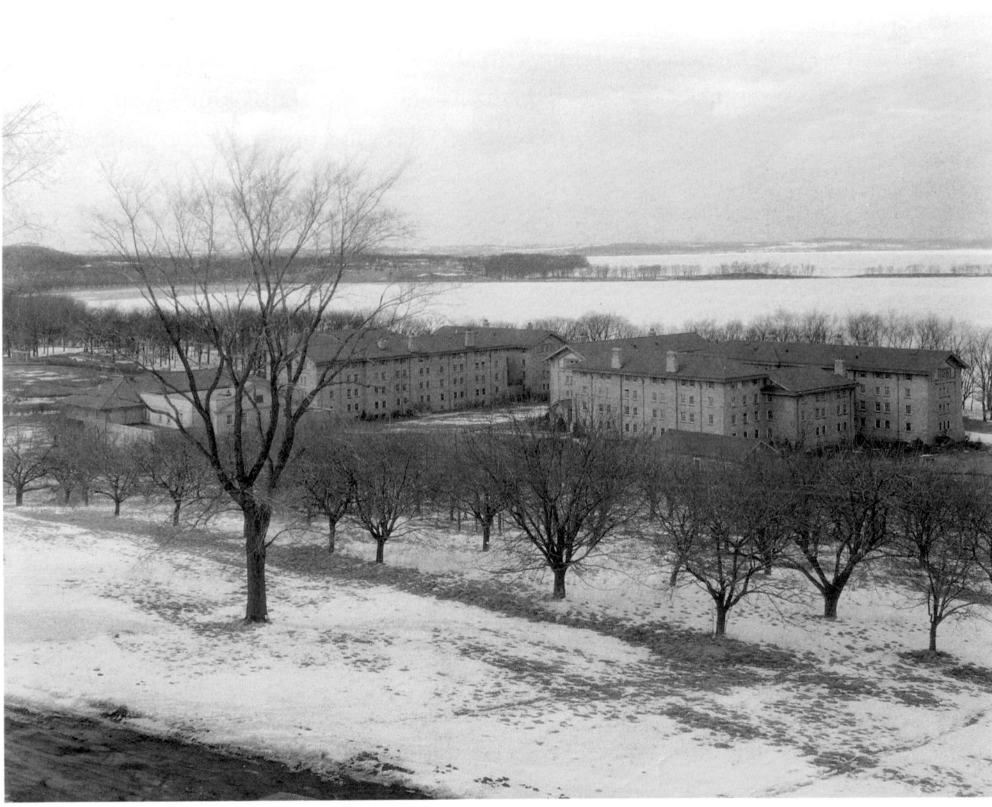

Figure 3.1. Adams and Tripp Halls with refectory, University of Wisconsin–Madison, 1924–26, Arthur Peabody, architect, view from the crest of a hill looking northwest toward Lake Mendota. Courtesy of the University of Wisconsin–Madison Archives (2018s00131).

linearity, orderliness, and clarity. Their choice for the location of the men's dormitories was the shore of Lake Mendota, north of the old campus and west of the north–south line of Charter Street, the spine of the campus. In contrast to his Anglophilic patron, Cret mustered no enthusiasm for English models:

> It seems to the advisers [Cret and Laird, referring to themselves] that a modern dormitory system should depart from the ancient monastic scheme typified in the old English colleges and often copied in this country and should substitute for it a scheme in consonance with the modern love of freedom and horizons wider than those of medieval life.[38]

Cret saw the enclosed quadrangle as tainted by its physical and metaphorical link to medieval closed-mindedness. (It is not clear whether he meant Catholic or Anglican closed-mindedness. Perhaps he meant both.) His proposed dorms were U-shaped, with their open sides accepting the eastern sun and with all rooms having views onto the placid horizon. This scheme never came to fruition.

When UW eventually constructed Adams and Tripp Halls, which opened in 1926, the architect, Arthur Peabody, rejected Cret's notions and returned to the

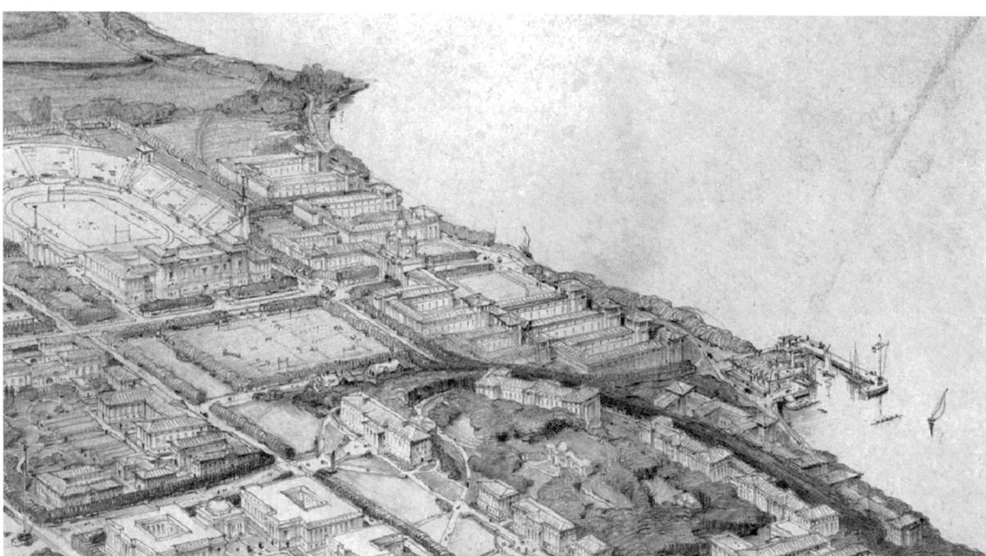

Figure 3.2. University of Wisconsin–Madison, 1908, Laird and Cret, architects, master plan, detail. Laird and Cret's master plan rejected the idea of closed quadrangles, which Cret regarded as old-fashioned. Instead, he proposed a series of U-shaped buildings facing Lake Mendota. Courtesy of the University of Wisconsin–Madison Archives (CLP-Z0006).

British quadrangles Van Hise had earlier praised. Peabody was the official Wisconsin state architect. He had designed many structures for the UW campus, and the men's dormitories were simply included in his portfolio of work for the state. Peabody worked closely with the Dormitory Committee, a group made up of faculty members who sought to understand the social needs of UW's undergraduates. The committee produced a detailed report using information gleaned by Peabody, who collected data on recent dormitories at eight schools: the University of Chicago, Columbia, Cornell, Harvard, Northwestern, the University of Pennsylvania, Princeton, and Yale. Shortly thereafter, John Dollard, a UW administrator who served as secretary of the Wisconsin Union, compiled a second report based on his own in-person tour of twelve universities, including the same ones that Peabody visited.[39] Dollard concluded that "the dormitories should be conceived as parts of the human and educational machinery of the university; that the object of dormitory building is more than to provide additional housing facilities, that it is designed to bring into the life of every undergraduate the cultural inspiration

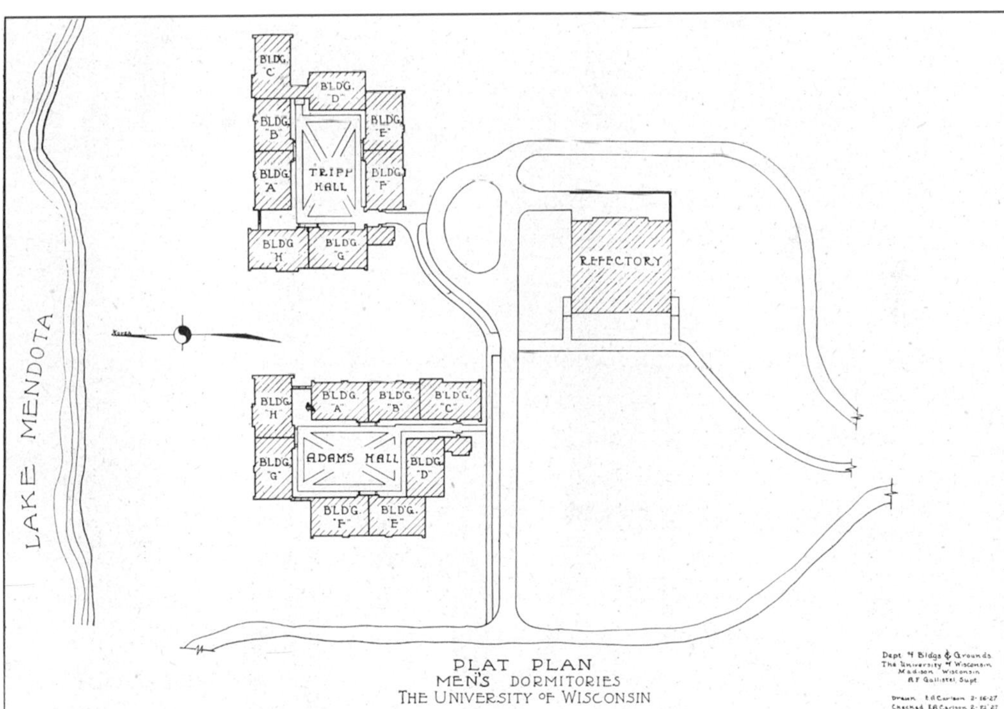

Figure 3.3. Adams and Tripp Halls, University of Wisconsin–Madison, 1924–26, Arthur Peabody, architect, site plan. Adams and Tripp had the same plan, but one was turned ninety degrees from the other. Courtesy of the University of Wisconsin–Madison Archives (2018s00140).

and force of the university."[40] In other words, these were more than just places to sleep. In fact, Dollard noted, "We are advised not to call a dormitory a dormitory, but rather a hall or a house."[41] The Dormitory Committee decided to construct beds for 500 men (250 in each dorm) along with one refectory and one kitchen.

On Peabody's tour of other colleges, he observed that both administrators and students preferred single bedrooms. For one thing, singles automatically eliminated roommate troubles. The experts he met with preferred the entryway type over the corridor plan, which was perceived as being noisy and offering too little privacy. Even though a building with a long corridor with one or two staircases and a group bathroom was cheaper to construct and maintain than an entryway plan building serving the same number of students, administrators still preferred the entryway, because it allowed them to limit the numbers of students and create what they considered to be manageable groups.[42] They well knew that construction of extra staircases was costly on a per student basis, just as they knew the plumbing for so many additional bathrooms (one per stair) was expensive. Even so, Dollard agreed with Peabody, noting that the benefits of the entryway plan far outweighed its shortcomings:

> The future plans of Harvard, Yale, Princeton, University of Pennsylvania, Cornell, Chicago, and Northwestern all provide for the entry system in their dormitories. The advantages of the integration of life into small groups, the lessening of noise and rough hous[ing], the development of a more home-like and comradely spirit, are fairly obvious.[43]

Dollard also noted another problem with long corridors: one person could cause a disturbance and then easily avoid detection.

The idea behind Adams and Tripp Halls was for each to create a closed-off space, the courtyard. The fact that the dorms faced away from the lake made them cozy and self-contained. These were true quadrangles, with courtyards inaccessible to anyone other than the residents. Each man had a single bedroom, and to create community the men were organized into houses, which formed vertically off of staircases, although the plan also employed a very short double-loaded corridor. Although Peabody referred to the plan as the entry type, it was actually a hybrid of corridor and entryway types, an arrangement akin to the women's dormitories at the University of Chicago in the 1890s (see chapter 2). A story about the dorms in the school's newspaper, the *Daily Cardinal,* noted small luxuries, such as extra-thick mattresses and mohair curtains.[44] One publication lauded

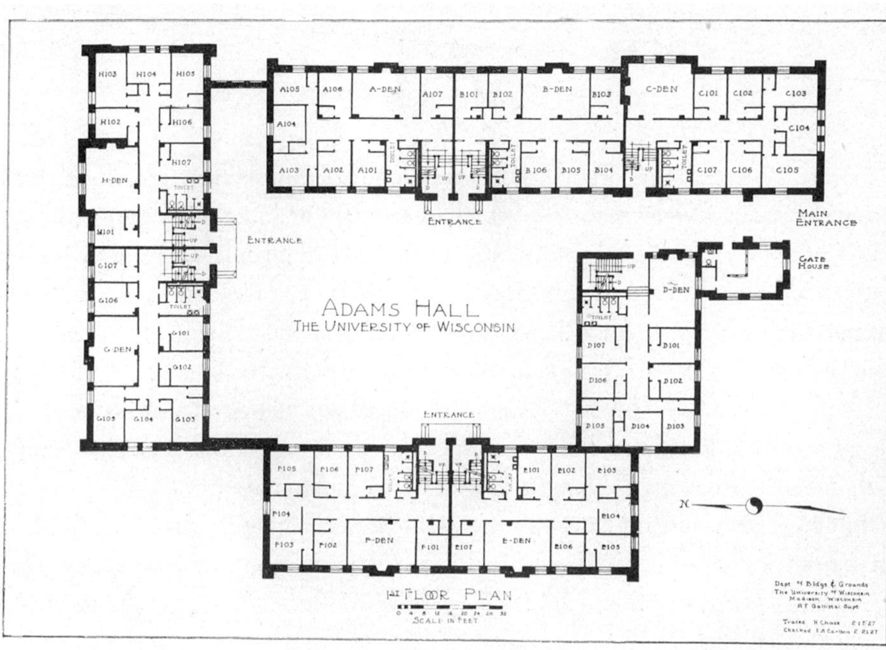

Figure 3.4. Adams Hall, University of Wisconsin–Madison, 1924–26, Arthur Peabody, architect, plan, first floor. The building was divided into eight units, each of which had a first-floor den with a fireplace. Courtesy of the University of Wisconsin–Madison Archives (2018s00141).

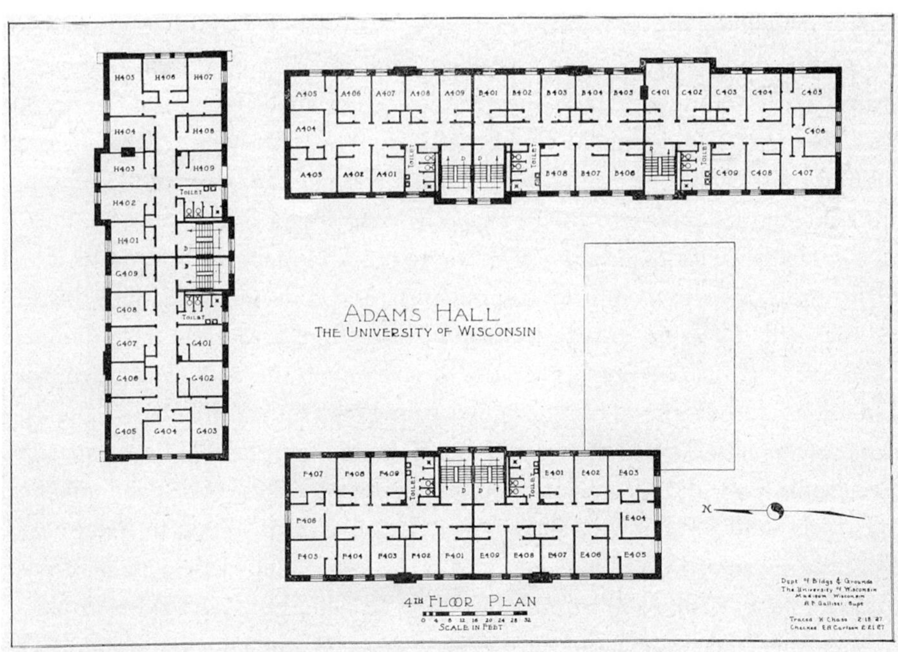

Figure 3.5. Adams Hall, University of Wisconsin–Madison, 1924–26, Arthur Peabody, architect, plan, fourth floor. Students would be grouped into houses; this floor would have had bedrooms for sixty-two students. Courtesy of the University of Wisconsin–Madison Archives (2018s00142).

the central heating and fireplaces for symbolic hominess and actual warmth.[45] (Rooming houses were notoriously badly heated.) On a fact-finding mission, the UW Dormitory Committee came up with the idea of placing doors between the single bedrooms, not for reasons of security, as had been the case in the design of women's dorms, but so that these rooms could later be turned into suites. The committee called this arrangement "the convertible type."[46]

Peabody's quads embraced the spirit of Van Hise's inaugural address from two decades earlier, but there were differences as well. At Oxford and Cambridge, each college had its own dining hall, which was integrated into the quadrangular architecture. But here, in a cost-saving measure, a separate refectory was built to serve both dormitories.[47] The refectory had two dining rooms (one for each dorm), however, so the young men could still eat with their friends. There was also additional space for another five hundred diners. All of the diners were serviced by one kitchen, with a storage facility on the lower level.[48]

For the exteriors, Peabody employed a stripped-down, round-arched style, with rusticated blond Madison sandstone in irregular bond complemented by roofs with large overhangs and visible brackets (Plate 5). The style showed a Romanesque influence but contained a heavy dose of American Arts and Crafts. Red-tiled roofs granted a slightly Tuscan appearance. In plan, the two compact quadrangles had porter's lodges in a nod to Oxbridge.[49] But once again, the quadrangles at Oxford and Cambridge were formed from series of linked rectangular units, not the single, freestanding square donut used here. The importance of the enclosed outdoor room cannot be overemphasized, as it was intended to create community by forcing the residents into a shared space.

The challenge for the deans at UW was to produce men's dormitories that had all the esprit de corps, comfortable furnishings, and convenient locations that fraternities had, but at the cost of a cheap boardinghouse. And the dorm builders could not easily use economies of scale to save money, because to compete with fraternities, dormitories needed to gather young men into small groups. The *Wisconsin State Journal* noted that fraternities provided comfortable living quarters, wholesome food, and "democratic community living." These were good qualities, the article went on, but "not all the men can or wish to belong to fraternities." The phrase "can or wish" was a not-too-subtle way of acknowledging that a Jewish student might "wish" to join a fraternity, but he could not, and neither could an African American student, or even a white Protestant student who was poor. The article then cited a 1925 report that observed that for those "who do not have the fraternity connection the dormitories will be a boon."[50] In 1927, at the annual national meeting of deans of men, one attendee observed: "I think we all realize

Figure 3.6. Adams Hall, University of Wisconsin–Madison, 1924–26, Arthur Peabody, architect, porter's lodge. Photograph by author.

Figure 3.7. Adams Hall, University of Wisconsin–Madison, 1924–26, Arthur Peabody, architect, interior of courtyard. Photograph by author.

that our social life at universities centers pretty largely around our fraternity and sorority life."[51]

An elegant color brochure stated UW's aspirations for the new men's dormitories: "Parents and university officers now agree that beauty and comfort in students' everyday surroundings play an important part in better health, better work, and richer lives" (Plate 6).[52] Each section of the dormitory was called a house and had a "group leader" who was either a young faculty member or graduate student; he would act more in the capacity of an older brother than as a tutor, master, or head of house.[53] The booklet laid out the entire planning process, explaining the seven needs of university men that would be generously met by Adams and Tripp Halls. It claimed in flowery and optimistic prose that dorm living would alleviate class differences:

> Here, too, the man from the well-to-do home and the man who tends furnaces to buy his text-books will learn respect for each other across a common table; and the son of banker and farmer will find mutual understanding, of a winter's evening, in give and take to the crackling of logs in a wide fireplace.[54]

All the aspirations of student life deans were summed up in "The Seven Needs," which were spelled out in the same recruitment brochure:

> I. For inviting, comfortable, individual living quarters for Wisconsin men
> II. For wholesome food, healthfully prepared, pleasantly served
> III. For democratic community living and the opportunity for friendship
> IV. For experienced counsel and leadership in making the most of university life
> V. For adequate athletic fields, conveniently at hand
> VI. For quarters at the center of University affairs—the Hill, Memorial Union, Camp Randall
> VII. For reasonable living expense, made possible without burden upon the taxpayers of the state[55]

From the grandiose to the banal, the pamphlet celebrated the ascent of democracy and the nice blue-green color of the dormitories' painted metal furniture; the ensemble was touted as "masculine in design marked by substantial simplicity."[56] The document also extolled the central location, the nearby athletic fields, the advantages of having a single room, and the specific brand of mattress provided, all of which (apparently) contributed to the dormitory as a positive cultural influence.

A social room is a feature of each entry in Tripp Hall

Figure 3.8. Illustration from a 1926 brochure directed to prospective residents of the University of Wisconsin's Tripp Hall. The fireplace and its potential for cross-class interaction was a key recruitment tool. Courtesy of the University of Wisconsin–Madison Archives (2018s00143).

The dorms opened in 1926. In 1929, the university's yearbook, *The Badger,* boasted that Adams and Tripp Halls, now three years old, offered amenities that no other organization (meaning fraternities) could match: informal chat sessions with prominent men, six new tennis courts, and intramural fields nearby, as well as self-government and good conditions for studying. The dorms held six dances per year and provided plenty of opportunities for singing Wisconsin songs.[57] In contrast to *The Badger,* the *Daily Cardinal* spun a different tale: it reported that rather than developing the habits of collegiate gentlemen as was intended, the young men who lived in the dorms had "ribald" table manners, roughhoused late at night, and mutilated university property.[58]

This is not to say that the university leaders were in agreement about what constituted bad behavior. For example, depending on whom one asked, smoking was a nasty habit or a sign of normal manhood. When the Facilities Department wanted to ban smoking in the dining hall, Professor H. C. Bradley (head of the Dormitory Committee) was not pleased. Writing to Dean Halverson, director of dormitories, Bradley insisted that smoking created a homelike environment. Smoking was not a sin, he pointed out. And since smoking was already allowed in the bedrooms, it stood to reason that smoking should be allowed in the refectory. Furthermore, he argued, "prohibition [of smoking] robs the dining room of a certain charm." Adults get to smoke, so why not college boys? "Imagine the University club, or any club, without its smoke." Bradley believed that students should be encouraged to spend time in the refectory, and if they could not smoke there (indeed, if they could not replenish their supplies of tobacco there), they were likely to be lured to the bright lights and jazz clubs of the city.[59] There was a national upsurge in smoking premade cigarettes around this time, and the students were (not surprisingly) enchanted by the highly addictive and heavily marketed "ciggies." The university constructed Adams and Tripp Halls in order to create community, and driving the students off campus with a tobacco ban was counterproductive. Home was where the smoke was, and so it remained in the dining hall.

In 1930, Alex L. Trout, an architect, speaking at the annual meeting of the Association of Deans and Advisers of Men, asserted that the time had come for universities to phase out the "closed court," by which he meant the completely enclosed quadrangle. In its place, Trout argued, the H, U, E, or T plan should take command. He warned that if a courtyard were too small, the building would cast shadows on itself, making the open space dark and dank. In a likely reference to Adams and Tripp Halls, he quipped, "I know of one group built near a lake with a splendid view *possible,* [but] less than a quarter of the students in the building get a glimpse of the lake." In fact, his snide remark was generous—at most, one-eighth of the residents of the UW halls had views of the lake, since half of the rooms on the north side faced into the court. In Trout's view, if the quadrangle was merely an aesthetic gesture—merely a tired, knee-jerk reference to a historical association with Oxford and Cambridge—then it had no meaning or purpose in the present. It was, he said, "like buying random books with red bindings merely to fill out the color scheme of a library."[60]

As we have seen in earlier chapters, for all the university's claims of egalitarianism, the dormitory existed as a space of exclusion. The residence hall was certainly more democratic than the fraternity, but it still created barriers, and in this way it was a microcosm of the world outside the university. Adams Hall provides a compelling example. Under Jim Crow, in the decades before the Fair Housing Act of 1968, it would have been nearly impossible for an African American professional to find a place to live in Madison, Wisconsin. That is how Carson Gulley, the chef for the refectory and a beloved figure at the college, came to live in the basement of Adams Hall. Gulley was later a cookbook author and pioneer in broadcasting who hosted cooking shows on radio and television. The Facilities Department at UW, in an effort to keep the chef employed on campus, carved out an apartment for him and his family in Adams Hall. One can read this extraordinary situation in two ways. On the one hand, that the college allowed an African American family to cohabit with white men might seem progressive. On the other hand, Gulley and his family lived in the basement and entered through their own door; they were clearly not viewed as equal to the collegians, but rather existed in a subservient relationship to them. Gulley later became a prominent spokesman for fair housing and was a founder of the Madison chapter of the NAACP.

THE WOMEN'S DORMITORY AT HOWARD UNIVERSITY: "A WELL-ORDERED HOME"

Chef Gulley's apartment at Wisconsin was shoehorned into a dormitory designed by white men for white men. In contrast, nearly every space at Howard University was built by black architects for black students in anticipation of creating a model world of high achievement. When black architects built for black clients, both groups wanted the best value for the limited funds available. Kendrick Ian Grandison notes the important public identity of black colleges during this time, with the colleges representing in physical form the acquisition of land, aspirations for education, and success in business that supported the uplift of African Americans.[61]

Indeed, black college leaders wanted structures on their campuses that would match or exceed those of white institutions. As architectural historian Ellen Weiss, chronicler of the Tuskegee Institute, explains:

> Black-built structures do not differ significantly from those by white architects for white clients. Bricks and mortar do not change with the makers' ethnicity. Programming is the same for black or white usage. Rooms and their arrangements fail to betray skin color even though race certainly conditioned the lives of those who built and inhabited them.[62]

For African Americans building important institutions, the difficulty in achieving the necessary wealth to construct monumental buildings made their accomplishments in the architectural realm intensely felt.[63] Weiss argues that "the Tuskegee campus succeeds in evoking another era's gentility" and that it furthermore reflects "heroic efforts for racial identity."[64] Her characterization of Tuskegee accords well with the architecture of Howard University: "The buildings that remain are monuments of creativity, devotion, and determination in the face of great odds."[65] Howard's administrators knew that their actions were watched by white Americans, and that they were constantly being judged. As the 1922 handbook for Howard students said: "Always remember that a Howard student is a marked student. Each represents more than himself or herself, because the University entrusts its honor and reputation to each student."[66]

Howard University, the premier African American university at the time, boasted the leadership of Lucy Diggs Slowe, a nationally respected educator. Her accomplishments were many. In addition to being a tennis champion, writer, and a founder of the first African American sorority (Alpha Kappa Alpha), Slowe served as dean of women at Howard for fifteen years. She was the first African American member of the previously all-white National Association of Deans of Women and the first African American to address a meeting of the association. When the still mostly white NADW held its 1932 meeting in Washington, D.C., the deans also went to Howard to get a tour of the new state-of-the-art women's dormitory designed by African American architect Albert Cassell. Decked out in furs and winter coats, they posed for photographs in front of the brand-new building, now known as the Harriet Tubman Quadrangle, but at the time known simply as the Women's Dormitory.

As dean, Slowe's job included many functions: monitoring the academic progress of women students, keeping their health records, supervising the women's student government, providing career counseling, distributing fellowships, and

Figure 3.9. Women's Dormitory (now Harriet Tubman Quadrangle), Howard University, 1929–31, Albert Cassell, architect. Scurlock Studio Records, Archives Center, National Museum of American History, Smithsonian Institution.

Figure 3.10. Women's Dormitory (now Harriet Tubman Quadrangle), Howard University, 1929–31, Albert Cassell, architect, courtyard, photomontage. Scurlock Studio Records, Archives Center, National Museum of American History, Smithsonian Institution.

passing out on-campus jobs.[67] But constructing and managing dormitories was a chief plank in her platform, because she believed that the dormitory shaped the student's cultural life:

> Experience has shown us that much of the student's leisure-time is spent in the dormitory and if he is supervised by a person who challenges his mind, he can find opportunities in the dormitory for supplementing his classroom work. In other words, the dormitories can serve not only as laboratories in human

relations but also as places for the development of those cultural pursuits that ought to be part of every college student's life.[68]

Before the Women's Dormitory was built, Howard's female students lived at home or in boardinghouses or sorority houses. The office of the dean of women inspected the boardinghouses.[69] Given that Slowe was one of the founders of Alpha Kappa Alpha, the first African American sorority, it is clear that she was no enemy of Greek organizations, but she did seek to regulate their activities. At Howard, students could not join fraternities or sororities until their sophomore year, and to qualify they had to submit proof from the registrar's office of high academic standing.

Slowe asserted the importance of the dean in the construction of new dorms: "In planning the building of college houses, it is absolutely necessary to think first of the educational ideals which are to be fostered in them; therefore, it is necessary that the educational adviser in the college and the architect work in co-operation."[70]

Figure 3.11. Lucy Diggs Slowe (front row, fourth from left), dean of women at Howard University and highly regarded educator in the nascent field of student affairs, in front of the newly completed Women's Dormitory at Howard with other members of the National Association of Deans of Women, February 18, 1932. By posing in front of these state-of-the-art residence halls, the deans of women showed that they equated their work with the safe housing of their charges. Scurlock Studio Records, Archives Center, National Museum of American History, Smithsonian Institution.

Almost certainly calling attention to the lack of support from other administrators, Slowe wrote: "It is my opinion that college officials have never realized how important it is to house students properly in the light of their total education. Dormitories for too long a time have been considered places to sleep rather than places to live."[71] Slowe also held strong opinions about the professionalization of deans:

> [Dormitories] should be administrated by persons who are as well trained academically as classroom teachers, for the head of a dormitory will be in much more intimate contact with a student than the classroom teacher. . . . At Howard University, we have persons as educational directors of our dormitories who have the same qualifications as those persons selected for the faculty.[72]

Slowe was a leader even among the earliest women deans who consistently argued that they possessed useful professional expertise.

The Women's Dormitory at Howard was similar to Adams and Tripp Halls at UW in that it was designed to be a completely enclosed quadrangle; the courtyard of the Howard quad was larger, however, and had fewer points of entry from the courtyard to the inside of the dorm. The Women's Dormitory existed in a decidedly urban context; it was closed off from the city for the protection of the young women. The building was partitioned into five sections, although it framed a rectangular space. One side was made up of two connected blocks. In the initial construction phase, there were three ranges that formed an L.

On the first floor of one range, the architect, at Slowe's behest, supplied a panoply of social spaces, including parlors, a music room, and a social hall that could be used for special parties or every day as a dining room. At the University of Chicago in the 1890s, Dean Marion Talbot had noted that the additional spaces for socializing in the women's dormitory were useful because hospitality was part of the young women's educational experience. The same was true at Howard in the late 1920s, and Slowe's opinions echoed those of her predecessors. "A dormitory should be as much like a well-ordered home," Slowe wrote, "as it is possible to make it." A ladies' dormitory was where young women learned about the refinements of carefully managed domesticity. Students entertained guests in order to learn to be good hostesses and (later) good wives and mothers. They were being trained in "thoughtfulness, courtesy, and hospitality."[73]

Another reason for the many rooms on the main floor was that, according to housing experts, women simply needed more space than men did.[74] A partial explanation was that women did not go inside men's dormitories, and thus if a woman

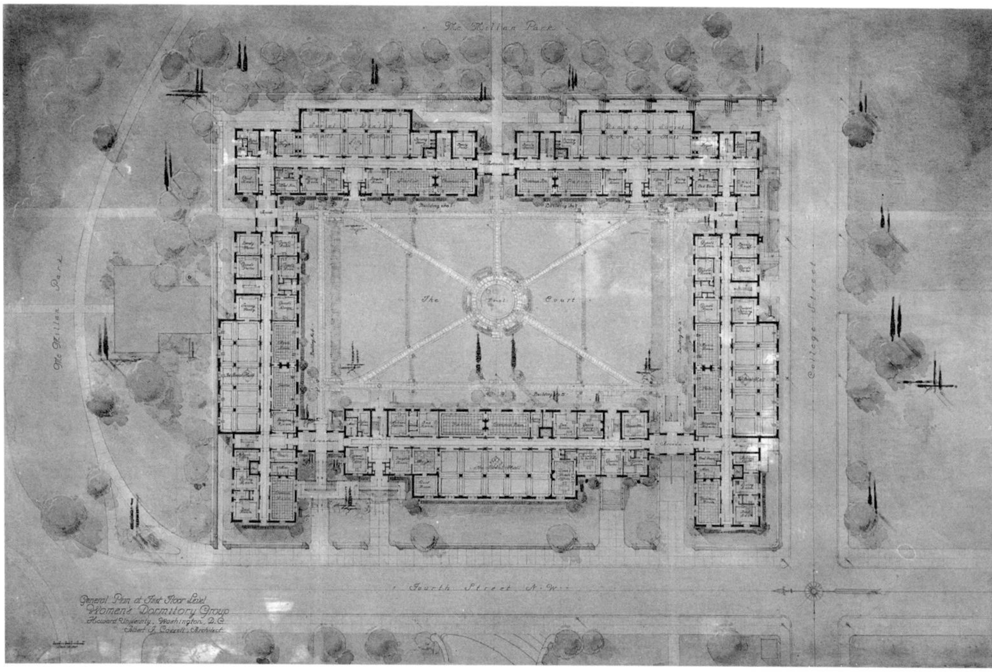

Figure 3.12. Women's Dormitory (now Harriet Tubman Quadrangle), Howard University, 1929–31, Albert Cassell, architect, plan of quadrangle in five parts. At first, only three structures (forming an L) were built. Later, the whole was enclosed following Cassell's designs. Full sets of these plans are found in Drawings Role 230, Cassell Collection, Springarn Archive Center, Howard University. Scurlock Studio Records, Archives Center, National Museum of American History, Smithsonian Institution.

was meeting a date (chaperoned, of course), he had to come to her dormitory. Residence halls required public spaces where young people of opposite sexes could talk with each other. Furthermore, the girls without dates needed quiet places to study outside their rooms.[75]

The rooms at Howard were doubles, and each had a sink. A leading dean of women, Harriet Hayes at Teachers College, Columbia University, noted in 1932 that double rooms were both economical and good for student development: "They possess the practical advantage of a saving in space and expense per student housed. They are also conducive to a type of companionship and social training that may sometimes prove invaluable in the social discipline and personal development of individuals."[76] On the downside, double rooms "provide more administrative problems than single rooms."[77] Hayes recognized that not all students were suited to being roommates, but she believed that, on balance, the experience of sharing a room was good for a student's development. She credited "American college youth" with making double rooms so successful:

> After the first few weeks of a term are over and obvious misfits are taken care of, the students settle down in general peace and harmony, accepting with good humor and contentment the situation they face in common. Life in the average dormitory is ordinarily lived on a basis of genuine good will, fair dealing and democracy.[78]

Like Hayes, Slowe emphasized the democratic potential of the dorm, seeing it as offering students the possibility of self-advancement outside the classroom. The university's students were self-governing, and students ran the residence hall's government. Slowe found that without guidance, students tended to spend too much time dancing and playing cards. She romantically assumed that exposure to lovely collegiate buildings would unconsciously "quicken the students' love of beauty."[79] There was nothing specific about the architecture at Howard that would call attention to its African American origins. Indeed, the Women's Dormitory was standard for a college in the midrange of wealthy institutions. It was a model for its many social rooms, its understated exterior, and its role as an extension of the job of the dean of women. Unlike the dormitories at UW, where graduate student leaders

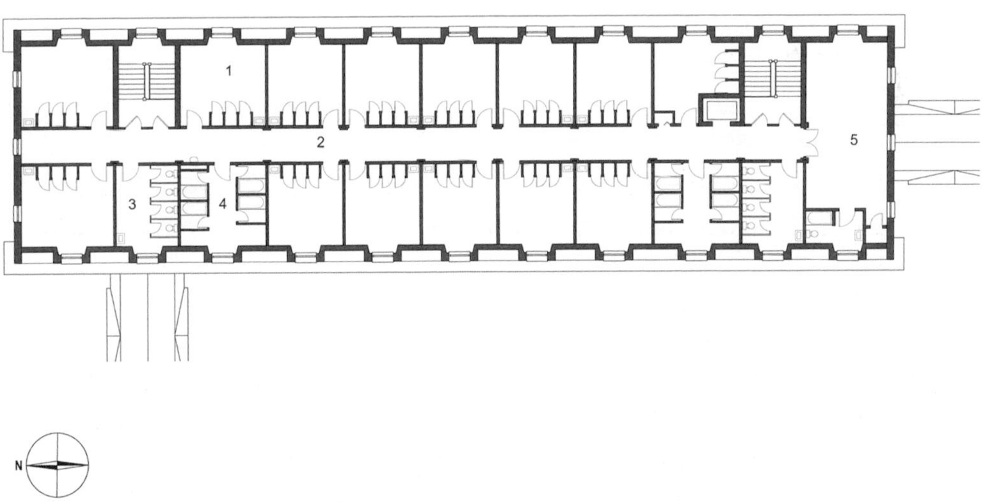

Figure 3.13. Women's Dormitory (now Harriet Tubman Quadrangle), Howard University, 1929–31, Albert Cassell, architect, plan, one floor of one section of the quadrangle originally known as Building I (in the northeast corner of the plan in Figure 3.12). 1 = bedroom; 2 = corridor; 3 = toilets; 4 = showers and bathtubs; 5 = supervisor's room. Drawing by John Giganti.

lived on-site, the Women's Dormitory employed professional assistants to Slowe. For another model, one that was almost unachievable for all but the top three or four wealthiest colleges in the United States, we turn to Yale University and its vigorous promotion of the residential college system in the late 1920s.

RESIDENTIAL COLLEGES AT YALE AND THE QUADRANGLE PLAN

In 1925, under the leadership of President James Angell, a committee of Yale professors and administrators proposed a new way of delivering education to undergraduates in which professors and students would be connected as they had been in the days of the colonial Yale.[80] The committee used an architectural term, titling its report "The Quadrangle Plan."[81] According to architectural historian Paul V. Turner, during this period "the English quadrangle came to be regarded by many people as the most appropriate embodiment of the principles of the residential college."[82] The relationship to medieval England was direct, given that Oxford and Cambridge had residential colleges with histories that stretched back centuries. The men who promoted residential colleges in the United States visited England frequently. Further, the compactness of the square donut plan promoted closeness among the students. As Turner notes, "The enclosed quadrangle seemed to provide a natural setting for a college community that valued intimacy and fellowship."[83] Characteristically, the members of America's ruling class took the British examples as colorless suggestions to be improved upon with Yankee wealth and extravagance.

Today, Yale's website boasts: "At the head of each college is a Head of College, the chief executive officer of the college. Working with each Head of College is the Residential College Dean, who serves as the college's chief academic adviser. The Head of College is responsible for setting the moral and intellectual tone of the college while the Dean is charged with maintaining university regulations. *Both Head of College and Dean live in the college with their families.*"[84] The term *residential college* is a slippery one. Today it implies an around-the-clock learning environment in which professors and students live together, dine together, and commune with each other as a subset within a larger university. By some definitions, professors must live on-site for the arrangement to be accurately called a residential college. Today, the residential college concept (at Yale, Harvard, the University of Pennsylvania, and elsewhere) is enmeshed with the idea of the on-site professor, but that was not always the case. During the early decades of the residential colleges at Yale, for example, the masters, deans, or heads did not live with the students, although a selection of fellows did.[85] Fellows were young male assistant professors or advanced graduate students. Their energy and enthusiasm did much to carry off the major effort of establishing the residential colleges, each of which housed between 250 and 300 men.[86]

Other proponents of the residential college concept consider the actual dwelling to be less important than the body of people brought together under the guiding hand of an adult who is committed to nurturing undergraduates. Preferably, a selection of students (fewer than three hundred) will stay together for more than one year, an arrangement that promotes loyalty to the group, as once students held loyalty toward their class years.[87] Many educational theorists consider the creation of a manageable cohort within a big university to be more important than any specific type of building, quadrangular or otherwise.[88]

Historian of education Alex Duke observes that the presidents of Harvard and Yale fell in love with the architecture of Oxford and Cambridge at an opportune time, when a confluence of factors allowed this wildly expensive educational idea to catch fire. Undergraduate populations were growing, students were flocking to fraternity houses, and faculty members needed a push from central administration to reconnect with students. College leaders argued that it was urgent for the focus of higher education to return to shaping boys into men, or girls into women. According to Duke, those who wished to import English collegiate ideals to the United States did not study the British universities systemically or scientifically, but instead relied on fictional accounts and house histories.[89] Accounts of Oxford were particularly impressionistic, rooted in the enthusiasm of Rhodes scholars rather than in hard facts. Furthermore, Duke argues, a racial hierarchy informed the supposedly strong connection between American Anglo-Saxon Protestants and the Gothic colleges of England, an interpretation that never fully surfaced in the 1920s and 1930s. (This argument falls apart, however, when one considers that the white American educators who designed Colonial Revival colleges in the 1920s and 1930s also believed themselves to be superior to members of other races.)

Thanks to the generosity of the Harkness family, Yale's residential colleges were among the most impressive dormitories in the land, and far more luxurious than their English precedents.[90] When the University of Wisconsin's Dormitory Committee visited Yale in 1924, the members learned that while a recent dormitory at Cornell cost $1,600 per bed, Yale's Harkness Memorial Quadrangle cost $10,000 per bed.[91] Yale had spent more than six times Cornell's cost per bed, and Cornell was not a poor college. One aspect of the early twentieth-century dormitory building boom was shared by UW and Yale, however, and that was the perceived need to push back against fraternities. Yale's benefactor Edward Harkness himself felt like an outsider, and it "trouble[d] his thoughts in later years, that some of the men he knew and liked—'average men' like himself—had not been chosen [for fraternities and societies], and so had been excluded from experiences that would have been rewarding and constructive."[92]

Harkness was friends with fellow alumnus and architect James Gamble Rogers, who from 1918 to 1920 had already designed a single large-scale dormitory, Harkness Memorial Quadrangle. Paid for by Harkness's mother, Anna Richardson Harkness, Memorial Quad was built in memory of her son Charles (Edward's brother), who died in 1916 without heirs. The building's tower was a focal point for the whole Yale campus; the source for the design was the tower of St. Botolph's Church in Boston, Lincolnshire, England. At the time he designed Memorial Quad, Rogers had never been to England, although he traveled to Britain later.[93] In addition to influence from architectural periodicals, Rogers's design sources likely included Princeton, the University of Pennsylvania, and Bryn Mawr.

Memorial Quadrangle marked a new investment in housing Yalies.[94] It did much to alleviate overcrowding, but it was not specifically designed as part of the new residential college program. The massive building added many needed beds, but it did not include dining facilities, a library, or social spaces for student gathering.[95] Memorial Quad was Rogers's first building at Yale, and the start of a lifelong client–architect relationship of lasting importance in the history of American architecture. The plan shows that it was a dense student environment, with rooms for six hundred students crammed within its stone walls. It was much more urban than UW's Adams and Tripp Halls, and thus a bit more like Tubman Quad at Howard. Memorial Quad faced inward, turning away from the city, much like the buildings at the University of Chicago. There were very few entrances from the street to the internal world of the courtyard. A resident or guest could not go directly from the street to a room; he or she would first have to walk into the courtyard and then take one of many staircases up to the rooms. The vast majority of the square footage was taken up by bedrooms and studies, although there were a few common areas or lounges. The rooms were arranged so that two single rooms adjoined a study (Plate 7).

Four years after Memorial Quad opened, President Angell and his supporters concluded that Yale needed to go further to improve the life of undergraduates. Thus they wrote "The Quadrangle Plan," although the report's recommendations were not immediately accepted. Harkness offered funds for a series of residential colleges, but when Yale did not act quickly enough, he gave an enormous gift to Harvard instead. This launched Harvard's house system, another series of residential colleges.[96] The ideal for Yale's "colleges" (as for the "houses" at Harvard) was to have fellows and students live together in intellectual communities enriched by lectures, music, clubs, sports, and dining. Harkness revered these qualities in ancient British colleges and sought to counteract the atomized social atmosphere of early twentieth-century Yale. The demise of social life for undergrads at Yale had many causes: increased enrollment, curriculum updates that allowed for electives (and thus made it less likely that particular groups of men would meet on a regular basis in core classes), a housing shortage that pushed students into boardinghouses in New Haven, and the popularity of fraternities and secret societies. The great value of residential colleges was that they enabled students to develop acquaintances over a long period; these were stable communities in which undergraduates spent multiple years of their lives. They had the potential to correct the fragmentation of the social fabric of Yale.

The scale of the project of building Yale's residential colleges is almost unimaginable in the context of university planning today. It would be like designing, constructing, furnishing, and opening for business several enormous five-star hotels, all in the space of two years. (I say hotel instead of dormitory because these buildings had large staffs: cooks, janitors, laundresses, groundskeepers, and so on.) The dedicated team of Angell, Harkness, and Rogers, with input from John Russell Pope, was uniquely suited to pull this project together.

In March 1927, Angell went to England, allegedly on a vacation, but in fact to look at architecture.[97] In spite of some difficulties between Harkness and Angell, Harkness agreed to donate over fifteen million dollars to endow the whole residential college system.[98] According to Brooks Mather Kelley, who assessed the situation in 1974, the residential colleges were a success: they broke down divisions among science, engineering, and liberal arts students, and each college had its own newspaper, clubs, sports teams, and singing groups. Through this arrangement, "Yale recaptured some of the closeness of the old, smaller college, while at the same time enjoying the privileges of a great university."[99]

The first college, Jonathan Edwards Residential College, was cobbled together of existing buildings. Rogers designed new spaces for a dining hall, common rooms, library, fellows' suites, and a master's house, and even though it was retrofitted, it became the template for later colleges.[100] The next two colleges to open, in 1933, were Branford and Saybrook; these were situated in the renovated Memorial Quadrangle.[101] Pope designed and built one of residential colleges (Calhoun) in a Gothic Revival style. Rogers designed and built the rest using a range of styles from Colonial Revival to neo-Gothic; Davenport College was Colonial on the inward face, but Tudor on the street side.[102] Davenport, Pierson, and Trumbull Colleges also opened in 1933, as did Pope's Calhoun College. Berkeley and Timothy Dwight

Colleges followed in 1934 and 1935, respectively. Yale added two more colleges in the 1960s, as will be explored in chapter 5.

The architects used the quadrangle plan for all of the projects, regardless of exterior style. Each residential college had a group of fellows, all of whom had offices in the building, and about one quarter of them lived on-site.[103] Student rooms were arranged in a variety of ways, from two bedrooms with a study in between to singles, singles with studies, and larger suites for four men. The designers took great care with the dining halls; each of the residential colleges had its own china and flatware patterns. The colleges also featured lounges, common rooms for students, common rooms for fellows, squash courts, music rooms, and other spaces for recreation.[104]

CALHOUN COLLEGE

Harkness knew Rogers from his undergrad days, which helps explain why Rogers designed so many more of Yale's colleges than did Pope, even though Pope had been engaged to devise a master plan. Pope's contribution to Yale's college system was Calhoun, which stood out visually for its use of materials. Although the style was Tudor throughout, the exterior walls facing the city were gray and tan stone with rough surfaces, while the walls facing the courtyard were variegated brick. Facing the street, generous rectangular windows and warm yellow coloring projected the ancient Oxbridge mode. Calhoun College, named for nineteenth-century southern politician John C. Calhoun, was four stories beneath a sharply pitched slate roof. Many of the windows were not pointed, but rather square-headed, making this an excellent example of the perpendicular style of English Gothic. The gable facing the courtyard included diamond patterning in the multicolored brick; although the patterning was not as pronounced as in Butterfield's Keble College at Oxford, Keble was nonetheless a probable source. The gable with the brick polychromy demarcated the master's house. There were crenellations in whimsical locations, and chimneys (both stone and brick) pierced the sky. The plan of Calhoun employed a mix of suites (two bedrooms with an attached, shared study) and singles.

Remarkably, Yale's colleges created a sense of esprit de corps not by selecting men with similar interests but rather by assigning them randomly. Students lived with other freshmen for their first year, and then, at the start of sophomore year, moved physically into their residential colleges, with which they remained affiliated until graduation. The colleges were not thematic or based on curricular similarities; rather, each captured a wide swath of undergraduates. The architecture

Figure 3.14. Calhoun College (now Grace Hopper College), Yale University, 1932–33, John Russell Pope, architect. Photograph by Peter A. Juley; copyright Peter A. Juley and Son Collection. Smithsonian American Art Museum J0101388.

supplied many common rooms and lounges to ensure that students had ample space to relax in each other's company.

The sharing of meals was essential. As Provost Charles Seymour wrote to a close friend in the days just after seven of the colleges opened:

> I do not think I realized until Saturday afternoon the magnitude of the undertaking. It is just as much as starting seven new good-sized hotels. The atmosphere of the halls was a cross between an English hall and an American club, but there was very little in it reminiscent of our traditional commons manners, and a great deal was added by the beauty of the table service; the plates and the silver are lovely.[105]

No expense was spared, not on the china, the silverware, or the stained-glass windows, which included themes that romanticized the Old South; one window portrayed slaves carrying baskets of cotton on their heads. This window, and

Figure 3.15. Calhoun College (now Grace Hopper College), Yale University, 1932–33, John Russell Pope, architect, courtyard. Yale Manuscripts and Archives.

another in the Calhoun common room, became the subject of controversy in recent years, and (as discussed in the Epilogue) Calhoun College was renamed Grace Hopper College in 2017, in acknowledgment that Calhoun's name, a painful reminder of racism, is not a suitable one for an inclusive college home.

Turner sums up the architectural achievement at Yale: "The buildings . . . at Yale exemplified the era's desire for collegiate intimacy, clubby good humor, and the confirmation of an ancient and noble institutional heritage."[106] At Yale, the establishment of the residential colleges was administered at the highest level: the president, the donor, the provost, and the members of the Yale Corporation (the university's governing body, equivalent to the boards of trustees at other universities) were all deeply involved. Yale's dean of men, a position founded in 1919, was the person responsible for student conduct, discipline, and other undergraduate problems.[107] He was not involved in dealing with architects or managing Yale's construction projects. Indeed, the goal of the residential colleges was to place

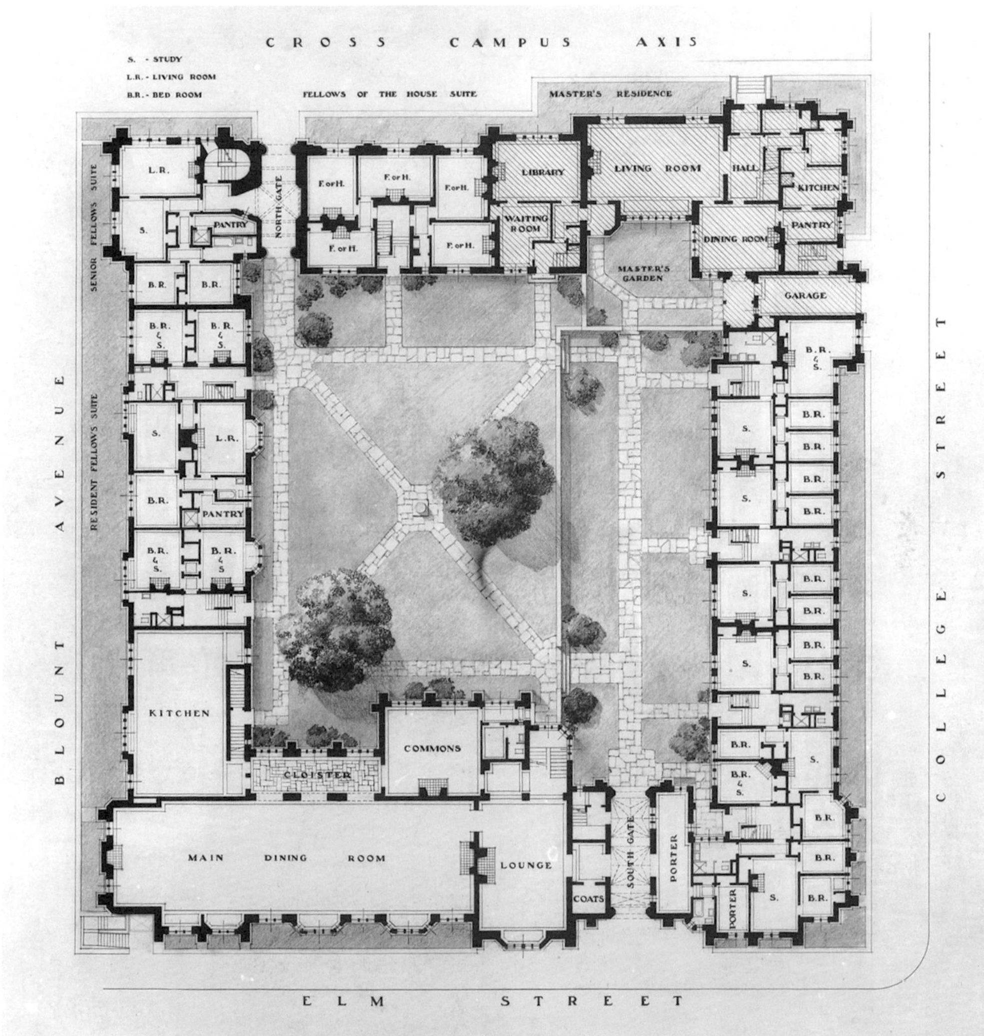

Figure 3.16. Calhoun College (now Grace Hopper College), Yale University, 1932–33, John Russell Pope, architect, plan. Photograph by Peter A. Juley; copyright Peter A. Juley and Son Collection. Smithsonian American Art Museum J0101389.

scholars in a role where they could care for students directly; these professors would take on the pastoral role played by their English forebears, and by instituting a whole administrative rank of advisers, Yale lessened the importance of the stereotypical dean of men: a disciplinarian with a coach's cajoling personality.

In contrast, at state universities, especially in the Midwest, deans of men had established themselves as essential to the smooth running of their institutions.

Figure 3.17. Calhoun College (now Grace Hopper College), Yale University, 1932–33, John Russell Pope, architect, common room, photograph from 1933. The stained-glass windows in this room (and the dining room) contained mythologized scenes of pre–Civil War life in the American South. This room included a window showing a chained black slave kneeling next to John C. Calhoun (see Figure E.1). Yale Manuscripts and Archives.

By 1940, their jobs were secure. Deans of women were victims of their own success. The job was so important that the professional deans expanded their purview to include the care of students, regardless of gender. In turn, deans of *men* were elevated to the new position of dean of *students,* which is how men took over a profession that had been invented by and for women. Gradually both titles, dean of women and dean of men, were phased out, and the positions were transformed into the high-ranking vice president of student affairs and the lower-ranking director of housing.

Deans of men in the Midwest were not cowed by East Coast schools. In fact, more than a whiff of criticism may be found in their writings. One dean, for

Figure 3.18. Calhoun College (now Grace Hopper College), Yale University, 1932–33, John Russell Pope, architect, dining hall. This room included a stained-glass window depicting two slaves carrying baskets of cotton on their heads (see Figure E.2). Yale Manuscripts and Archives.

example, noted that the Gothic style of Yale's recent building boom was not the best approach for creating interior space: "The historic styles that make the exterior monumental might lead to dark interiors, deep shadows, [and] insufficient light."[108]

In 1932, Harriet Hayes published a major book on the design of dormitories. It was unlike any single publication that came before it, in that it treated every aspect of dormitory design. Hayes had on-the-ground experience with the construction of dorms and had visited many operating dorms. She identified the essential paradox on her book's first page, saying that a dormitory "is institutional in character, yet it must serve as a home."[109] She also stated plainly that women needed more space than did men.[110]

Two of the universities featured in the case studies in this chapter relied on the concept of adult supervisors living in dormitories with the students: at Wisconsin, graduate student "leaders" lived in the dorms, and at Howard, paid professional female educators did so. While some fellows lived in the Yale colleges, Yale did not require masters and deans to live in the residence halls until the 1960s.

From the vantage point of student deans, the period before World War II was one of evident improvement. Dormitories had become widely accepted as part of the educational experience, while fraternities had been knocked down a peg. And deans of students had an increasingly large role to play in the development of the whole student. In 1950, Robert Moser, an expert on counseling in residence halls, quoted Donald L. Halverson, former director of housing at UW, who was present at the annual meeting of student housing experts. Moser celebrated Halverson's principles from the 1920s and 1930s, when Wisconsin's well-known dean had celebrated the "social values of living together":

> Personally, I can see little or no justification for the University's going into the rooming and boarding business. But, there is much justification in bettering housing and living conditions, in giving students the protection and security of a well-conceived system where living in the hall will be an education and a privilege, a system . . . which stresses the social values of living together, or getting the other fellow's viewpoint, of learning to get along with one another, and to respect one another's opinions, of benefitting by the daily give and take, of learning to live with the group and appreciate the value of associated effort . . . of rubbing elbows by the city boy and the farm boy. . . . All these experiences are cultural and educational and thus worthwhile.[111]

Yale, Wisconsin, and Howard all relied on romanticized notions of Oxbridge in their creation of low-rise quadrangles in historical styles. All three hoped to create small social groups within large universities. They saw the undergraduate experience as one that took place both inside and outside the classroom, with the dorm or residential college a key aspect of the student experience. In the next chapter, we will explore the extension of these ideas into an architectural form that could not be any further from the quadrangle: the skyscraper.

4

Dorms on the Rise

Skyscraper Residence Halls

After World War II, college administrators in the United States faced a flood of new students. In 1961, Harold Riker, a student dean and author of several books on dormitory design, stated that "the most pressing problem in student housing is that there isn't enough."[1] There were many reasons for the lack of housing and the upsurge in students, but the GI Bill of 1944 ranks highest among them. Formally titled the Servicemen's Readjustment Act, it created the biggest federal program affecting education since the Morrill Act's land grants of 1862. Like the earlier act, the GI Bill resulted in a demand for all types of campus buildings to meet the needs of the swelling numbers of students. But unlike the Morrill Act, which corresponded to a decrease in college officials' enthusiasm for living on campus, the GI Bill sparked an embrace of on-campus living. In the years after the war, the economy expanded, Cold War politics led Americans to place their faith in education as a means of defeating communism, and middle-class families expected to send their children to college. State legislators embraced the principles of the federal education bill and directed funds to state universities with an eagerness that is unfathomable today. Americans valued higher education as never before. For a while, it seemed as if everyone could get a college degree. The expansion of the student population was accompanied by increasing diversity, if only among whites. As Scott Carlson notes, when Congress passed the GI Bill, "ethnic European Americans from Irish, Italian, Polish, Jewish, Greek and Slavic background went off to college, joined the professional class, and moved to the suburbs."[2] Blacks and Hispanics, however, did not benefit as much from the bill, for a range of reasons, including that blacks were barred entry at many southern public universities and that historically black colleges were underfunded.

The number of undergraduate students nearly doubled.[3] With the upsurge of students on campus came the increasing professionalization of the student affairs administrators who oversaw housing. Housing officers formed a professional group, the Association for College and University Housing Officers, or ACUHO, which met for the first time in 1949. Architecture loomed large on the meeting's agenda. Touting a central tenet of student affairs philosophy, Dean Lloyd Morey of the University of Illinois gave the welcome address: "We realize that the place in which we house students is not merely a place in which to eat and sleep, as important as they are, but is a vital contribution to the whole intellectual and social development of our students."[4] Public universities, answerable to taxpayers, often rejected historical architectural styles for their new dormitories. The Gothic spires and neo-Georgian pediments of the previous generation seemed wasteful and old-fashioned in a time of explosive social change. The architectural manifestation of the postwar period was the modernist skyscraper dormitory.[5]

Just after Morey's opening remarks at the 1949 ACUHO meeting, James W. Hammond, of the architecture firm Skidmore, Owings & Merrill, took the podium. Hammond preached to the converted when he identified a crisis in university housing, a shortage that led to unfair advantages for some students. He said that only the "small number belonging to a well-equipped fraternity" could reap the benefits of close contact with the campus and with other students. The rest of the students were "on their own," facing the complicated challenge of "finding clean, well-heated, cheerful, safe, and well-ordered rooming houses."[6] At the second ACUHO meeting, architect John Merrill spoke, further proof that the built environment dominated the organization's agenda. In a workshop with housing officers in 1950, Merrill was asked, "Is there a comparison of the cost of dormitories relative to their height?" He answered that "a four story building will probably cost less per square foot or per cubic foot than a two or three story, for the reason that your foundation, basement area, and the utility tunnels . . . take up a smaller percentage of the total area."[7] A foundation, a basement, and utility tunnels had to be built anyway, he explained, so a fifth floor might as well be added on the top to increase maximum capacity. There was general consensus about practical height limits: "Five stories is about the limit that you will ask people to walk up and you will put in elevators. There is an additional cost." The same logic that pertained to the foundation also applied to the vertical circulation—once an expensive bank of elevators was added, there was no economic reason to stop at five stories. One might as well add a few more floors.[8] The skyscraper dormitory solved some of the overcrowding problem at the same time it represented progress. This chapter explores the advantages and disadvantages of this brazenly new way of housing students by focusing on residence halls at Rutgers, New York University, and the Ohio State University.

At state universities, the numbers of students in undergraduate courses increased, and students sat in large halls listening passively to lecturers. Many professors prided themselves on giving dynamic, meticulous presentations, but, even so, students lost the close relationships with professors that had once been typical in smaller classes.[9] According to Thelin, University of California president Robert Gordon Sproul justified large class sizes by claiming that students gained more from big courses taught by the best scholars than they did from weaker scholars in smaller settings.[10] The Cold War turned universities into knowledge production machines, where researchers urgently sought answers to questions in basic sciences as well as practical knowledge for military uses. Federal funding for research in physics, chemistry, and mathematics shot up, and competition for grants and investment in prestigious graduate programs took hold. The research university, which dated back to Johns Hopkins in the 1870s, now definitively dominated higher education.[11]

Clark Kerr, an educator of far-reaching importance in American history, set the tone for much of the opening up of higher education. He believed that everyone should be able to attend college, even those with modest financial means. He celebrated the "multiversity," as he called it, which was his formulation of a large research university that was somewhat like a metropolis. The multiversity would be large and dynamic; its students would be met with almost unlimited opportunity. Kerr recognized that a giant research university, like a great city, could be both anonymous and isolating. Many observers have noted that just as universities swelled with undergraduates, university policies shifted away from undergraduate teaching, because the prestige of winning big grants and running graduate programs drove undergraduates down to the bottom rung of the collegiate ladder.

THE RIVER DORMS AT RUTGERS

Although Rutgers currently is a large, state-funded university of the type that Kerr promoted, before World War II it was a small liberal arts college for men. The human scale and courtyards of the previous generation of dormitories contributed to the convivial atmosphere of Rutgers College. For the first ten or so years after World War II, Rutgers remained a medium-size liberal arts college. It was primarily a place where New Jersey citizens could send their sons for an affordable education.

After the war, enrollment at the college surged (especially from 1947 to 1949) and those years were followed by a period of sustained, permanent growth.[12]

Figure 4.1. Temporary housing for students at Rutgers College, 1946. Returning veterans lived in crowded conditions like this on many campuses. R-photo, buildings and grounds, box SL07 student life, folder "veterans," Special Collections and University Archives, Rutgers University Libraries.

During the initial student housing space crunch, the men lived in makeshift quarters, where they slept in tightly packed bunk beds and studied at tiny desks. There was almost no privacy. Most of the newly enrolled young men were veterans, so they were familiar with the conditions, which resembled those in military barracks.

This kind of overcrowding could not endure—a few more permanent dormitories were essential if the college was to grow into the state university that it had recently become.[13] Demarest Hall, a student residence designed by York & Sawyer and built in 1951, demonstrated the continuing ambience of a small school and recalled the colonial period of Rutgers's heritage in its red brick, white trim, and cupola.[14] Even more specifically, the gambrel roof (a roof with an upper slope that is shallow and a steeper slope below, thus giving more ceiling height in the attic) signaled the Dutch Colonial Revival style. Because Rutgers traced its roots back to the Dutch Reformed Church, the choice of this style was appropriate.

Although the exterior of Demarest resembled the nearby dorms, known as Bishop Quad, in plan Demarest employed a hybrid version of the entryway scheme, which included interior corridors: students entered the building from the courtyard, and, from there, staircases took them to their rooms. Once inside, students could circulate freely, using corridors that completely traversed the halls. Demarest's common rooms soon became magnets for social activities. (During this time, Rutgers had no student center, and the only space available for large social gatherings, such as dances, was the gymnasium.) As the yearbook, *The Scarlet Letter,* put it: "The spacious well decorated lounge [of Demarest] is the scene of freshman mixers with the [female] Douglass frosh, dances, parties, bull sessions, card games, and even studying."[15] When Demarest opened, nostalgia for lost Netherlandish roots still melted the hearts of administrators. But this low-rise brick building was not sufficient to solve the problem of crowding. Revolutionary changes required bold moves.

Figure 4.2. Demarest Hall, Rutgers University, 1951, York & Sawyer, architects. This C-shaped dormitory was built in a historical style just a few years before Rutgers administrators embraced modernism. R-photo, buildings and grounds, box 9, Special Collections and University Archives, Rutgers University Libraries.

The Rutgers deans predicted that the undergraduate student population would grow from five thousand in 1954 to nineteen thousand by 1970. Eager to solve the ongoing housing shortage, Rutgers officials planned three nine-story dormitory-and-classroom buildings on the banks of the old Raritan. Clean-cut Rutgers College men moved into urbane structures that announced the arrival of the forward-looking state university. The River Dorms, built in 1955 and 1956, went up only a few years after Demarest and a stone's throw from it—but in terms of architecture, they came from a different, decidedly modern world.[16]

The shift in style and scale did not come easily. Based on university projections, Rutgers had to find space for a thousand men on a campus closely bounded by private homes, a river, and the headquarters of a major corporation, Johnson & Johnson. The dean of men, Cornelius Boocock, did not at first welcome the idea of high-rises. In 1953, he suggested demolishing Bishop House (built in 1852 and now on the National Register of Historic Places) so that Rutgers would have enough space to build a series of low-slung, U-shaped buildings in the vicinity of the existing dormitories. He also wanted the university to purchase land for the construction of several more residence halls, again because he wanted to place one thousand students into low-rise buildings. It need hardly be stated that building low requires more land than building tall; thus, owing to the added expense of the land purchase, Boocock's suggestions about the site were ignored. Boocock stated his preferences (which reflected those of his staff): the new dormitories should be sited close to Demarest, should be low (three or four stories), should have entryways instead of corridors, and "must necessarily follow the traditional type of architecture to harmonize with existing buildings."[17]

Although the architects later took some of Boocock's suggestions seriously, at this stage they ignored every one of them. In January 1954, at the first meeting between President Lewis Webster Jones and the architectural firm Kelly and Gruzen, the architecture team confirmed that the buildings would not be next to Demarest, they would not be low, they would not have entryways, and they would not adopt a traditional style. The long, thin site along the Delaware and Raritan Canal—land that Rutgers already owned—emerged as the most desirable and least expensive space. The choice to build high-rises was generated in part by the small site and the fact that Rutgers already owned the land, but it was also entirely in keeping with the fashion in dormitory design in the 1950s. From tall buildings in this appealing location, on a clear day, students on the upper floors would have been able to see the Manhattan skyline. The three buildings would be angled to allow maximum sunlight and the best views.

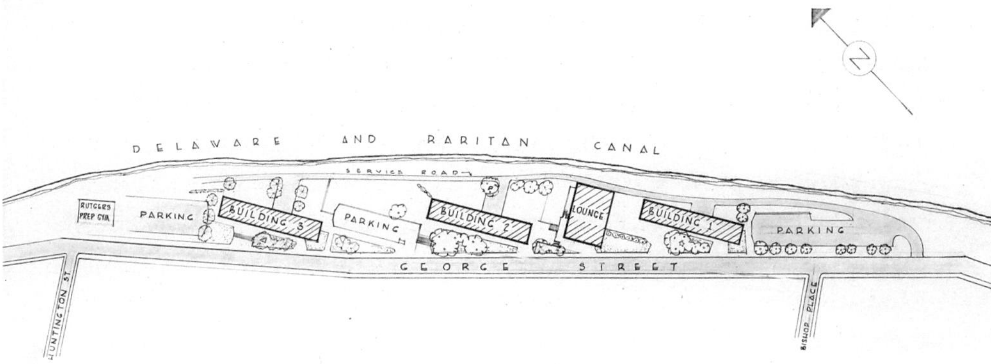

Figure 4.3. River Dorms, Rutgers University, 1955–56, Kelly and Gruzen, architects, site plan. These three slab dormitories (labeled Buildings 1, 2, and 3) housed one thousand young men on a sliver of land adjacent to the Delaware and Raritan Canal. The freestanding recreation center was a low-rise building, and the parking was at grade. R-photo, buildings and grounds, box 9, Special Collections and University Archives, Rutgers University Libraries.

The lead architect, B. Sumner Gruzen, lobbied for tall buildings when he told the Buildings and Grounds Committee of the board of trustees that the new dormitories, taking advantage of modern materials, would be cheaper than old-fashioned Demarest. He estimated the cost of Demarest at $2,400 per student and that of the new dorms (which were also more spacious) at $2,100 per student. Gruzen said it was any architect's responsibility to insist on "1954 architecture for 1954 students."[18] He was supported by Marie Hilson Katzenbach, a member of the board of trustees, who noted that the buildings at Oxford and Cambridge were diverse in style but always indicative of the periods in which they were built.

President Jones was present when the architects pitched two alternative skyscraper schemes. The first was denser and taller, with three thirteen-story buildings. The second comprised six seven-story buildings. University officials rejected the three thirteen-story buildings because the scale was far too big. Furthermore, because the footprint of the six seven-story buildings was larger than that of the three thirteen-story towers, the shorter buildings allowed for more classrooms on the lower levels, which was a desired outcome, as the demolition of temporary classrooms (on this exact site) had caused a critical lack of instructional space.

Boocock was not the only one concerned about the new style. Former Rutgers president Robert C. Clothier (a Princeton graduate) wrote privately to Lansing P. Shield, who chaired the Buildings and Grounds Committee, arguing that skyscraper dormitories would lead Rutgers away from the "traditional atmosphere of academic quiet (don't smile) which has prevailed in our dormitory areas heretofore and which is characteristic of Dartmouth, Princeton, and other non-urban universities."[19] Although his parenthetical comment "don't smile" suggests that he knew college boys could be boisterous, he was nonetheless perfectly serious about maintaining "a contemplative and reflective experience," which he felt was essential for undergraduate life. He further noted that the University of Pennsylvania and Columbia were envious of rural and suburban campuses. Rutgers, in Clothier's opinion, would be mistaken to build what he called "city dormitories."[20] The former president's opinion was not surprising; given that Demarest was built during his tenure, his preference for small-scale historicist structures was clear. For Clothier, the turn away from a small-college atmosphere toward the ruckus of densely packed dormitories came with a sense of loss.

The architecture firm concentrated its efforts for part of 1954 on a plan that included six buildings, each with a complex internal arrangement in which groups of sixty students would occupy individual "houses," with each house occupying two floors. Skip-stop elevators (elevators that stopped at every other floor) would deliver students to their so-called houses. The *Daily Targum,* the student newspaper, noted that "this staggered elevator system will eliminate half of the stops an ordinary system would have to make."[21] (Another way of putting that might be that if the elevators made 50 percent fewer stops, the occupants would be inconvenienced 100 percent of the time.) By August 1954, the architects reduced the number of residences to three. Also around that time, they scrapped the complicated double-height units, owing to their anticipated expense, and instituted a much simpler plan in which the student groups were arranged on single floors.

Martin Beck, the project architect, accepted Dean Boocock's advice on several important design matters. Boocock argued for an apartment for a supervisor or a married couple who would act in the role of houseparents. Housemothers were required by university policy in all residence halls and fraternities, and Boocock explained that the "control of resident students rests on this system."[22] The architects added the apartment.

Without uttering the word *suicide,* Boocock argued against balconies high off the ground, saying such a feature in a college dormitory was "not desirable and might even be dangerous."[23] One set of plans included a balcony outside each lounge, which was enough to concern Boocock; when another set of plans showed balconies on every room, his memos seethed with frustration. In one memo he wrote to President Jones, he ticked off many reasons this multiplicity of terraces was a terrible idea: students would store food and drink (one can speculate that he meant beer) outside; the doors opened inward and would waste valuable floor space in the small rooms; the plate glass of the doors might shatter during "sudden squalls or high winds"; and students would dry their clothes on the railings, which would demonstrate their disorderly habits to onlookers.[24] Indeed, the dean implied, the balconies were an invitation to slovenliness and mischief. The balcony-laden design ended with a compromise—the lounges had outdoor terraces, but the individual rooms did not (Plate 8).

As irritated as he was, Boocock did tell Jones that he sympathized with the architects, who were trying to avoid the look of "a low-cost housing project."[25] This loaded comment criticized the whole skyscraper concept (which we know Boocock disliked from the beginning) and amplified the critique mounted by Clothier. A single slab-shaped modernist building with a repetitive facade made up of rows of identical windows would bring to mind public housing, and three such buildings would summon up images of housing projects even more readily. In that regard, Boocock's remark was apt. On the other hand, as the architects could have reasonably countered, tall modernist housing had been built in wealthy urban neighborhoods, such as Greenwich Village in New York and Society Hill in Philadelphia. One difference between low-income public housing and middle- and high-income apartment blocks was that the latter tended to have balconies, which is probably why the architects included them in the first place. The architects made only one gesture toward the academic context, which was that the steel-framed buildings were clad in red brick.

The three slab-shaped River Dorms eventually came to be known as Campbell, Frelinghuysen, and Hardenbergh Halls, named for founders of the college. The plan of each residential floor of the River Dorms was a double-loaded corridor, with doors exactly opposite each other. Given that the three dorms were built on the same plan, and the stacked residential floors were identical, this construction was streamlined and made operation of the halls efficient. Such corridors were inexpensive to build and allowed for fifty-six people to form one social group per floor. Each room was for two students. Wardrobes for clothing were placed against the corridor wall to provide soundproofing as well as storage space. Lounges, kitchens, stairs, and elevators were at the midpoint of the hall, and the locations of these common spaces were marked on the exterior by the projecting balconies. One additional suggestion from Boocock was that the architects should use the River Dorms as an opportunity to "come up with a new type of bathroom and toilet for public buildings." He suggested that other than the savings of having

Figure 4.4. River Dorms, Rutgers University, 1955–56, Kelly and Gruzen, architects, interior hallway. Photograph by Laura Leichtman.

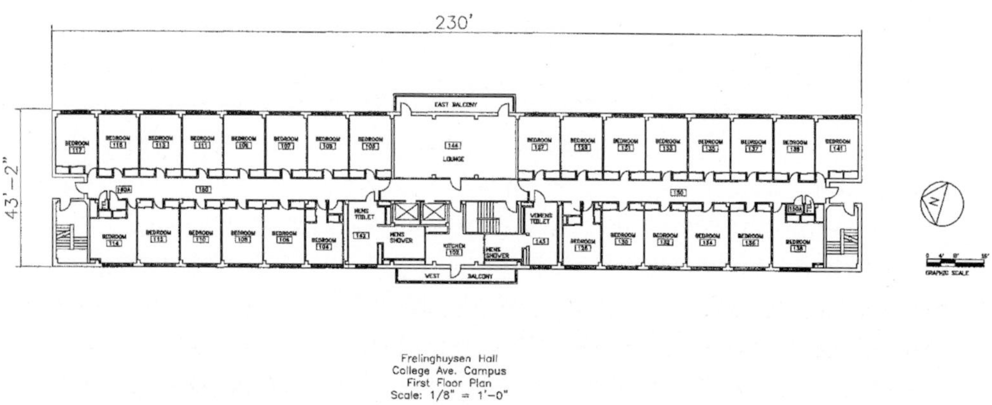

Figure 4.5. Frelinghuysen Hall, River Dorms, Rutgers University, 1955–56, Kelly and Gruzen, architects, plan, first floor of residential space (above the ground floor). The architects employed a basic double-loaded corridor plan. The elevators and one set of stairs were in the center, adjacent to the kitchen and bathroom and opposite the lounge. Additional stairs were at either end of the corridor. All rooms were doubles, except the supervisors' rooms, which were singles located at either end of the hall. Special Collections and University Archives, Rutgers University Libraries.

Figure 4.6. River Dorms, Rutgers University, 1955–56, Kelly and Gruzen, architects, interior rendering of a double room. Special Collections and University Archives, Rutgers University Libraries.

plumbing grouped together in vertical columns, there was no good reason to have showers and toilets together. "There is no reason why steam from a shower bath should cloud mirrors of a man trying to shave, nor is there any reason why ablutions should be connected so intimately with the calls of nature."[26] He made a good point, but the architects did not follow up on his idea.

In a common modernist strategy, Sumner and Gruzen lifted the building off the ground on pilotis, showing the influence of Le Corbusier and ensuring that the first level of living space was not at grade. A more unusual strategy was their placement of the classrooms below street level, cut into the canal's bank.[27] These sixty instructional rooms were not exactly underground—they were below grade on the street side but above grade on the canal side. The northernmost building had one floor of classrooms, and the other two had two floors of classrooms. Each classroom was square and designed for the traditional small class size of twenty-five persons. The classrooms looked out at the trees and brush above the Delaware and Raritan Canal. The university boasted that the seating capacity for teaching was fifteen hundred students. Oddly, university officials did not see the sharp increase

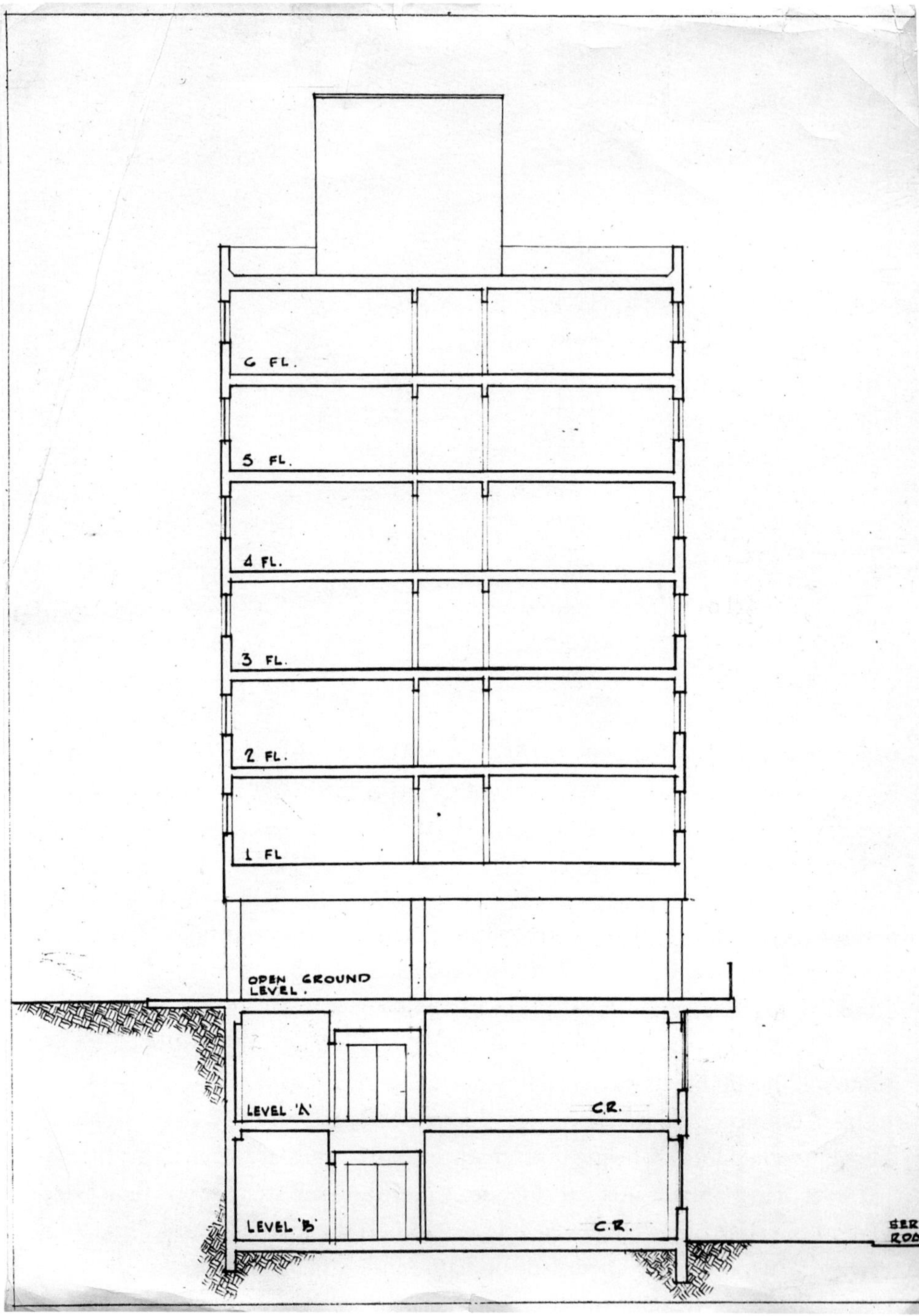

Figure 4.7. River Dorms, Rutgers University, 1955–56, Kelly and Gruzen, architects, section showing two levels of classrooms below grade (levels A and B). The ground floor was open to the outdoors and held aloft by pilotis. There were six floors of identical student housing above. The box on top was for mechanicals. R-photo, buildings and grounds, box 9, Special Collections and University Archives, Rutgers University Libraries.

in student population as a reason to build larger classrooms at this time. Either that, or the long, thin shape of the River Dorms did not lend itself to large classrooms, a fact that was lost on later architects who renovated the instructional space by combining square classrooms into nonfunctional rectangular ones. Only 18 percent of the land on the site was used for building, with the rest left free for circulation, terraces, and parking. Parking was relegated to the north and south ends of the long, thin site. In its time, this was a cutting-edge program for combining parking, instructional space, dwellings, and a recreation center.

Located between two of the River Dorms was a recreation center, with a large lounge, snack bar, and music room. The Ledge, as it was called, was a good place for Rutgers men to meet ladies from Douglass College, the all-female college located in New Brunswick. Originally the Ledge was designed to include a roof terrace, accessible from a side staircase. The main room was a unified, high-ceilinged volume, with a wall of windows that looked out over the Raritan. Gracious and open, the space was a point of pride for the student life staff, who had argued against using the building for a bookstore and post office, which would have cluttered the open hall. The Bruce Springsteen Band (as it was once known), among other major musical groups, played there. The placement of a student center among high-rises became standard in site planning during the 1960s. By pressing students into high-rises, planners could save real estate for student centers, dining halls, and other places for student activity.[28]

Beck wrote an essay on his architectural design philosophy that demonstrates his concern for the psychology of students, if not great skill in communication:

> Throughout the planning of these residence halls, the architects have approached the many problems involved with a concept that has become basic in present day educational building. This is the belief that today's student, no matter at what level, is a social being, and that he functions best, academically, physically and socially, when he feels at home.[29]

There was nothing homelike about the River Dorms, however—unless the students had grown up in the so-called projects.

One of the first freshmen to live in Hardenbergh Hall was also the founder of the River Dorm Club. Although he was enthusiastic enough about the residences to start a club, he was unimpressed by the architecture, which he described as "functional yet sparse."[30] Rutgers's division of public relations produced a special publication to mark the opening of the River Dorms; it employed watery metaphors to promote its theme of the democratization of higher education. A human deluge—a "tidal wave"—of students was washing up on the river's edge, lifting the floodgates of higher education so that students of all social classes could earn degrees at the first state university that could trace its roots to the colonial period.[31] (This claim was in fact an error. William and Mary was also a colonial college with state affiliation.)

The River Dorms soared above everything else at Rutgers. The three identical slabs were uncompromising in their modernity. The simple, sleek, money-conscious style was a statement of the future-focused goals of state-funded higher education. The River Dorms announced Rutgers's arrival as a state university; it was no longer a cozy liberal arts college. While there was a dramatic change in style from Demarest to the River Dorms, there was no equivalent change in the students—there were just more of them. And they were all men. Rutgers did not

Figure 4.8. River Dorms, Rutgers University, 1955–56, Kelly and Gruzen, architects, view from across the Raritan River during construction, showing steel frames. R-photo, buildings and grounds, box 9, Special Collections and University Archives, Rutgers University Libraries.

become coeducational until 1972, because Douglass College's leaders wanted a cooperative but not coeducational system. Midwestern colleges had been coed since the nineteenth century (see chapter 2), but East Coast schools were slow to adopt the practice.

Observers of Ivy League colleges tend to see the late 1960s as the moment when coeducation finally took hold. Resistance was strong: educating women in the Ivies' hallowed halls would diminish the contribution these institutions made to the nation as whole. The assumption was that each admission slot given to a woman was one taken away from a man, and since a woman would not put her education to use in public service or corporate stewardship, the country would have lost that one potential leader. As we saw in chapter 2, however, many midwestern state universities and two Ivies (Cornell and Penn) had been coeducational for decades by the late 1960s. Indeed, the well-adjusted, cheerful female undergraduate—managing her schoolwork without descending into the bluestocking blues—was a stock character in popular culture. In 1949, *Life* magazine produced a cover story that compared a happy-go-lucky sorority girl at a coed university to a sober, studious student at Smith. The author made no attempt at balance, almost openly mocking the "Smithie," Janet, for having to rely on "other girls for fun," and for taking her schoolwork too seriously. In contrast, the magazine depicted the coed at the University of Missouri, Jane, as lighthearted, sociable, attentive to her own appearance, and attractive to men. Jane's world revolved around activities with her boyfriend, Dick: getting "pinned," going to formal parties, having a Coke during the day between classes, and smooching in the front seat of a car. "Missouri girls think the all-feminine atmosphere of a women's college is unnatural and dull."[32] The article was more than an advertisement for coeducation—it was a condemnation of women's colleges. This kind of popular culture imagery reduced the Smith student to an academic drudge, perpetuating nineteenth-century stereotypes. Jane's boyfriend's fraternity association was celebrated in the article: fraternities remained popular postwar, although their influence on campuses lessened when undergraduate populations soared. The reporter directly addressed socioeconomic class when he noted that Missouri was "set up to give the best possible education to all comers," whereas Smith students were carefully screened for greater wealth. The Smithies were even shown riding horses. Since the yearly tuition and room and board at Missouri was listed as $700, compared with Smith's $1,600, the article left the reader with the clear impression that the state university in Missouri was not only more fun but also a bargain.[33] Covers sold magazines—and there was only one smiling girl on the cover, the wholesome and confident Jane from Missouri.

Figure 4.9. A student at Smith, an all-women's college, sits on the floor of her room typing a paper. *Life*, May 9, 1949. Photograph by Peter Stackpole, 1949.

Figure 4.10. A student at a coeducational state university enjoys her time with her boyfriend. *Life*, May 9, 1949. Photograph by Peter Stackpole, 1949.

SILVER RESIDENCE CENTER AT NYU UPTOWN: A COED RESIDENCE HALL

Many all-male colleges admitted women after World War II, but the process proceeded in fits and starts. Whereas Rutgers did not admit women (officially) until 1972, Douglass College women were taking courses on campus long before that. Many graduate programs were coed. Seeing a young woman on campus would not have surprised anyone in the 1950s or 1960s. New York University presents a different and even more complicated example. Women had been allowed to enroll in certain departments at NYU as far back as the 1870s, but they were not included in University College, an all-male internal-to-NYU undergraduate liberal arts college. This academic unit was located on the Bronx campus (also called University Heights or the Uptown campus). The Bronx setting (today the site of Bronx Community College) was considered bucolic compared to Greenwich Village, the original location of NYU, and when the Gould family donated land for a new suburban campus in 1894, the university used the site for a male-only liberal arts college. The premier architectural firm of McKim, Mead & White produced a measured, elegant essay in classicism, modeled on the 1893 World's Columbian Exposition in Chicago and contemporaneous with Columbia University's classical campus in Morningside Heights. The original NYU Uptown was an orderly assembly of buildings with uniform cornice heights, buff-colored brick, and a domed structure as its focus.[34] This suburban all-male enclave went through major changes in the 1950s. The college expanded in size, and university officials chose an internationally known architect to completely reimagine McKim, Mead & White's campus, adding a modernist set of buildings that would make a statement equivalent to the neoclassical setting.

Both NYU Uptown and Rutgers had good reasons for pressing hundreds of students into tall buildings. Both institutions faced long and narrow sites bounded by rivers. Building tall meant that half of the rooms had striking views. When NYU hired Hungarian immigrant and onetime Bauhaus instructor Marcel Breuer in 1956, he added a series of modern buildings in the vicinity of the McKim, Mead & White structures. NYU officials gave Breuer great freedom in the design, and his scheme employed all parts of a difficult site that dropped off steeply to a highway below. The new complex included a science building, a community center, lecture halls, and a dormitory for six hundred students (later named the Julius Silver Residence Center), all of which cascaded down a hill sloping toward the Major Deegan Expressway.

When Breuer got the job, NYU Uptown was all male, but in December 1958, the university announced its plans to make the Bronx campus coeducational. The engineering school, which was located in the Bronx, already accepted women into evening classes and graduate programs. Although NYU's officials might have asked Breuer to rethink his plan completely in order to produce two separate dormitories, one for each gender, they did not.[35] Instead, they asked him to adjust the six hundred–bed, seven-story high-rise residence, shaped to curve along the river, so that it would accommodate both men and women. In a 1959 article about new college buildings, *Architectural Record* anticipated the frayed nerves this coed dorm might cause when it made a point of noting that "rigid division and control will of course be maintained."[36] NYU fund-raisers simply stated that the time was right for coeducation, even in the sciences: "Women, with their great creative capacity, will be encouraged to enter careers in science and engineering as well as the liberal arts—to participate fully in the exciting and awesome work of the Age of Science in which we live."[37] Construction on the dorm began in May 1959.

The building's community hall was designated as the space for men and women to socialize during this important early phase (for NYU, anyway) in coeducation, when student affairs officers argued that men and women needed common areas such as dining halls and lounges. The community hall sat on relatively high ground, but three levels of the dorm were below the floor of the community hall. From the common room above the dining hall, the plan directed men and women into their own separate pedestrian bridges, which in turn led to the men's and women's ends of the slab. The contemporary architectural press, no doubt prompted by the architect, emphasized that costly elevators were unnecessary because the entrance level was on the fourth (or middle) floor, and so the maximum vertical communication was three flights, either up or down. On the other hand, if a first-floor student had the misfortune to strike up a friendship with someone on the seventh floor, the pair had to meet in the community hall in the middle, or one of them had to walk up or down seven flights of stairs.

Inside the men's section, the services (stairs, elevators, and bathrooms) were in the center, bounded on both sides by parallel corridors. In contrast to the men's side, the women's end of the hall included a double-loaded corridor; every two bedrooms shared one bathroom. Members of ACUHO took it for granted that units for women had to provide more space per student than did those for men. As the architect Hammond explained: "This may be due to a feeling that women demand—and even deserve—the luxury of more space, or due to the very real fact that women come to college with more belongings to be stowed away. A closet perfectly adequate for a man's clothes may be very cramped indeed when two bouffant evening dresses and three crinoline petticoats are hung in it."[38] These bulky feminine garments gobbled up closet space, but clothing storage was nothing in

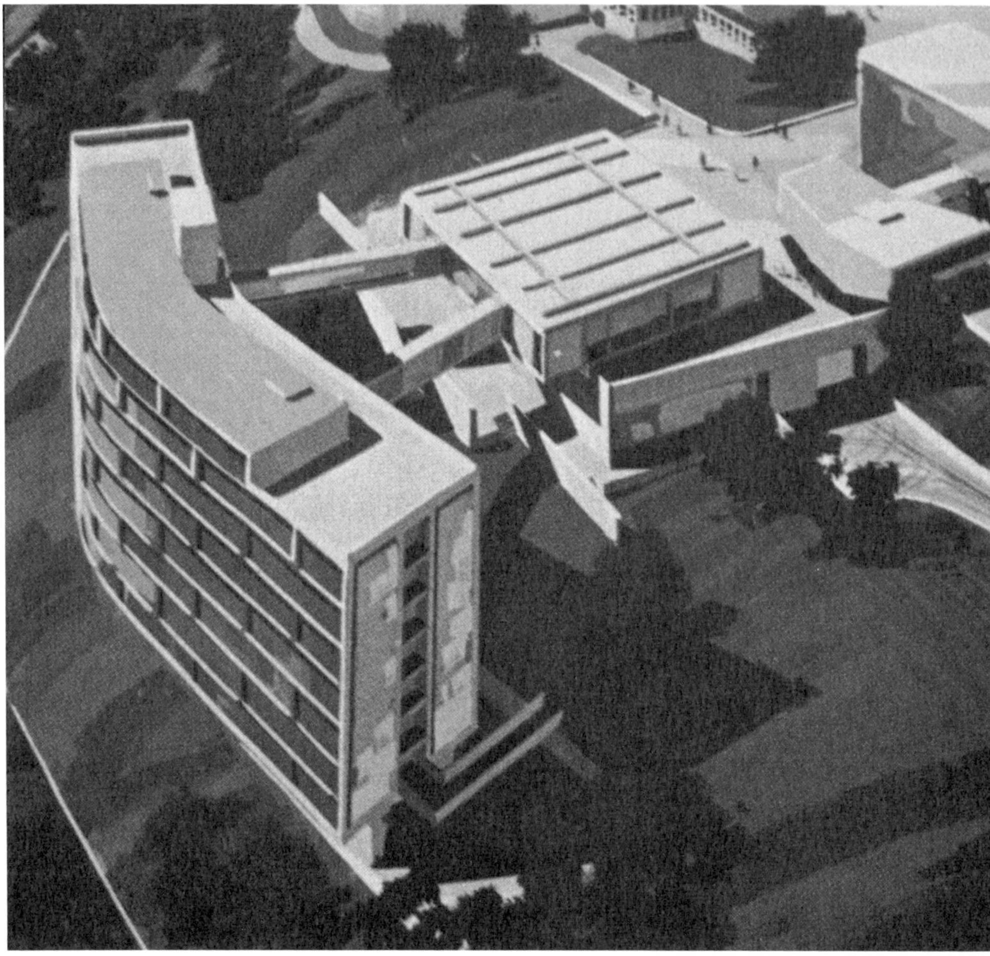

Figure 4.11. Julius Silver Residence Center, New York University Uptown, 1956–61, Marcel Breuer and Associates, architects, bird's-eye view. This drawing is from a pamphlet produced by the New York University Office of Food and Dining Services. University Buildings, box 14, folder 25, New York University Archives Collection.

comparison to the space that women needed for preparing snacks, laundering, ironing, sewing, and shampooing their hair.[39]

The scheme of pedestrian bridges funneling men and women from the recreation rooms into a divided skyscraper was a diagram of reluctant coeducation. The building did much of the work of social control, but not all of it: curfews, check-in procedures, and the usual array of parietal regulations governed residents' visits with members of the opposite sex. To cite one of many examples, the student handbook from 1963 explained that women visitors were not permitted on the

Figure 4.12. Julius Silver Residence Center, New York University Uptown, 1956–61, Marcel Breuer and Associates, architects, view of pedestrian bridges. Photograph by author.

men's side of the dorm, with the exception of mothers or guardians, who were allowed to visit on Sundays between 2:00 p.m. and 5:00 p.m. The handbook advertised the dorm as a "place where the resident continues his education in an informal and personal manner."[40]

The fire stair tower on the women's end appeared almost as a freestanding column, a stunning and avant-garde effect. But Breuer was also attuned to historical precedent. As he remarked, "We 'modern' architects don't hate tradition—the opposite is true."[41] Although most of the buildings were formwork-revealing concrete, the cream-colored Roman brick, precisely the same brick used on the nearby neoclassical McKim, Mead & White buildings, was a nod to context (Plate 9).[42] As the *New York Herald Tribune* reported, perhaps overstating the case: "The architects, Marcel Breuer and Associates, are using the same rough-stone foundation and brick as that in the adjacent Hall of Fame of Great Americans, so as to blend the structures optically."[43]

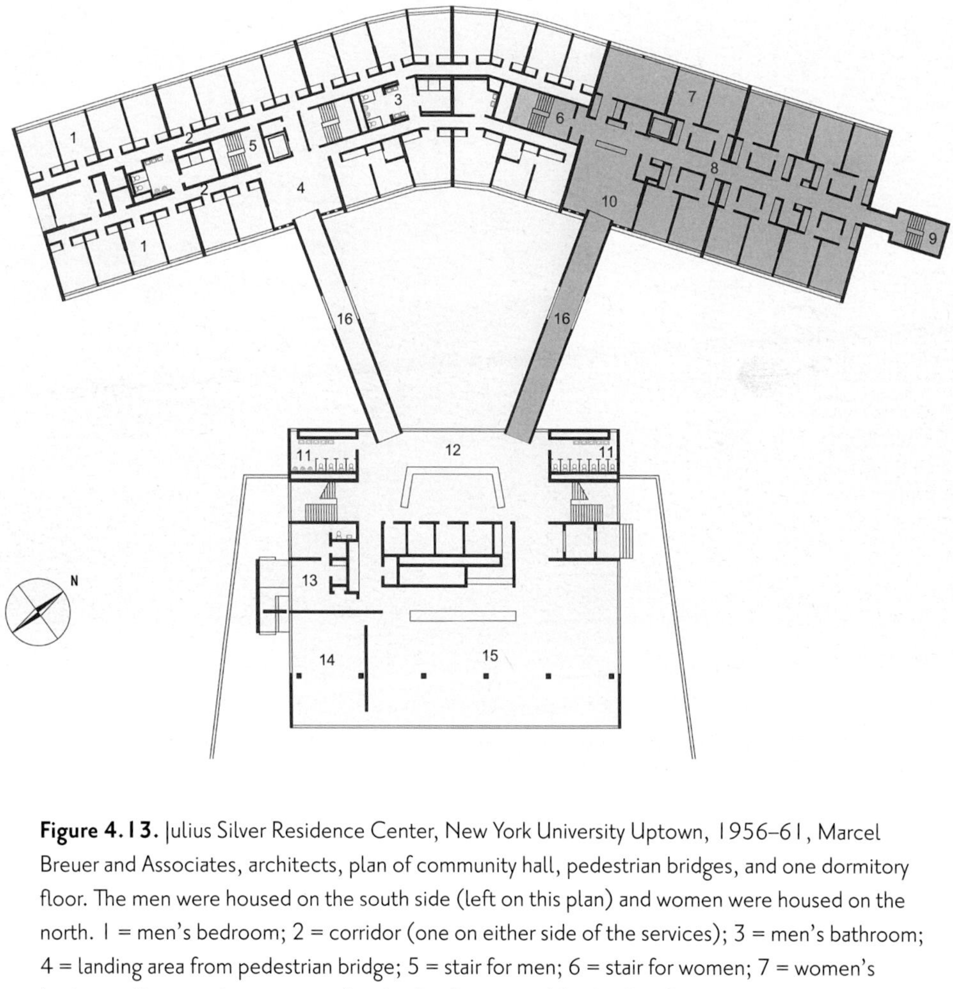

Figure 4.13. Julius Silver Residence Center, New York University Uptown, 1956–61, Marcel Breuer and Associates, architects, plan of community hall, pedestrian bridges, and one dormitory floor. The men were housed on the south side (left on this plan) and women were housed on the north. 1 = men's bedroom; 2 = corridor (one on either side of the services); 3 = men's bathroom; 4 = landing area from pedestrian bridge; 5 = stair for men; 6 = stair for women; 7 = women's bedroom; 8 = corridor on women's side; 9 = fire stairs; 10 = landing for pedestrian bridge on women's side; 11 = lavatories (serving the dining hall downstairs as well as the lounge and residence hall); 12 = reception desk; 13 = supervisor's apartment; 14 = television room; 15 = lounge; 16 = pedestrian bridge, one for men and one for women. Drawing by John Giganti based on Max Fengler, *Students' Dormitories and Homes for the Aged* (New York: Universe Books, 1964), 10.

Figure 4.14. Photograph from a 1963 New York University student handbook features the newly coed Uptown campus and the Silver Residence Center. The dining hall is on the left, one pedestrian bridge is visible, and the dormitory is in the background. Handbook produced by the NYU Resident Halls Student Government Activities Council, University Buildings, box 14, folder 25, New York University Archives Collection.

NYU began construction with a government loan of three million dollars, and fund-raisers added another million from a variety of donors when the structure was almost complete. Eventually, Julius Silver, vice president, general counsel, and member of the board of directors of the Polaroid Corporation, topped off the account. A plaque in his honor bore the following statement, written by Silver: "It is my hope that this center of brotherhood and learning, dedicated to the democratic way of life, will assure to all equal opportunity to cultivate those qualities of intellect and character which provide the ferment for progress and thus contribute to the advancement, the power, and the dignity of a free society."[44] In the 1960s, the college residence hall was seen as a bulwark against communism. Ironically, while the Soviets forced whole families to live in dormitories (something that was considered grotesquely antidemocratic), Americans encouraged students to live in dormitories to promote individualism.

Breuer patterned the interiors of the NYU dorm with repetitive diamond-shaped lozenges, creating dark, moody stairwells. Silver and others considered the sculptural forms and cutting-edge creativity of the architect's design to be signs of the freedom of expression that was afforded to artists in the West but denied to those in the Soviet Union. Breuer dominated the architectural scene at that time. By selecting him, NYU officials communicated their institution's elite status in architecture—not with historicizing styles, as the previous generation might have done, but with contemporary architecture.

OHIO STATE UNIVERSITY: TOWARD A MORE HUMAN BEEHIVE

One can understand why a college would build a high-rise on a cramped urban site in the Bronx or New Brunswick, but why build a skyscraper when a lot of land is available? In Columbus, Ohio, many reasons surfaced, including confidence in air-conditioning, trust in fast elevators, and the desire to create nice views from student bedrooms while also preserving green space for playing fields. In 1962, the OSU campus planner added another reason: he stated that he preferred tall buildings on that side of campus to balance the bulk of the football stadium, and he wrestled with a metaphor to describe the relationship: "[Morrill and Lincoln Towers] did compete with the stadium . . . as a matter of fact, they are slightly higher, but by putting them slightly higher, they stand up on their own two hind legs."[45] OSU officials chose the color of the concrete for the towers specifically to match the stadium's concrete color. The size and color of the football stadium set the tone for that entire area of the campus (Plate 10).

Morrill and Lincoln Towers (also known as the Olentangy and River Towers, and sometimes referred to as the River Dorms), both twenty-four stories, housed 3,840 students. No attempt was made to lessen the impact of the buildings' considerable mass. OSU's president, Novice G. Fawcett, lauded the project for being "economical in terms of space and in terms of cost; it was at the time the largest single building project ever undertaken by OSU."[46] Originally, university officials planned for two towers for men and one for women, which accurately reflected the student body's gender ratio. Although the deans of students eventually got involved in the planning and endorsed the innovative plan, the first programming meetings were held without the knowledge of John Bonner, the head of housing at OSU.[47] But when the whole project was scaled back to save costs, rather than building

Figure 4.15. Morrill and Lincoln Towers, Ohio State University, 1963–67, Schooley, Cornelius, and Schooley, architects, view from fields west of campus. Drawer 114, Morrill and Lincoln, 1966–67 December, Photo Archives, The Ohio State University Archives.

Figure 4.16. Morrill and Lincoln Towers, Ohio State University, 1963–67, Schooley, Cornelius, and Schooley, architects. Drawer 63, folder "Lincoln and Morrill Towers (2)," Photo Archives, The Ohio State University Archives.

three shorter towers, the decision was made to build two and maintain the twenty-four-story height. Administrators faced an elementary math problem: there were not enough women to fill a whole tower, and yet the architects dictated that the towers be identical in height. The genders needed to be separated, so the student deans invented a system in which each tower would house men in the lower two-thirds and women in the upper third. To keep the genders apart, they hired an elevator construction specialist named Charles Lerch, who engineered separate elevators for men and women that would not stop on the other gender's floors.[48] Each tower had a coed dining hall. As at NYU Uptown, student affairs experts promoted the internal public rooms, such as lounges, cafés, and cafeteria, as acceptable spaces for coed socializing.[49]

The design inspiration for the plan of each floor was the geometrically compelling domicile of the honeybee. OSU's student affairs deans enthusiastically endorsed the honeycomb plan, because it eliminated the double-loaded corridor. According to the student newspaper, the dean of men and the dean of women "thoroughly investigated" the unique plan.[50] In 1954, Walter A. Taylor, director of

Figure 4.17. The elevators in Morrill and Lincoln Towers at OSU kept men and women separate: the elevators for men stopped only on the men's floors, and those for women stopped only on the women's floors. These dormitories were racially integrated. *The Makio* (yearbook), 1967. The Ohio State University Archives.

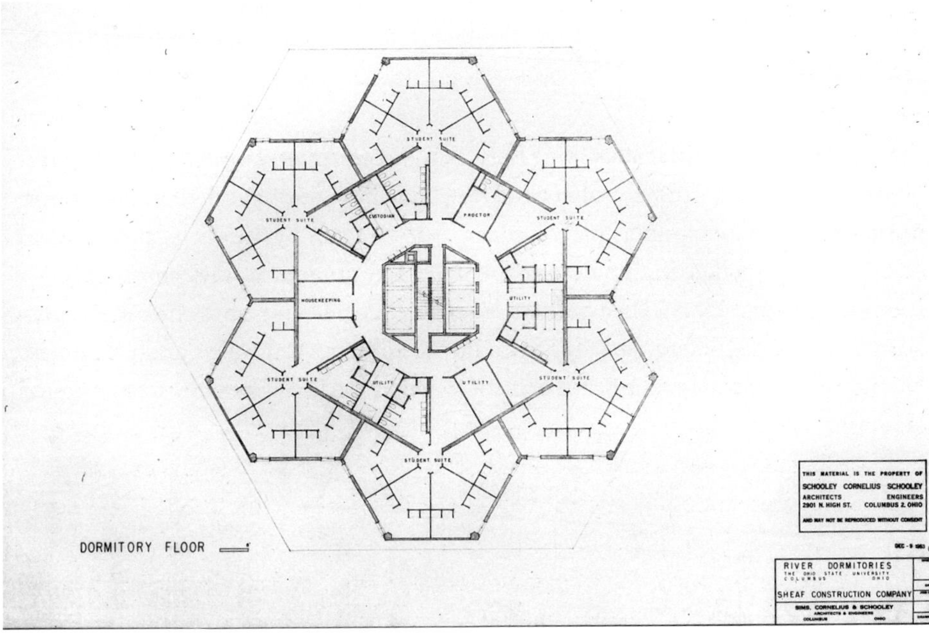

Figure 4.18. Morrill or Lincoln Tower, Ohio State University, 1963–67, Schooley, Cornelius, and Schooley, architects, plan of one floor of one tower. The design inspiration for this dormitory was the beehive. RG10/B-7 Office of the Planner, The Ohio State University Archives.

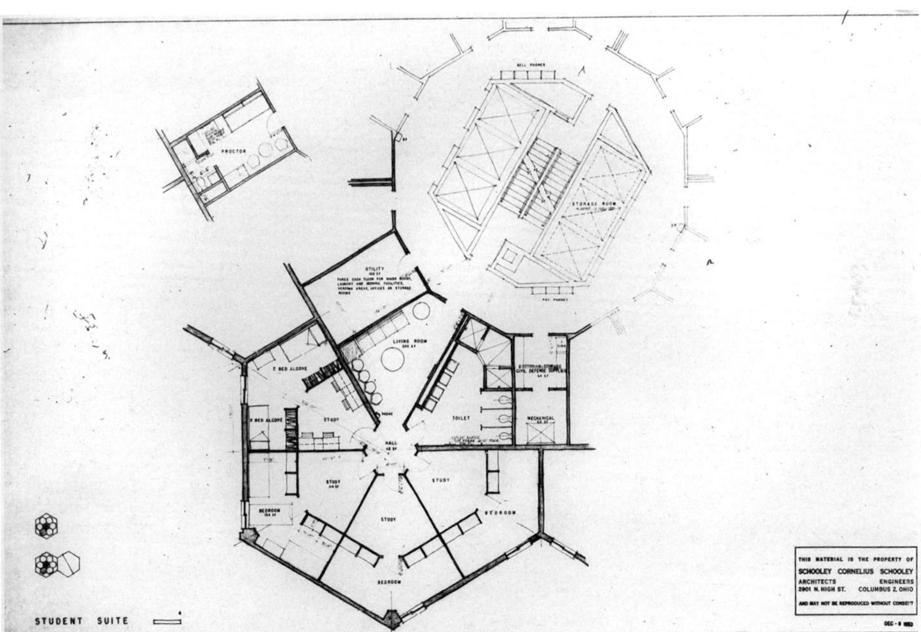

Figure 4.19. Morrill or Lincoln Tower, Ohio State University, 1963–67, Schooley, Cornelius, and Schooley, architects, plan of one suite on one floor of one tower. The complete lack of internal double-loaded corridors was considered a great advance in planning. There were ninety-six students per floor, sixteen per hexagonal lobe, and four per wedge-shaped suite. RG10/B-7 Office of the Planner, The Ohio State University Archives.

the Department of Education and Research of the American Institute of Architects, described the corridor plan as a "bowling alley" and said that "corridor dormitories were in increasingly bad repute."[51] A 1963 study by the deans' professional society found such corridors dehumanizing: "The student studies and sleeps in a room exactly like every other room in his residence hall and where he cannot possibly be alone anywhere; he steps from it into a long, windowless and pictureless corridor that represents the acme of institutionalization."[52] The OSU deans argued

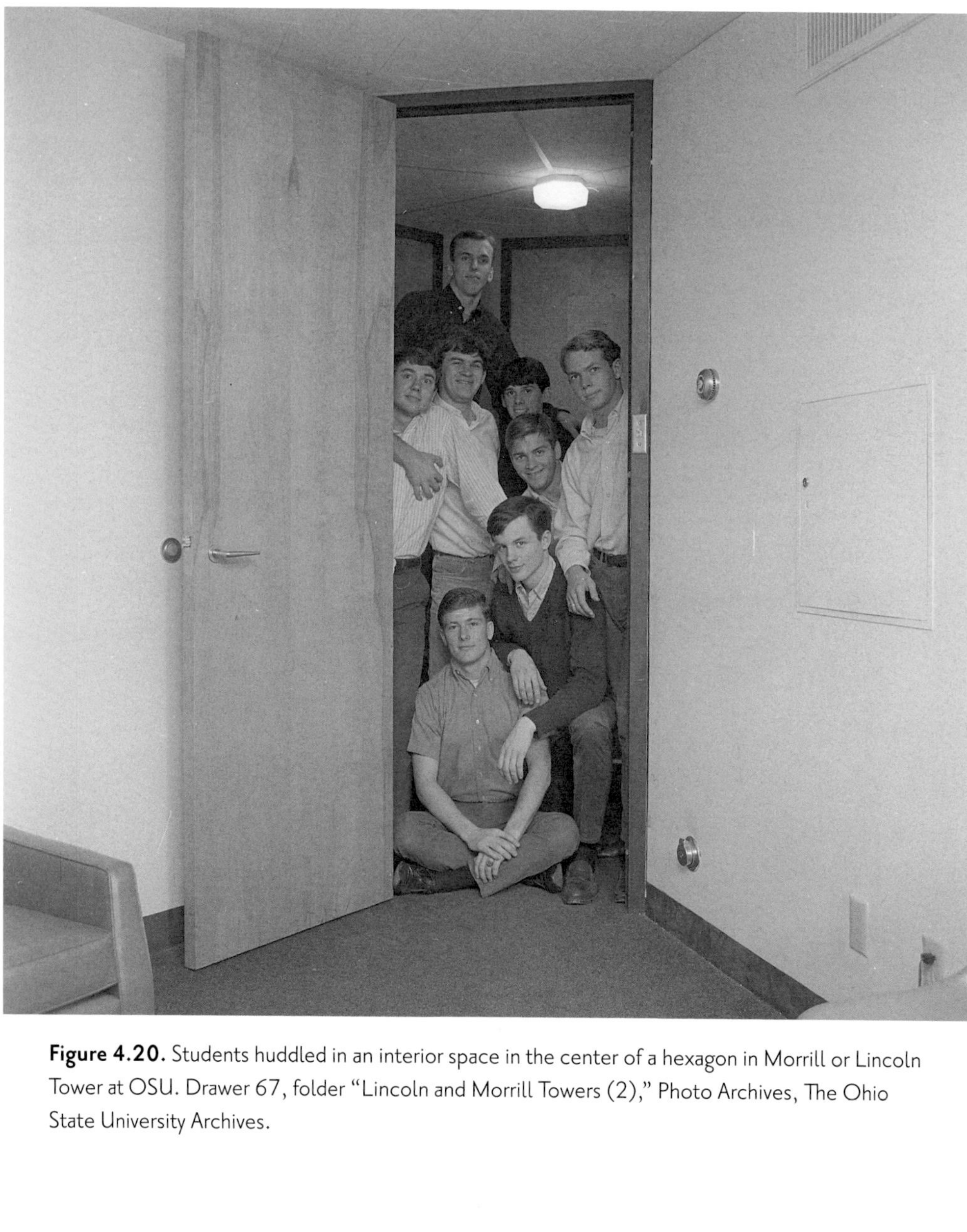

Figure 4.20. Students huddled in an interior space in the center of a hexagon in Morrill or Lincoln Tower at OSU. Drawer 67, folder "Lincoln and Morrill Towers (2)," Photo Archives, The Ohio State University Archives.

that the honeycomb plan would "promote better communication and higher student morale," and they found it to be particularly promising for students with "problems of social adjustment," who would be "more easily absorbed in units of 16 students than in units of only four students."[53] The beehive was considered *less* dehumanizing than the corridor.

Morrill and Lincoln housed blacks and whites together. On-campus housing at OSU was not racially integrated until the 1940s, even though the university's first black graduate completed his degree in 1892. Like many universities, OSU had almost no effective means of fighting any racial discrimination that its students experienced in the town. Landlords could simply refuse to rent rooms to black students. In 1963, the university's Office of Student Affairs set up a hearing board to make it possible for students to file official complaints about off-campus housing. Thereafter, if a landlord was found guilty of discrimination, the board reported this finding to the dean of women or the dean of men, and the landlord's property was removed from the approved list of rooming houses.[54]

Figure 4.21. Morrill or Lincoln Tower, Ohio State University, 1963–67, Schooley, Cornelius, and Schooley, architects, view from the study area of a four-man suite into the sleeping area beyond. The sleeping area had two sets of bunk beds. Drawer 67, folder "Lincoln and Morrill Towers (2)," Photo Archives, The Ohio State University Archives.

Not surprisingly, integrated housing came with strife. One openly racist parent, Martin Krumlauf, an attorney, complained about an interracial couple he had seen publicly displaying their deeply felt affection in the lobby of Morrill Tower. This particular complaint was lodged in a longer rant against coed housing in general. After first pointing out that he had several friends in the state legislature, Krumlauf explained that he, his wife, and their fifteen-year-old daughter went to visit his niece in Morrill Tower, where they found "sprawled on the floor of the lobby, four or five couples, mostly of the 'hippy' type, doing what I would call for lack of a better word 'petting.'" He went on: "I believe it wrong to have boys and girls domiciled in the same building; I believe it wrong to have a lobby full of petters; and I believe most people will agree with my views."[55] The dean dithered. He defended coed housing on the basis that other universities' student affairs departments supported it, and he claimed that mixed-gender dining and programming enabled students to gain valuable skills, in spite of the temptations they invited.[56]

At the end of the first year that Morrill and Lincoln were open (1966), a graduate student conducted research for a master's thesis on Morrill Tower and its effect on students. She was a student in the personnel assistant program, which was nested within the psychology department and was among the first master's programs for the professional training of deans of students. Echoing the standard philosophy, she wrote: "The residence hall is more than a dormitory or building with sleeping accommodations. . . . It is also a social and recreational center which fosters and develops the extraclass life of students. Finally, it is an educational community, a place where learning goes on outside the classroom."[57] She distributed a survey and received an astonishing 388 responses. She found that 95 percent of the students identified Morrill Tower's third-floor lounge and lobby as "attractive or very attractive," noting especially the spaciousness and the view. According to 53 percent of men, the best feature of the building was the fact that it was coeducational, an opinion with which only 20 percent of women concurred. Only 2.5 percent of the students said that Morrill Tower looked like a residence hall. More common comparisons (choices provided by the questionnaire's author) were to a prison (7.8 percent), a grain silo (17.8 percent), and a spaceship (6.9 percent).[58]

The deans at OSU argued strenuously for on-campus living, pointing out that commuters missed out on many of the most important aspects of college life: "Resident students have some real advantages such as the constant proximity to library facilities, opportunity for widening their circles of friendship through out-of-class participation in student organizations, the developing of leadership talents through the many and varied contacts with other students."[59] Although the word *diversity* was not in vogue at the time, Dean M. W. Overholt did allude to the global nature of the university when he wrote: "Casual and frequent contact with students from other towns and cities from the state, nation, and foreign countries has proven a valuable and culturally broadening experience for resident students."[60]

In May 1968, as the school year was coming to a close, and just eighteen months after the towers opened, two female students died in a fire on the eleventh floor of Lincoln Tower. A fellow student was charged with arson, found not guilty by reason of insanity, and committed by the state to a psychiatric hospital. An arsonist can set a fire in any dormitory, or any building for that matter, but the fact that these were unusually tall buildings struck at the hearts of Ohioans. Skyscraper dorms worried parents, made firefighting difficult, and aggravated state inspectors.[61]

Fire safety was one of many issues raised by those who objected to large dormitories. Another was the negative effect such dorms had on local rental markets. For decades, the rentals in college towns were mom-and-pop (mostly mom) operations. So when a new dwelling for thousands of students opened its doors, the household budgets of elderly women who ran boardinghouses took a major blow. In 1965, a local man, R. R. Fling, complained to OSU's president, wanting to know why the university was spending funds on something that the private market was already providing. He asserted that university officials were not modeling good business practice if they built tall structures that were both ugly and a waste of money. The university leaders asked the people of Ohio to believe that they were men of "integrity, responsibility, and leadership," yet they had the gumption to steal the livelihoods of their "neighbors, some of them old and relatively helpless," who had long sustained themselves by renting rooms to students. Who was paying for these "austere but unnecessarily expensive dormitories"? He answered his own question: the parents.[62]

Although high-rise dormitories are now common on college campuses, they are not well loved by modern-day deans of students. C. Carney Strange and James H. Banning, student affairs experts, summarize decades of opinion: "Gifford (2007), in a review of thirty years of research on the effects of high-rise living, concluded that 'high-rises are less satisfactory than other housing forms for most people, . . . social relations are more impersonal and helping behavior is less than in other housing forms, [and] . . . crime and fear of crime are greater.'"[63] Strange and Banning conclude that although skyscraper dorms are "economical in the short run, [they are] antithetical to the end goals of education."[64] In their view, high-rises are unwelcoming, do not lead to inclusion, are difficult on newcomers, and do not encourage people to help one another.

Clark Kerr evoked the spirit of the age when he told the audience at his 1958 inauguration as president of the University of California, Berkeley, "The world has changed—from an emphasis on tradition to an emphasis on progress—and the universities have changed, albeit at first reluctantly, to become the architects of progress instead of the protectors of tradition."[65] This shift from tradition to progress was decidedly reflected in residence hall architecture. But the skyscraper did not last long as the dominant mode of student housing. In the next chapter, we will explore alternative schemes, the hill town and the return of the quadrangle, both of which represented the rejection of high-rise living.

5

Rejecting the High-Rise

Quadrangles (Redux) and Hill Towns

If Americans turned on the radio in 1964, they were likely to hear a youthful, scratchy voice relaying a message they surely already knew: the times were a-changin'. Bob Dylan's purposeful anthem scolded parents for failing to understand their offspring: "Come mothers and fathers throughout the land . . . / Your sons and your daughters are beyond your command." Those sons and daughters, unmanageable baby boomers, transformed colleges. Back in the 1950s, however, few educators anticipated the seismic shifts that lay ahead. As historian Helen Horowitz has observed, "No one surveying the campus scene in 1959 could have predicted the 1960s."[1] Some of the behavior of college students associated with the 1960s actually started earlier, such as their demands for greater autonomy and complaints against in loco parentis. Yet the cultural shifts that took place around 1968 were so significant that the date offers a reasonable framework for ending this chapter.[2] Protests against the Vietnam War, sit-ins, the Free Speech Movement, antagonism toward business interests and colluding universities, opposition to the military draft, uninhibited use of birth control, recreational drug use—these were all evidence of a forceful youth culture that made college officials rethink higher education from the ground up. In spite of the fast-paced change swirling around them, deans of students persisted in maintaining that the residence hall was essential for building student character.

The fact that modernist architecture was, by its very nature, rigid and repetitive became a metaphor for the misery that dorm dwellers felt about their lives as subjugated students. Deans and students objected to skyscrapers with long, echoing corridors. Harold C. Riker, a student affairs dean, noted that the "corridor plan is the most common and the least satisfactory way to arrange student rooms." The arrangement "poses perennial noise and conduct problems."[3] Students argued that greater diversity was the key to student acceptance of on-campus housing. They complained that modernist skyscraper dorms undermined the individuality of students.[4] Cookie-cutter dorms, both low-rise and high-rise, in which every room was identical to every other left them feeling anonymous. Different architectural solutions were in demand.

This chapter explores two new residential colleges at Yale University, an early residence at the University of California, Santa Cruz, an experimental college that was part of Rutgers in New Jersey, and, finally, Kresge College, also at UC Santa Cruz. In all of these cases, administrators and builders sought to make the ever-growing research university manageable for undergraduates. College officials tried to find alternatives to skyscrapers and rejected modernist urban planning. I am not, however, suggesting that there was a linear progression from skyscrapers to later forms of student housing. (Indeed, some of high-rises described in the preceding chapter overlapped in time with this chapter's examples.) Yale looked to the medieval town plan. Cowell College at UC Santa Cruz and Livingston College at Rutgers both embraced the quadrangle. UC Santa Cruz's Kresge College, which was approved by the University of California regents in 1968, looked again toward the hill town.

To comprehend the powerful responses demonstrated by these four projects, one must understand the stranglehold that modernist urban planning had on the 1950s college campus. The Illinois Institute of Technology in Chicago was the foremost example of modernist campus planning. Under the direction of Ludwig Mies van der Rohe, the campus took shape as a series of rectilinear boxes in orthogonal relationships to one another. While Mies's campus in Chicago did not have high-rises, it used strictly functional zoning. As Michael H. Carriere describes it: "Mies's designs for his IIT buildings, often described as 'clean,' 'crisp,' and 'ordered,' provided a tangible symbol of the university's rational approach to technological innovation."[5] Planners copied mainstream modernist zoning principles on thousands of campuses. Residential areas, academic areas (with classrooms and faculty offices), athletic zones, and places for artistic performances were kept separate. Student centers were developed as their own freestanding building type.[6] Libraries held books and not much else. Riker reported in 1960, with surprise, that some colleges were "experimenting with formal classrooms in the residence halls."[7] The functional division of space was a modernist zoning principle that was widely employed in both cities and colleges.

But such rigid zoning became a target. The younger architects who took part in the influential International Congresses of Modern Architecture (known as CIAM, from the organization's name in French, Congrès Internationaux d'Architecture

Figure 5.1. Illinois Institute of Technology, Chicago, 1941–55, Ludwig Mies van der Rohe, architect. Photograph by Ann M. Keen.

Moderne) were wary of the modernist urban planners' fixed zones and preference for high-rises. Members of this generation of architects who formed the self-named Team X (or Team 10) found modernist urban planning to be almost as dogmatic as the academic architecture that preceded it. They wished to replace the anonymous, car-oriented, disingenuous universality of modernism with a kind of architecture that would meet the needs of specific communities. In its disregard for the individual and uncritical acceptance of high-rise housing, modernist planning had lost any connection to the people it was supposed to serve. The members of Team X felt that one of the problems facing architects was how to balance the need for communality with the desire for individuality. The same ideas were popular on college campuses.

The first informal meeting of the architects who would form Team X was in the Dutch village of Otterlo in 1953; the group's first official meeting was in southern France in 1960. The hill town emerged as a pervasive paradigm in the 1950s and

1960s. Hermann Schlimme has observed that Alison Smithson, Peter Smithson, Aldo van Eyck, and Georges Candilis "traveled individually to Greece, Spain, Italy, or North Africa," and that Giancarlo De Carlo lived in an Italian hill town.[8] The hill town was a precedent that captured the imagination of architects because it offered opportunities for casual interaction and seemed like it would generate "social spontaneity."[9]

In 1966, the Team X architects met in De Carlo's Urbino. At that time, they saw De Carlo's Collegio del Colle, a residence for students that he designed in 1962 and completed in 1966 as part of his urban plan for the whole town. The Collegio del Colle made an enormous impact on contemporary architecture; van Eyck lauded it for treating each student as an individual, rather than subsuming students into a lumpen crowd.[10] De Carlo defined spaces by the activities he hoped would take place there, rather than by superimposing idealistic forms on the landscape and then shoehorning functions in afterward. In this way, De Carlo's design for the university in Urbino was the opposite of Mies's at IIT. At the top of the hill was the college hub, a dynamic large-scale concrete structure that served as a gathering space for large groups. In contrast, the spaces for individuals (the student bedrooms) cascaded down the hillside, each one identified by its own window. Parking for the town of Urbino was tucked inside the belly of the hill.

YALE UNIVERSITY'S NEW RESIDENTIAL COLLEGES OF THE 1960S

One of the first experiments with the hill town concept for residential colleges took place at Yale, among the revered 1930s-era Yale colleges, which were by the postwar period creaky, crowded, and run-down. Even worse, they seemed like a sad breeding ground for a generation of dull and unsettled men like the dreary capitalists depicted in Sloan Wilson's 1955 novel *The Man in the Gray Flannel Suit,* which spoke to the conformity demanded by the business world. The architect of Yale's pathbreaking new colleges, alumnus Eero Saarinen, cogently explained: "We have tried to avoid the sense of standardization which is so prevalent in twentieth-century architecture and in twentieth-century 'man-in-the-gray-flannel-suit' life."[11]

First, Yale officials had to decide whether to choose the cost-saving route, which would have been to construct traditional residence halls containing student bedrooms and a smattering of lounges and laundries, or to go full out and build more residential colleges, with apartments for masters and fellows, libraries, dining halls, common rooms, and snack bars. They chose the latter.

Yale president A. Whitney Griswold formed a committee to explore the question, and the resulting report reiterated Yale's commitment to residential colleges.

Figure 5.2. Morse and Stiles Colleges, Yale University, 1958–62, Eero Saarinen, architect. Saarinen is seen here with a large model of the two residential colleges, which he designed to have the rambling plan of an Italian hill town. Yale Manuscripts and Archives.

The committee members looked to the United Kingdom for guidance and found that British universities had recently decided to house their students in a panoply of newly expanded colleges:

> For a time it was anyone's guess whether the British universities would elect to solve their problem by going the way of European universities, which are non-residential, which confine their education effort almost wholly to the classroom, and which place little or no limit on the size of their classes; or, on the other hand, by cleaving to the residential tradition represented by Oxford and Cambridge. Certainly it would have cost far less money and effort for them to have chosen the European way. Instead they chose the Oxford–Cambridge way. They did so only after prolonged study and re-appraisal of the residential principle *in an educational context.* Their conclusion was that the *educational* value of this principle was so great that it was worth all the effort and sacrifice to extend it at least in the

> form of halls of residence to the provincial and Scottish universities as well as preserving it in the colleges of Oxford and Cambridge.[12]

At Yale, the report claimed, residential colleges would help the university to avoid the difficulties that were bound to arise when lower-class men attempted to join the "Elis" in New Haven. The document rallied support in classist terms. Referring to the GI Bill, it continued:

> In both countries [the United Kingdom and the United States], the war and its aftermath have brought to the surface and into circulation in higher education young men and women without any previous background or experience in such education or any truly cultivated or carefully reasoned conception of its purposes. The British Education Acts of 1944–45 admitted for the first time a whole new class of citizens to educational privileges heretofore largely enjoyed only by the aristocracy and the wealthy. In the United States, a comparable increase in the demand for higher education brought similar elements into our colleges and universities. At the same time, in both countries, a widespread collapse of moral and aesthetic standards and a deterioration of taste, which affected even students from well-educated and prosperous homes, followed the war. . . . These trends have put a premium on the residential college as means of cultivating and refining students in moral and aesthetic terms as well as preparing them for responsible membership in society after graduation.[13]

The residential college was considered crucial for transforming certain "elements," meaning middle- and working-class men, into refined and cultivated gentlemen. Furthermore, the networking aspect of the residential college was key. It would help prepare Yale's "thousand leaders per year" for the world of work—not the routinized, hollow business world populated by men in identical suits, but some not-yet-known brighter American future.

Griswold was fortunate in striking a deal with philanthropist and Anglophile Paul Mellon, who embraced the living–learning concept and valued modern architecture. Griswold, Mellon, and Saarinen set out to meet the challenges of the 1960s with revolutionary and grand architecture. They were tackling a fundamental problem: How do you create architecture for unstructured learning, the kind of informal, morality-refining education that takes place outside the classroom? The answer lay in nonstandard spaces.

Later named Morse and Stiles Colleges, Yale's two new residential colleges exemplified Griswold's commitment to modern design: "A great university should look at modern architecture as a way of expressing itself."[14] Griswold held an appreciation for individual contributions to culture. He gave architects, including Saarinen, Paul Rudolph, and Gordon Bunshaft, artistic freedom for reasons he made clear: "Could *Hamlet* have been written by a committee, or the 'Mona Lisa' painted by a club? Could the New Testament have been composed as a conference report? Creative ideas do not spring from groups. They spring from individuals."[15] Needless to say, architects loved Griswold. And even though Saarinen was known as an audacious contemporary architect, he sought imagery and materials that would respond to the architectural context of Yale. The outcome was, paradoxically, daring and nostalgic at once (Plate 11).

The planning principles that distinguished Morse and Stiles from their squared-off forebears were significant: Saarinen was not guided by the quadrangle. The gentle convex curve of the north face of the Morse and Stiles complex, with its oval lawn, was open to the city. The asymmetrical exteriors hit the sidewalk less ominously than did the walls of Yale's quads. Each college had its own dining hall, served by a single kitchen on the lower level. All the programmatic needs were met: student rooms, faculty apartments, libraries, and dining halls. Saarinen spoke to students about what they wanted in the new colleges, and they expressed an admiration for the nooks and crannies of neo-Gothic colleges over the predictable spaces of Georgian Revival ones; the architect therefore leaned heavily toward the erratic forms of the Middle Ages. Most of the structures at Morse and Stiles were three or four stories tall, but towers on the east and west created a picturesque silhouette, another reference to towns in Italy, such as San Gimignano and Urbino. Urbino was an especially relevant case, as it was home to a seventeenth-century university.

The *New Haven Register* reported on November 26, 1962: "Crowds thronged Yale's new Stiles and Morse Colleges this weekend to decide for themselves what they thought of the . . . daring design."[16] Visitors were greeted by curved lines and crooked streets. Sam Callaway, who lived in Stiles when it was new, later remembered this as a serious planning flaw; having also lived in a typical quadrangular Yale college, Saybrook, he found that he missed the natural way people met each other in the outdoor "room" created by the four walls of the courtyard.[17] But (of course) a perfectly square outdoor room was not in keeping with a plan inspired by medieval towns. As an architecture student, Callaway was prepared to appreciate the aspirational architecture of an internationally known designer, but he found the interior of Stiles "sterile" and the dining hall "like a tomb." On the positive side, he felt that the residential college system as a whole was "absolutely central to everybody's Yale experience."[18] Another Yale student from the early 1960s, one of

Figure 5.3. Morse and Stiles Colleges, Yale University, 1958–62, Eero Saarinen, architect, site plan. 1 = master's houses; 2 = dormitories; 3 = outdoor courtyards; 4 = dining halls; 5 = shops; 6 = graduate school (existing). Drawing by John Giganti based on Max Fengler, *Students' Dormitories and Homes for the Aged* (New York: Universe Books, 1964), 14.

modest means, found that the residential colleges made the socioeconomic disparities between the prep school men and the others less noticeable.[19]

The materials used for Morse and Stiles also inclined toward the medieval: Saarinen called the walls "masonry without masons." His idea was to place larger-than-usual stones in the reinforced concrete, then blast off the outer layer of concrete with water; this was supposed to allow the stones to emerge from the slurry. The technique was meant to be an efficient and high-tech way of attaining contextuality (a nod to the Gothic Revival surroundings) without copying old-fashioned construction methods like stone setting. Alas, as architectural historian Rejean

Figure 5.4. Stiles College, Yale University, 1958–62, Eero Saarinen, architect, westernmost entry to the college's residential portion. Workers created the rough surfaces of the building's outer walls by using unusually large stones in the concrete and power-washing the outer layer before the wall was set. When this technique did not prove effective, workers hammered away at the concrete to reveal the stones. Photograph by author.

Legault has pointed out, these walls were neither efficient nor high-tech; workers had to chip away at the concrete with hammers to reveal the large stones.[20]

There remained great loyalty to the staircase type at Yale. As one college master put it, "I feel strongly that the entry system should be preserved and that we do not go to elevators and corridors."[21] The plan of Morse and Stiles was a hybrid of the two most popular dormitory plans: the entryway and the double-loaded corridor. The plan for Nassau Hall at Princeton from the mid-eighteenth century combined these two types, as did Adams and Tripp Halls at the University of Wisconsin–Madison in the 1930s. This compromise or hybrid plan had its own history.

About 70 percent of the rooms in Morse and Stiles were singles. This was an unusual luxury, even at Yale. It reflected the ideas of the patron, Paul Mellon, about the individual in the group. As Mellon explained it, the funds he provided were "to support Yale's purpose of improving opportunities for each student to develop as an individual in the educational environment of a great university."[22] Saarinen echoed this sentiment.[23] Each room on a given floor had an irregular, angular outline. Although the overall shape of the dormitory included a curve, inside there were few curvilinear spaces. The walls of the corridors were not parallel to one another (in plan), but the walls did meet the ceiling in the normative way. Many well-educated people have perpetuated the claim that there are no right angles in Morse and Stiles, but such people are apparently blind to the angles formed by the walls and floor, the walls and ceiling, and the corners of the windows.

Saarinen was particularly enthusiastic about continuing the Yale traditional of providing so-called butteries. (A butte was a barrel for holding beer; the word is medieval in origin, and the term *buttery,* meaning a place to get drinks inside college, is still used at Oxford and Cambridge.) At Morse and Stiles, the butteries took the shape of informal basement snack bars with round oak tables. The *New York Herald* celebrated these subterranean common rooms with the breathless

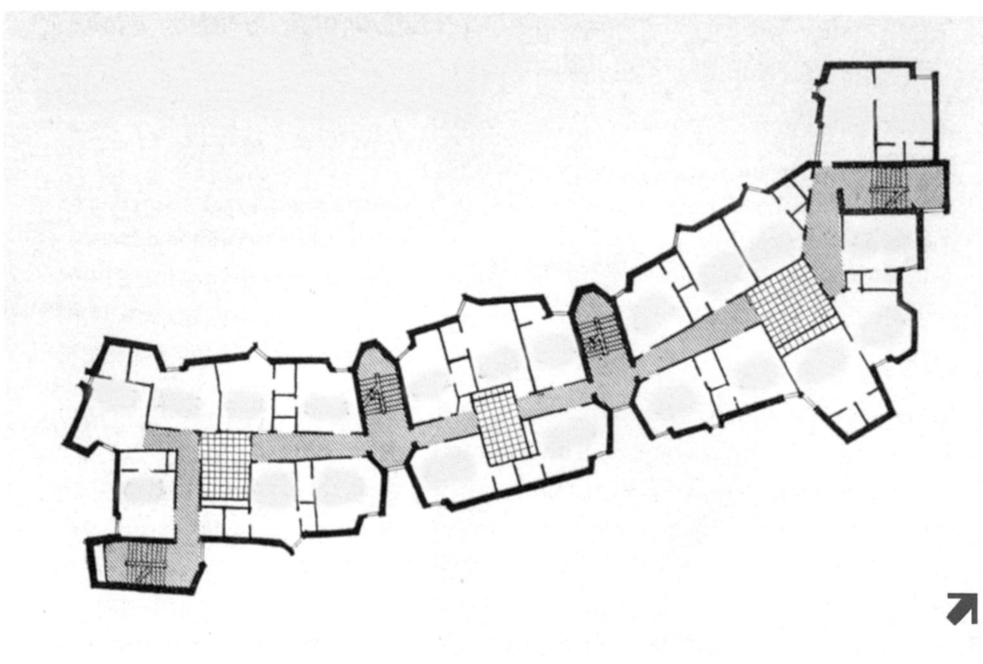

Figure 5.5. Morse College, Yale University, 1958–62, Eero Saarinen, architect, plan of one floor, showing a hybrid of the entryway and double-loaded corridor systems. Drawing by John Giganti based on Max Fengler, *Students' Dormitories and Homes for the Aged* (New York: Universe Books, 1964), 14.

Figure 5.6. Morse and Stiles Colleges, Yale University, 1958–62, Eero Saarinen, architect, interior of a single room. From *Yale College Introductory Information, 1966–67*. Collection of the author.

headline "2 New Yale Colleges Will Have Butteries." Quoting Saarinen, the reporter explained that "fellows and students can make conversation and argue 'until the long hours of the night.' Without TVs, [butteries] will become 'centers of conversation rather than areas where people sit drugged by canned entertainment.'"[24] These cavern-like cafés were not charming afterthoughts or out-of-touch references to Oxbridge. They were intentional: their purpose was to facilitate the character building that came out of interactions between young faculty members (or graduate students) and undergrads.

Griswold owed Mellon a debt of gratitude. Mellon's gift made it possible for Yale to continue the residence college tradition and add to the overall number of undergraduates. Griswold's thank-you letter to Mellon began, "Repeatedly during the past few months I have sat down to write to you about your wonderful gift to Yale only to abandon the attempt with the sense of my own inadequacy." Then his modesty slipped away and he continued: "I believe that your gift will truly affect the course of Yale as profoundly as any benefaction in its history. . . . Not only will it ensure the future of the kind of education we are all concerned to preserve at Yale, but also the kind that is most in danger, and yet most desperately needed in our country."[25] The goals were lofty, and the stakes were high—the dream was that fellows and students would dwell in harmony, share meals on fine china, and revel in sizzling conversation in the buttery—and that this would foster a new generation of men whose finely developed character would allow them to act responsibly on the world stage. The buildings were individualistic and the students produced therein were to be equally creative and original. This concern for individuality and enthusiasm for the future are indicative of the Cold War ethos.

The energetic push for two new residential colleges at Yale came from the top: President Griswold was enamored of the college idea. He stated this fact on numerous public occasions, as in a speech in which he outlined his seven aims as president. Goal number 6 was "to preserve the residential principle in the fullness of its strength as the most powerful ally of formal education."[26] As we have seen in earlier chapters, with the rise of the research university, professors relinquished the role of providing students with moral guidance in favor of research and teaching. At large state universities, deans of students emerged to take over the counseling of students. At elite schools like Yale, however, faculty continued to guide students in their personal development. Not all professors wanted this role, nor were all fit for it. But some, the ones who chose to serve as masters in the colleges, accepted the job of pastoral care. Starting with the Harkness family's gift in 1932, Yale recommended that some adult dwell with the undergraduates in each residential college, although that adult could be a graduate student. Not every residential college

Figure 5.7. Morse and Stiles Colleges, Yale University, 1958–62, Eero Saarinen, architect. Library of Congress, Prints and Photographs Division, Balthazar Korab Archive at the Library of Congress.

had a live-in master until the policy was codified in 1963, at which time Yale clarified that each college must have a two-part administrative structure, with the "master" as the chief administrative officer and the presiding academic presence and the "college dean" as a person who would "assist in the administration of the college" and "bring [his] own intellectual and academic background" to the community. The master approached the student holistically; the dean was more of an academic adviser. Just as Morse and Stiles were coming into existence, Yale reasserted its belief in adults and students living together in the Oxbridge way.[27] Ideally, *both* master and dean would dwell in the college, but frequently only the master lived in.[28]

UC SANTA CRUZ AND THE CLUSTER COLLEGE

Yale was wrestling with some of the same issues as the University of California: how to make the big research university seem small. From his perch as president of the entire University of California system, Clark Kerr developed a vision of tiered levels of state universities, with two-year colleges focusing on vocational skills and remedial education, a state college system for ordinary undergraduate education, and the "UC" level, which would include the most prestigious research universities and boast the highest admissions standards. In his book *The Uses of the University,* first published in 1963, he described the large research university as a remarkable invention, but one perilously challenged by contemporary forces. He compared the vast offerings of the "multiversity" to an awe-inspiring city; like a metropolis, the multiversity could be overwhelming and dehumanizing.[29]

The University of California campus at Santa Cruz, a newcomer on the collegiate scene, had two founding fathers, Kerr and Dean McHenry; the first students arrived in 1965.[30] In 1961, Kerr appointed his old friend McHenry to serve as chancellor of UC Santa Cruz. Kerr cherished the smallness of Swarthmore, his alma mater, while McHenry valued the great library and cultural events at his alma mater, the University of California, Los Angeles. The two men believed that they could merge the best of Swarthmore and UCLA by using the concept of the "cluster college." Such a college would combine all the advantages of the research university (such as libraries, science laboratories, and venues for cultural performances) with the humane scale of the small college. One of the key ideas for the cluster college was the integration of academic and nonacademic activities. Students would study, but they would also join clubs and take a strong role in governance. The individual colleges within UC Santa Cruz were intended to be communities of students and faculty, which was an overt reinterpretation of the residential colleges of Oxbridge.[31] UCSC was experimental in other ways. It had no majors and no grades, only essay-like evaluations—and yet it had very high entrance standards. Learning for its own sake was paramount. UCSC students were a self-selected class of young people who were not interested in being cogs in the wheels of the grinding machine of capitalism.

Kerr was well aware of the importance of architecture for this educational undertaking, and he even contributed to an article in *Architectural Record* titled "California's New Campuses: Building Big While Seeming Small."[32] For this audience of architects and allied professionals, Kerr outlined the needs of the cluster college and pinned his hopes for the future of American higher education on the concept. The article described UCSC's innovative campus plan, the work of John

Carl Warnecke and Thomas Church, which was unlike any other in the United States at that time, reflecting the experimental nature of the college. According to the plan, every attempt had to be made to preserve the redwood trees that dotted the site. Furthermore, Warnecke and Church required that the generous Great Meadow, with its viewshed including the Monterey Bay, be left open. The buildings, rather than occupying that flat open space (which would have been the obvious choice for earlier generations of planners) were relegated to the hills and to the small valleys between the trees. As architectural historian Virginia Jansen has explained: "That Master Plan, which guaranteed the survival of the Great Meadow, both as a concept and an ecological fact, and awarded almost religious respect to trees, created a set of primary sites along the so-called 'ecotome,' where the redwoods met the meadow."[33] The best sites went to Cowell and Stevenson Colleges, the first two complexes. The long-range development plan of 1963 specifically called for the residential colleges to project "informality, intimate scale, and inward orientation" and noted that, in contrast, the public buildings could be more formal.[34] UCSC included several coeducational communities for approximately six hundred students and fifty faculty fellows each.[35]

COWELL COLLEGE: QUADRANGLES BY THE BAY

Cowell College, the first residential college completed at UCSC, opened in 1966. It was named for the historic Cowell Ranch and the family that donated the land. Cowell was designed for six hundred students: two hundred resident men, two hundred resident women, and two hundred commuting students. Wurster, Bernardi and Emmons, the architecture firm, planned an upper quad, a lower quad, a dining hall, and a wide terrace. The dining hall and terrace offered a vista of the bay. Obviously, Cowell looked back yet again to Oxbridge, Yale, and Harvard, and Wurster, Bernardi and Emmons interpreted the old chestnuts by tweaking the plans and introducing a more casual style. With its pitched roofs and white walls, Cowell looked vaguely Mediterranean, with particular influences from coastal Spain, but it also resembled the Spanish Colonial styles of the New World, thus giving the place an appropriate California flair (Plate 12). Inviting balconies, appealing in the mild climate, were cantilevered off the facades. Enormous redwood trees pierced the sky. In the plan, each side of the quad was formed by a rectangular block. A stair in the center gave access to very short corridors, producing a cross between the staircase and corridor plans.

Each rectangular section was divided vertically into two four-story sections, with a wide staircase between the two sections that was fully glazed. The staircases

Figure 5.8. Cowell College, University of California, Santa Cruz, 1963–66, Wurster, Bernardi and Emmons, architects, view across terrace looking toward the dining hall. G730uuc874 p467 GB, UCSC Special Collections and Archives. Courtesy of Special Collections, University Library, University of California, Santa Cruz.

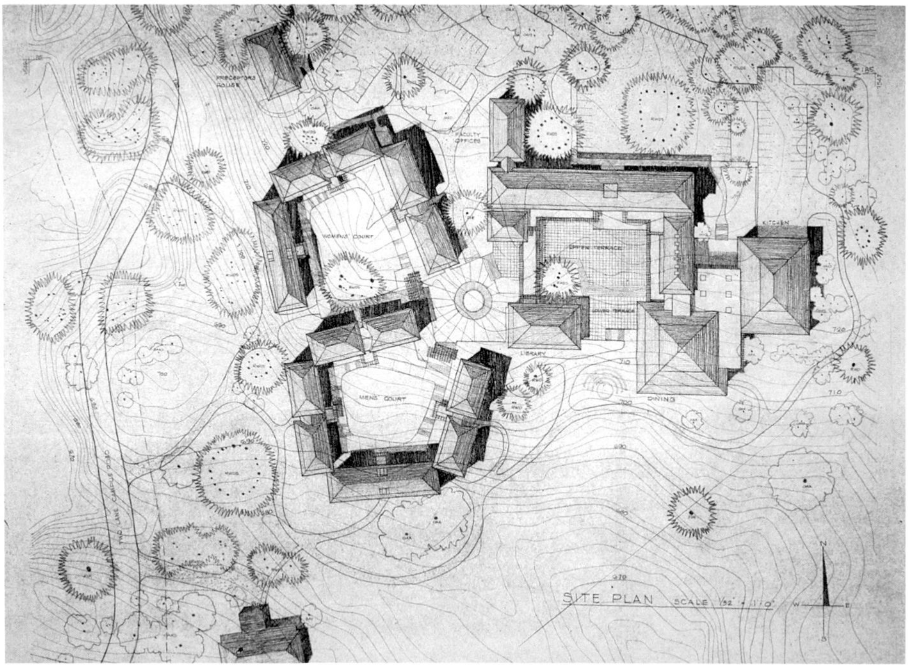

Figure 5.9. Cowell College, University of California, Santa Cruz, 1963–66, Wurster, Bernardi and Emmons, architects, site plan. Courtesy of Special Collections, University Library, University of California, Santa Cruz.

were encased in glass, a marked difference from cold-weather precedents. The relationship among the wings was not based on the right angle. Each four-story block was divided into two-story apartments, wherein eighteen students dwelled, and every two-story apartment had a lower level with a bathroom and living room, in addition to a mix of single and double bedrooms. The upper level contained only bedrooms but was still a mix of singles and doubles. These apartments required internal stairs to give upper-level residents access to the living rooms, although bathrooms were on both levels. In this somewhat complex but original plan, we can see Wurster working out a solution that would avoid the institutional double-loaded corridor. It landed somewhere between a row house and a duplex.

Cowell also included a generous open plaza with a low wall facing the bay. Beyond the plaza, a dining hall allowed for group interaction. Oddly enough, in spite of the incredible site, the housing turned in on itself.[36] (This is reminiscent of the decision made at the University of Wisconsin–Madison to forgo a lake vista in favor of creating a private outdoor space.) The architects dealt masterfully with complicated level changes and maneuvered around the redwoods. In these aspects,

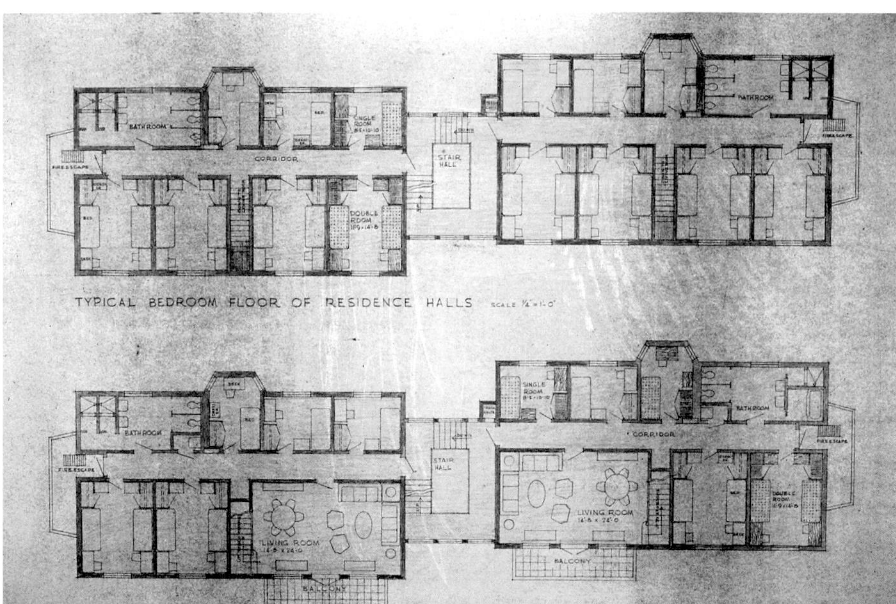

Figure 5.10. Cowell College, University of California, Santa Cruz, 1963–66, Wurster, Bernardi and Emmons, architects, typical bedroom floor plan (above) and typical living room and bedroom floor plan (below). The left side of this drawing shows one two-story unit. The glassed-in staircase in the center served both sides. Courtesy of Special Collections, University Library, University of California, Santa Cruz.

the architects faced existing conditions that were completely different from those at Oxford, Cambridge, or New Haven, and thus the outcome did not resemble English universities or Yale.

LIVINGSTON COLLEGE AT RUTGERS: "REPLACING THE IVORY TOWER"

UCSC was a direct influence on an experimental college on the other side of the country, one with far deeper historical roots. Rutgers traced its history back to 1766, but it had really only become a large, unwieldy state university in the 1950s. The founding of Livingston College within Rutgers, on the former site of Camp Kilmer, a disused military installation, was marked by an attempt to make the ever-growing university seem small and personal. Rutgers president Mason W. Gross counted the founding of Livingston among his greatest achievements, because it directed the state's attention to underserved sectors of society and indicated an effort to welcome disadvantaged students and focus on addressing social injustice through academics.[37]

Ernest Lynton, a physics professor who became the first dean of Livingston College, recruited faculty, fostered a contemporary curriculum, and promoted diversity. A *New York Times* article emphasized the novelty of this educational experiment, which the reporter said would seek to engage students with urban problems and social causes. Succinctly put, it was intended to "replace the 'ivory tower.'" The founders of Livingston wanted to transform the culture of higher education: student evaluations replaced traditional grades; students could initiate their own classes; affirmative action was the norm; faculty and students governed together. The intramural football team was called the Black Panthers.

The original program was an almost-utopian scheme for three small liberal arts colleges (called "unit colleges") on a 540-acre site across the Raritan River from the rest of the Rutgers campus. In 1965, the vision was for each new college to house three thousand, for a total of nine thousand students living on campus—and there would be a few more thousand commuters. By 1967, that vision had been limited somewhat, to Livingston Colleges I and II, each for three thousand. Eventually, the whole project was reduced to one college with a total of three thousand beds. Rutgers also built classroom buildings, a dining hall, and a library for Livingston during this phase. The values that stood behind Livingston College were such that the architecture needed to be innovative and expressive of the challenges of the 1960s.[38]

The three dormitories known as the Quads (the juxtaposition of the words *three* and *quads* has confused five decades of Rutgers students) emerged out of financial circumstances very different from those that gave rise to Saarinen's new structures at Yale, but Rutgers shared the wealthier school's interest in creating community within a research university. Livingston's design was more closely related to goings-on in Santa Cruz. Lynton kept a copy of Kerr's 1964 *Architectural Record* article about building big while seeming small in his files. In fact, Lynton and McHenry corresponded before Lynton visited California in November 1965. McHenry wrote to Lynton with enthusiasm after he had received Lynton's proposal for Rutgers: "Thank you for sending along the statement for the development of the Raritan Campus. After reading the first paragraph, I was sure you were describing our plans here at Santa Cruz!"[39] The plans at Livingston, then, were part of a national trend to use architecture to connect faculty to students.

Although not founded as a cluster college, Rutgers had an arrangement called the federated college plan that had much in common with the cluster college system, a major difference being that at Rutgers the dispersed colleges arose out of historical happenstance and administrative fiat. Students would have all the advantages of a large university but would live and study together in smaller social groups with faculty fellows. Another key theme was the integration of academic and nonacademic activities—in terms of both administration and the way the facilities were designed.

In early documents regarding the residential complexes on the Kilmer site, the architects were instructed to think of the dorms as "essentially quadrangles" grouped around the college hub, which would include classrooms, a dining commons, and a library. The aim was "to provide spontaneous contact between students and staff without formally organizing this and without destroying individual privacy."[40] The residences at Livingston were planned by the architecture firm Anderson, Beckwith, and Haible, which chose modernist forms, in the sense that there were no references to any historical styles. A less-than-modernist decision was to cover the frame of the buildings. The reinforced concrete frame, poured on-site, was veneered with nonstructural dark brick, and the windows were set within precast concrete panels. The local newspaper reported that the buildings at Livingston would be a "'concrete' expression of a specific educational concept—the small college atmosphere within the large university."[41]

Coupled with Lynton's commitment to build small to get bigger was an educational vision of a nontraditional college. Lynton argued that humanity was at a point where questions could be raised about "the viability of our civilization, because fundamental social, economic, and human problems are growing faster than their potential solutions."[42] Liberal arts education had to create an awareness of these problems, and a college's academic disciplines should direct their work and teaching toward finding solutions. In his initial iteration of what this might mean, Lynton wrote that scholarly and academic work at Livingston should focus on "the rapid, uncontrolled, and unbalanced growth of urban complexes," the development of the "former colonial countries," and "unassimilated scientific and technical progress."[43] He wanted a curriculum that would ensure that every student would address at least one of these problems and that interdisciplinary majors would be created to connect students and faculty across traditional boundaries for problem solving. He had begun discussions about interdisciplinary language programs (encompassing the languages of Asia, Africa, and Latin America), an urban studies program, and a liberal arts science degree. The last of these would be aimed at future civil servants, lawyers, and businesspeople, to inform them about the history, philosophy, and implications of scientific endeavors. Just as important to Lynton was that students should be empowered to shape their own educational experiences. Faculty members would serve as mentors, teachers, and advisers for their students, but the traditional hierarchical relationship between professor and student would be set aside. Lynton described the college as "essentially unique," having "some similarities to only the new campus of the University of California at Santa Cruz" and also some little similarities to the Claremont Colleges complex in Southern California.[44]

An early programming guide for the new college at Rutgers stated, "In the residence unit every effort must be made to avoid the hotel-like atmosphere so common in large universities today."[45] Residence life deans considered short, compact halls for ten or twelve people to be desirable for the social development of students, who would form family-like bonds. The preference for such small groups was a direct attack on the fifty-six-man corridors and looming skyscrapers that had burst into existence at almost all state universities, including Rutgers.[46] The interior arrangements of the Quads at Livingston reflected an antipathy toward typical institutional forms. There was no difference between the plans for the housing of men and those for the housing of women, and the dormitories were coed by floor. (In comparison, women were not allowed in the River Dorms at Rutgers College until 1964, and even then they were permitted in upstairs lounges on weekends only.)

In the Livingston "Annual Report" for 1965–66, the author (probably Lynton) summarized the chief goal of the college as combining the "flexibility and educational advantages of the medium-sized college with the intellectual strength and diversity of a large and growing university. . . . Rutgers is one of the very few major institutions which are tackling the problem of size in an intellectually meaningful fashion. . . . Two of these, the California campuses at Santa Cruz and at San Diego, are starting from scratch."[47] But Rutgers did not have to start from scratch. Rutgers–New Brunswick already had individual undergraduate colleges, each with its own identity: Rutgers College, Douglass College, and the agricultural and engineering schools. By adding a few more colleges, Rutgers would create an organization very similar to that of the highly regarded universities in California and, at the same time, mend fences with alumni of Rutgers College and Douglass, who feared that their private alma maters would be subsumed within a giant new state entity.

The influence of UCSC appeared in two ways: on the philosophical level of making the big university seem small and on the more fine-grained level of planning of dormitories. When Lynton visited California in November 1965, UCSC's Cowell College was under construction. It opened in September 1966, and the Livingston Quads opened in September 1969. In spite of the novelty of the educational philosophy behind these residential colleges, both UCSC and Rutgers returned to a historic plan, that of the low-rise quadrangle. The student life experts and college leaders at Livingston (like those at Cowell and those involved with Morrill and Lincoln Towers at OSU) asked the architects to eliminate the double-loaded corridor, and this the architects certainly achieved. Livingston was coeducational, and nothing was stated about differentiating between the sexes in the early programming documents, a mark of the equality of men and women in the eyes of the college's idealistic founders.

The plan of the Livingston Quads was very close to the one used at Cowell College. In both cases, the residential buildings were relatively low (from three to six stories), informally C- or U-shaped, and purposely varied to reflect the wide-ranging nature of the student body. At Cowell, the smallest social group was between seven and eleven; at Livingston, it was between nine and eleven. At both campuses, academic buildings and a dining hall were set a short walk from the housing. It need hardly be noted that Cowell students had better views.

The interiors of the Quads were extremely complex. On the north side of Quad I, a bar-shaped building included bathrooms, showers, janitors' closets, and a typing room in the middle of the bar, with bedrooms facing north and mechanical rooms facing into the courtyard. Partway around the C-shaped structure, a corridor ran along the inside of the buildings closest to the courtyard, taking many right-angle turns. The bedrooms, mostly doubles, were on the outside of the ring, with windows that looked out toward the remnants of Camp Kilmer and the woods beyond. On the east side, a table tennis room, a seminar room, and the lobby were placed on the courtyard side. On the south side, there was an apartment

Figure 5.11. Livingston College, Rutgers University, 1965–70, Frank Grad and Sons, architects, model showing the three Quads and an academic building, photograph dated April 20, 1966. R-photo, buildings and grounds, box 33, folder "Buildings and Grounds, Livingston College, Architectural Model," Special Collections and University Archives, Rutgers University Libraries.

for a faculty member. There were no clear views down any hallways, and the plan was totally incomprehensible to a first-time visitor. Steps and ramps were scattered throughout the structure. All of these design decisions were intended to encourage the creation of community among residents by causing unplanned interactions.

Lynton took the problem of size seriously, noting in an interview with the student newspaper the *Daily Targum* that Livingston would be "small where the dignity of the individual requires it."[48] An article in the *New York Times* about Livingston quoted Lynton as saying that the new college would have "a very swinging faculty, an exciting student body, and a real degree of orientation to everyday problems."[49] The planners designed the residence halls to accommodate groups of decreasing size: from fifteen hundred to five hundred to fifty to about ten. All three Quads together housed fifteen hundred students, but that was too big a number to form a coherent group. Each Quad provided shelter for five hundred, which was a

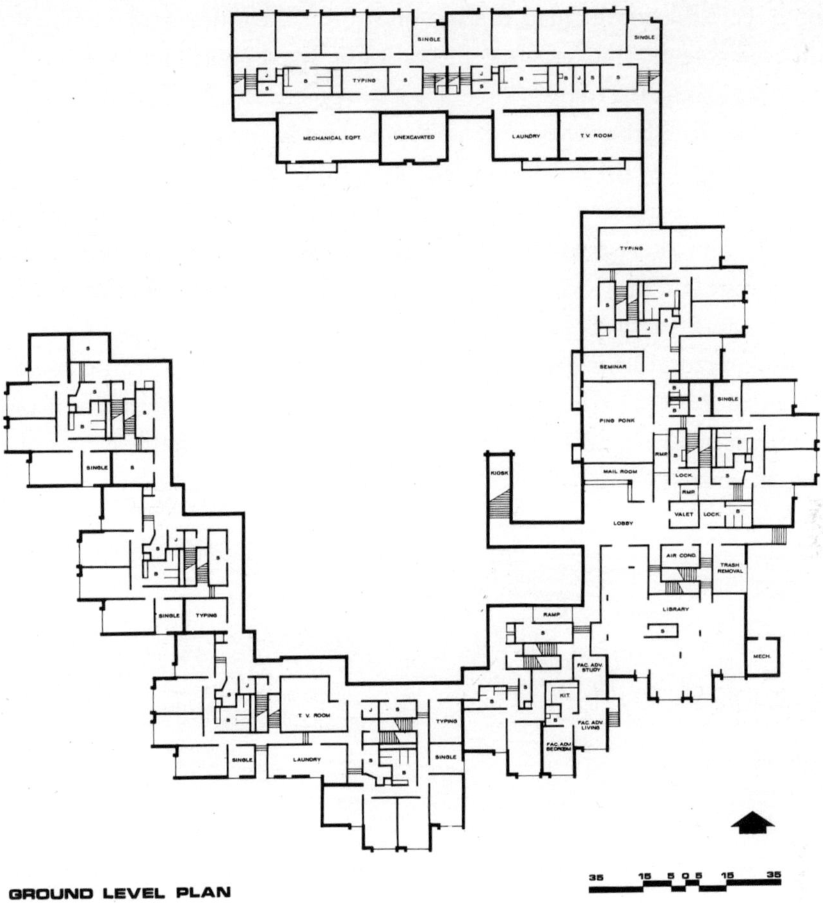

Figure 5.12. Quad III, Livingston College, Rutgers University, 1965–70, Frank Grad and Sons, architects, plan. Livingston College Papers (Office of Dean Lynton), RG 21/A0/04, box 18, folder "Livingston Campus Construction and Planning, Architects Drawings, Residence Halls, Plans Undated," Special Collections and University Archives, Rutgers University Libraries.

small enough number that the residents could at least recognize one another. This five hundred was then divided into ten "houses" of fifty students each, and within each house there were "floors" (originally called "small living groups") of nine, ten, or eleven students. While it was not possible to traverse from one Quad to another without going outdoors, a student could move from house to house within a Quad via underground tunnels. In each Quad, these tunnels provided access to a spacious lounge, laundry rooms, ironing areas, typing rooms, and storage. By placing large congregate rooms underground, the designers could minimize the overall height of the residence hall. In addition, because the facilities in the basement were meant to serve the entire Quad, not just one house, the tunnels (in theory) would act as social glue, holding together the variously sized social groups. Regrettably, the idealism behind the tunnels did not work in practice. According to philosopher and longtime Rutgers professor Peter Klein, who lived in Quad II as a resident adviser in 1970, the early residents were susceptible to burglary; if one student in a house propped open a door for a friend, anyone (including a thief) could get inside the house, from there into the tunnels, and then, by finding another unlocked door, move around freely within a Quad.[50] The tunnels turned out to be well suited to other nefarious activities as well.

As architectural historian Ricki Sablove has described, a visitor could not comprehend the Quads without walking into the outdoor courtyard of one of them and considering the structure from that space, which was the center of each residential unit: "While they were not quadrangles in the traditional sense of the

Figure 5.13. Quad III, Livingston College, Rutgers University, 1965–70, Frank Grad and Sons, architects, courtyard. The Quads were intended to be experienced on foot rather than by car. Photograph by Laura Leichtman.

word—but rather crescent-shaped clusters of buildings—the Quads were both a nod to the English collegiate model and an allusion to domestic scale. The Quads invited close inspection." These structures could not be comprehended from the street (in fact, they looked formidable). Instead, the Quads "had to be entered through courtyards, on foot.... The idea was to enclose the student in a sort of protective embrace."[51]

KRESGE COLLEGE: A RADICAL HILL TOWN

The year was 1968. The plans for College 6 at UC Santa Cruz were presented to the University of California regents and approved by them in March. Martin Luther King Jr. was assassinated in April and Robert Kennedy in June. It was a time of upheaval. College 6, later named Kresge College, asked: How could architects, students, and administrators put the calls for radical change being heard in the 1960s into permanent architectural form? Architecture is inherently conservative—it is long-lasting, relies on the past, requires tradition, and is slow to change. So how did radicalism manifest itself in architecture? Kresge was meant to be a place where the whole person could be educated, a place where the student would be nurtured both in and out of the classroom. This attitude toward teaching the whole student was not new. But the world of higher education was changing, and it required new ideas.

Where other universities tweaked their systems by making changes around the margins, at one specific college of UC Santa Cruz the problem of the residence hall was approached from the ground up. Kresge College, designed by the firm MLTW, made a sharp break from previous dormitory architecture. College students, faculty, staff, and architects created an unusual setting, guided by an almost antiarchitectural concept: flexibility. Furthermore, the process they used to get to that innovative design drove participatory architecture to new heights. One professor, Bert Kaplan, who taught psychology but whose courses were hard to categorize, said that "inchoateness" was the essence of early Santa Cruz.[52] Messy, multifunctional Kresge College was one way in which UC Santa Cruz built an anti-institutional institution.

Kresge College claimed the intimate urbanism of an Italian hill town as an inspiration. The basic *parti* was in place by 1967 and was almost certainly the work of MLTW's Charles Moore, although William Turnbull took over more of the design later. Moore was an engaging, erudite architect with a penchant for medieval and Renaissance art history. He certainly knew Morse and Stiles Colleges, because he had taken the position of dean of the Yale School of Architecture beginning in

1965, just three years after they opened. Moore could have met Giancarlo De Carlo at Yale in that year. De Carlo's scheme for Urbino, which included a car park underneath the plaza, was a likely source for Moore's suggested (but unbuilt) underground parking area beneath Kresge's little streets. The placement of parking inside the hill was guided by the plight of commuters. If a planner wants to create a pedestrian town, he or she has to get the people out of their cars, and the cars out of sight. (A village set within a sea of parking does not readily stir nostalgia for the Middle Ages.) Moore made this clear. In a planning meeting in 1967 that included McHenry, Church, and the architects Moore and Turnbull, Moore said: "The scheme departed from the current type of college plan, placing some of the parking under a portion of the college. The entire complex was organized around a pedestrian street system, with facilities of the college located to produce a heterogeneous activity pattern. The entire development was designed to develop the feeling of an older European village."[53] More generally, Michelangelo Sabatino has pointed out that Moore was familiar with De Carlo's and Saarinen's experiments with the hill town form.[54]

The faculty, staff, and students at Kresge College strongly supported the preservation of the site's redwoods, as dictated by the campus master plan. Moore's plan, which was by its nature rambling and inexact, made it easy to avoid the stately trees. An L-shaped street wound through groves of them. At the southern end, there was a fountain, the master's apartment, and the college office. A visitor would then walk up a street past the student dwellings, which were mostly apartments. The angle of the L was marked by a launderette and a classroom. A visitor continuing up the hill would find more student dwellings, again opening directly to the street. At the top of the hill, there was a café and meeting space. As we have seen with Saarinen at Morse and Stiles, the compressed street was an explicit rejection of the formal, square, confining space of a traditional quadrangle. Furthermore, medieval vernacular villages rebuffed the predictable and repetitive forms, bulky structures, and rigid geometry of modernist urban planning.[55]

Kresge's residents attempted to foster close social ties in their shared space; their hope was that students would live like families, with residents seeing and knowing each other. They settled on the idea of subdividing the college into "kin groups."[56] As described by a Kresge College leader in 1971:

> The organizational structure of Kresge centers around "kin groups"... [of twenty-five people]. Each group has a faculty woman and man as a member. Faculty wives are often members; some of the office staff have chosen to join groups. The faculty members serve as the academic advisers to each student in the group. The attempt is, of course, to make the groups into living-learning units.[57]

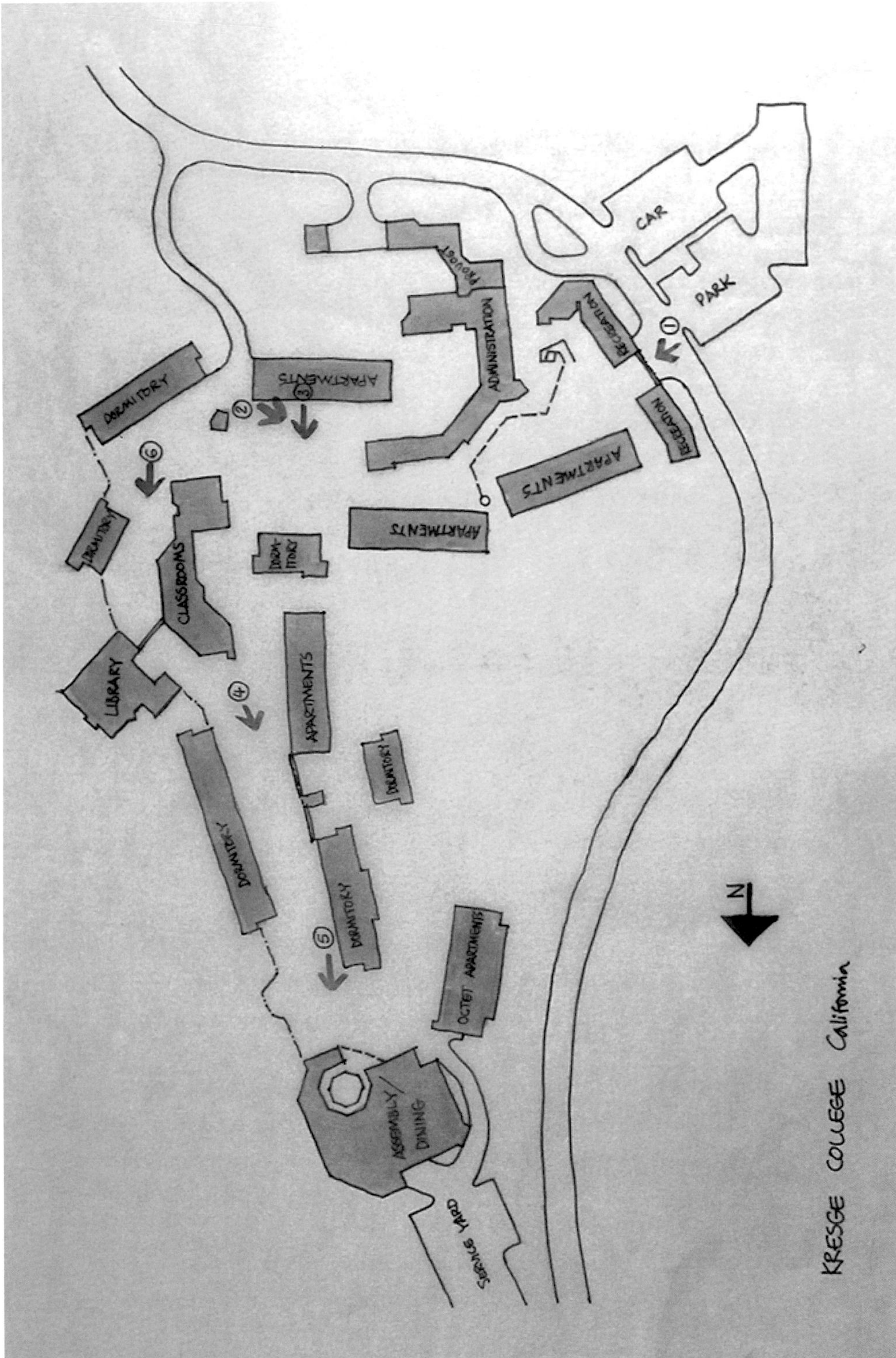

Figure 5.14. Kresge College, University of California, Santa Cruz, 1967–73, MLTW, architects, site plan. Collection of Marc Treib.

Professors, staff members, and students conducted a class called Creating Kresge College in 1970.[58] Some sessions of this class were conducted as "T-groups," something like loosely run group therapy sessions intended to increase individual self-awareness. The members promoted an ideal social realm in which "straight talk" and "being authentic" would prevail. In a report to the Ford Foundation, Bob Edgar, provost of Kresge College, presented T-grouping as an outgrowth of humanistic psychology:

> Over the past twenty years, work in the field of applied behavioral sciences has led to the development of a variety of techniques and approaches to facilitate and improve interpersonal communication. Some but not all of these techniques involve the use of small groups, sometimes called T-groups, sensitivity groups, or encounter groups, to help people explore and extend their communication skills.[59]

Emotional directness was valued over factual evidence. As one participant described it:

> Kresge has been a college with a heavy emphasis on *process,* both interpersonal and organizational. . . . The word T-group . . . designates a group of people . . . who have assembled, without an agenda, for the purpose of studying the interaction among *these* people and *this* time and *this* place.

The same writer noted that the ideal was to "never lay a trip on anyone."[60]

One modest-looking building was the site of students' most extreme example of how to use architecture to create community: it contained housing units with no interior divisions. The arrangement of interior spaces within the octets, as the units were known, was left up to the eight residents, who built the interiors *after* they got to the college. One group left the entire interior open and had only two private spaces, a bathroom and a meditation room.[61] (This was not widely copied in future residence hall construction, and the fire marshal turned out to be very petty when it came to certain kinds of student construction practices.)

Other suites and apartments (not the octets) furthered the kin-group, family-like association. They were low-rise, partly to mimic a Mediterranean village and partly to appear, once again, noninstitutional. MLTW designed the apartments to have a two-level arrangement, creating open interiors. All the activities of a student's life—going to class, visiting with friends, sleeping, eating—were jumbled together to encourage casual interaction among faculty, students, and staff.

Figure 5.15. Kresge College, University of California, Santa Cruz, 1967–73, MLTW, architects, original octets. Photograph by author.

(Archival documents demonstrate a complete blurring of those traditional hierarchical categories anyway; as one report concluded, "It's taboo to mention any subgroup, e.g. faculty, students, . . . or student leaders.")[62] Privacy was in short supply, and some rooms were plainly visible from the narrow street, hence their nickname, "the Zoo." Since the apartments opened directly onto the street, the plan eliminated the interior, double-loaded corridor. As I have argued, double-loaded corridors—those long, masonry block halls with rooms on either side, known to UCSC students from UC Berkeley and countless other colleges—signified the subjugation of students.

The specific curriculum at Kresge College was based on the theme "Humans and Their Environment," a concept reflected in the architecture. The buildings were painted an earthy brown on the outside walls, those that faced the forest (equating the outer edges of the buildings with nature), while the interior street-like spaces were painted bright white with colorful accents (defining those areas as human-made, constructed, and artificial) (Plate 13).

Figure 5.16. Kresge College, University of California, Santa Cruz, 1967–73, MLTW, architects, view of apartments nicknamed "the Zoo" because the occupants felt like they were on display. Photograph by author.

About halfway up the hill, there was a speaker's platform that also served as the cover over a storage shed used by the maintenance people. One student remembers the speaker's platform fondly:

> The one shed, that would normally have been there for facilities and maintenance and the garbage can, was actually set up there as a speaker stand looking over the lower part of the street, and so it was a very nice area for a group of people to gather and to watch people coming up and down and easily connect with everyone as they moved around. That was one of the most effective things, they tried to keep the buildings connected to the street, so that it was very easy to socialize and feel like there was a community rather than [people in] isolated individual dorms.[63]

Food was another flash point, as has historically been true in residence halls. Students objected to being served cafeteria food in a dining hall. Many students wished for the option of a family-style restaurant and an all-night café. Most of the students wanted to be able to prepare their own meals in their own apartments. Apartments are not particularly good for community building, which may be one reason the students consented to join kin groups. (Apartments are now a common option for upper-class students at many universities, but they were atypical for on-campus housing in 1970.) Initially Kresge provided kitchens, a restaurant, and a café.[64]

Kresge students wanted to express themselves. They asked for a sauna; they got one. There was no question about the sauna being coed—that was a given.[65] The only debate was whether it would be coed *and* naked, and that decision was handled by the students on a case-by-case basis. The architects were probably enthusiastic about the sauna because it evoked a domestic Scandinavian milieu, which was then in vogue. Another Scandinavian influence may be seen in the furniture, if it can be called that. The architects, students, and the provost requested furniture that students could arrange however they liked, creating individualistic rooms. In the previous decade, most dormitories included built-in industrial furniture, which was sturdy, cheap, and space-saving but offered little in the way of poetic revelation. In 1973, against the wishes of the university's purchasing department, UCSC purchased twenty thousand individual red, white, and brown polystyrene cubes, called Palasets, from the Finnish company Treston Oy.[66] Each student was supplied with twenty or so cubes, which he or she could organize to serve as dressers, bookcases, Frank Zappa album storage, and the like. The company warned that the boxes could survive in temperatures up to "160 degrees F, after which [they would] begin to soften gradually."[67] A student at the time, Steve Menagh, remembers that gradual softening differently: "So . . . we got the first batch of them in and [we were] sitting around yacking . . . [and] figuring, you know, this is going to be great . . . then we took one outside and lit a match and discovered that you could . . . light one of them on fire without too much trouble."[68] It is a safe historical assumption that there was a lot of inventive smoking taking place, and the Palasets lasted only a few years. But the fact that they existed offers material culture evidence of the students' desire to create their own environments.

Moore's architectural concept was to monumentalize ordinary civic places. A number of postmodern flourishes, such as a phone booth with giant, stylized ears, were the aspects of Kresge College that attracted the most attention at the time. (The phone booth now contains garbage cans, as the importance of a public pay phone is quite lost on today's undergraduates.) The laundry was another

Figure 5.17. Kresge College, University of California, Santa Cruz, 1967–73, MLTW, architects, interior of an apartment in 1970. Photograph by Morley Baer; copyright 2018 The Morley Baer Photography Trust, Santa Fe. All rights reserved; reprinted by permission.

decorative, larger-than-life element, marked by a dramatic square cutout and a yellow wall. In contrast to the ironic and cartoonish aspects of postmodernism, however, the planning—both the physical outcome and the process—was sincere. It was in the planning that the authenticity of the Kresge student experience revealed itself. Administrators and architects paid an unusual degree of attention to the students' voices. Turnbull, in particular, experimented gamely with architecture that was collaborative and even attended some T-group meetings.[69]

Figure 5.18. Kresge College, University of California, Santa Cruz, 1967–73, MLTW, architects, interior of a bedroom in an apartment showing Palaset plastic cubes stacked on the right. The student who lived here decorated the room with posters celebrating Malcolm X and Salvador Allende. Photograph by Morley Baer; copyright 2018 The Morley Baer Photography Trust, Santa Fe. All rights reserved; reprinted by permission.

The form of Kresge College was unexpected in many ways. It was a street, not a quadrangle or a skyscraper; it was playful and cheaply built, not serious and durable. Students wanted control; they resented architecture itself. As architectural historian Marc Treib, the graphic designer for Kresge College, has explained, the students were "hooked on the idea of flexibility . . . this was the era of the nondirective."[70] Students found in loco parentis insulting to their dignity. The year that the UC regents accepted MLTW's plan, 1968, was the same year the Beatles released "Revolution" in response to increasingly intense student protests against the Vietnam War in the United States and the May uprisings in Paris. The lyrics, written by John Lennon, disagreed with violent tactics ("But when you talk about destruction / Don't you know that you can count me out") but acknowledged that "we all want to change the world."

If we take a step back from this chapter's four extraordinary case studies and look at higher education as a whole, we can see some national trends leading to the present day. Although living–learning environments are costly, they are held in high esteem by today's student affairs professionals. Yale, Harvard, Rice, and a few other universities have maintained their residential colleges with faculty living in apartments under the same collective roofs with students. The University of Pennsylvania recently joined their ranks. More typically, however, professors do not wish to live on campus. University rankings depend partly on faculty productivity, and promotion at research universities depends on publication and so-called grantsmanship; self-sacrificing instructors who wish to live in the same buildings with undergraduates are not thick on the ground. And although many universities (both state and private) have a few token living–learning communities, these are seldom staffed by professors; instead, they offer cheap housing for housing directors and graduate students.

The four examples in this chapter, as different as they are, are linked by a common desire to create dwellings conducive to learning. All were innovative in their architecture, yet at the same time maintained a continuity with standard practice, in that they were based on the conviction that living on campus was part of the educational program. And they were constructed by educators who accepted that networking is a justifiable reason to go to college. Whether behind the lithic walls of Morse and Stiles, inside Cowell's and Livingston's nonlinear quads, or amid the theatrical townscape of Kresge, all the participants agreed that architecture shapes the morality of students and that character development is central to the university's mission, even as the era's ethos of peace, love, and understanding melted away.[71]

Epilogue

Architectural Inequality and the Future of Residence Halls

In this book I have argued that living on campus is an artifact of three centuries of American educational ideology that placed enormous value on socialization. In the seventeenth and eighteenth centuries, students were boys who needed moral guidance; in the nineteenth century, women began attending college in large numbers, always under protective eyes; as the concept of the adolescent emerged around 1900, youthful males were encouraged to delay adulthood; in the 1950s, students were military veterans eager to return to civilian life; in the 1960s, they were members of a youth culture that administrators almost feared. This mad dash through the centuries is obviously oversimplified, and yet it nonetheless demonstrates that today's students bear little resemblance to their predecessors, which makes it all the more remarkable that the residence hall still thrives.

The twenty-first-century student body is far too diverse to characterize in a few sentences, but one can begin to suggest the range. We find wealthy students on one end, those whose families are willing to pay for a traditional collegiate experience at a private institution—an experience that typically includes a residence hall, at least for one or two years. There are also some less affluent students who receive aid or outright grants to attend pricey private colleges. Then we can identify middle-class students who attend public universities to take advantage of in-state tuition. They can achieve even greater savings by commuting. At the bottom of the economic ladder are community college enrollees and those who wend their way through the taxing labyrinth of for-profit higher education, with its empty promises of easy employment. Since the demise of Trump University, the piratical nature of for-profit institutions has been widely recognized. Of course, with the rise of online learning, it seems reasonable to ask: Who needs dormitories? What role do they play in the future of higher education?

Some college graduates feel oppressed by the whole idea of the dormitory, because they were once introverted dorm dwellers or resentful commuters. Others wax eloquent about their freshman halls—from the safe distance of twenty or thirty years. Parents of college-age children are often particularly animated about this issue, since their funds are on the line: some see living on campus as an essential part of college, while others find fault with lavish residence halls, which they view as a probable cause of mounting costs. Experience tells me that people have strong opinions about dormitories, even if those opinions are not rooted in historical fact—a problem this book is intended to help solve.

WHY LIVE IN A RESIDENCE HALL TODAY?

Typical answers to the question of why a student should live in a residence hall include to "experience personal growth with opportunities to gain independence and display leadership," to "meet students with a diversity of life experiences," and to "learn principles of civility among roommates and neighbors."[1] Student life experts note: "For a significant number of students each year, moving into a residence hall is the signature moment of their entry into a postsecondary experience."[2] In other words, the watershed event of leaving childhood behind takes place in the shadow of the residence hall, on move-in day. That is the day when parents cry and offspring cringe.

Although many housing officials would like to require undergraduates to live on campus, families resist because of cost. Universities have to sell the idea that on-campus living is better than off-campus living. "As a university, [your job is] to make the living situation so attractive and such an important and integrated part of the college experience that everybody is going to want their kid to live on campus, at least for a year," says Susan Painter, a behavioral psychologist. Painter also recommends roommates, because "students who are in single rooms are more likely to drop out of housing and drop out of school."[3] She cautions that high comfort need not be the goal. Students should not be coddled, or they might never leave their rooms. Instead, residence halls need spaces that Painter calls "crossroads," where residents can casually meet other folks. Once again, the justification for the dormitory is a social one: planned activities allow students to make new friends, and new friends will become part of future networks for business and the professions.

The dormitory is a softer landing pad than an off-campus apartment and thus makes the transition to adulthood easier. Someone, usually a parent, pays a single bill for the whole semester. The housing fee covers cleaning services for the common areas and community bathrooms, so the residents need only make their beds and wash their clothes, chores that they may or may not perform routinely. Utilities and amenities are also included. Almost all residence halls, even old ones, have up-to-date game rooms and large-screen televisions plus old-school foosball and pool tables. Living on campus cuts down on travel time and provides added security. There are swipe cards to manage entry, and residence halls offer a safety net in the form of resident advisers and their supervisors. RAs are available to provide counseling, offer comfort, and handle emergencies. The entire apparatus of the student affairs department can step in if an RA refers a problem up through the ranks, whether to a counseling center, office of disabilities, or dean of students.

From the point of view of students' parents, official on-campus housing offers peace of mind. Student affairs departments were once staffed with retired military people, "discarded football coaches, elderly housemothers, and random others who had . . . scout-like qualities."[4] In contrast, today's student affairs experts are highly professional. For example, it is now recommended that anyone aiming for a career as a vice president of student affairs earn a doctorate in higher education. Currently, fifty U.S. universities have doctoral programs offering a specialization in student affairs.[5] The profession is powerful and entrenched. In 2011, one vice president of student affairs explained: "Students spend 80 percent of time outside of class. Student affairs professionals need to be there for that." He continued: "It's a complex setting today that needs great expertise. . . . Student affairs plays a huge role in developing the student that graduates from our college[s] today."[6] Student affairs deans commonly point out that because students are in the classroom only twelve or fifteen hours per week, a trained professional should be shepherding their personal development during the rest of the time. In other words, someone should be responsible for their education *outside* the classroom, and a lot of that time is spent in the residence hall. College deans of the early twentieth century were not wrong when they claimed, as we learned in chapter 3, that dormitories were more democratic and less exclusive than fraternities. This is a truth about college housing that has persisted.

THE PERSISTENCE OF GREEK LIFE

In the 1978 film *Animal House,* the Delta Tau Chi fraternity at Faber College is in trouble with the dean, who threatens to revoke its charter and hurl its members off campus. At a disciplinary hearing, Otter, a smooth-talking Delta brother, gives a rousing speech:

> Ladies and gentlemen, I'll be brief. The issue here is not whether we broke a few rules, or took a few liberties with our female party guests—we did. But you can't hold a whole fraternity responsible for the behavior of a few sick, twisted individuals. For if you do, then shouldn't we blame the whole fraternity system? And if the whole fraternity system is guilty, then isn't this an indictment of our educational institutions in general? I put it to you, Greg—isn't this an indictment of our entire American society? Well, you can do whatever you want to us, but we're not going to sit here and listen to you badmouth the United States of America.[7]

At the emotional apex of the speech, the brothers file out of the room humming the national anthem.

The screenwriters revel in portraying the brazen sexism, phony patriotism, and irrationality of the spoiled fraternity boys while skewering the fraternity as a microcosm of America. More recently, social critic Caitlin Flanagan has written that today's fraternity supporters defend Greek life by linking it to the deep history of American constitutional law. She notes that many fraternities attempt to assert their legitimacy by tracing their roots to the federal period:

> They emanated in part from the Freemasons, of which George Washington himself was a member. When arguments are made in their favor, they are arguments in defense of a foundational experience for millions of American young men, and of a system that helped build American higher education as we know it.[8]

The freedom of assembly for members of private clubs is protected by the Constitution, and the exceptionalism of the fraternity is inseparable from this fact.

Flanagan's takedown of fraternities might have been written in any decade, except for her use of a new kind of evidence: legal documents from civil suits. For most of American history, fraternity rituals were clandestine. Brothers would not reveal the details of hazing accidents, because to do so would be to deny the sacred trust of their union. But now researchers can use published legal documents that expose fraternity practices. In recent years there has been an uptick in legal cases involving fraternities, possibly because parents are unwilling to accept that crimes committed under the cloak of secrecy cannot be litigated.

Observing a bitter irony, Flanagan points out that the baby boomers (who were not angels themselves as college students) have become censorious and litigious parents:

> Boomers, who in their own days destroyed the doctrine of *in loco parentis* so that they could party in blissful, unsupervised freedom, have grown up into the helicopter parents of today, holding fiercely to a pair of mutually exclusive desires: on the one hand that their kids get to experience the same unfettered personal freedoms of college that they remember so fondly, and on the other that the colleges work hard to protect the physical and emotional well-being of their precious children.[9]

Today's hyperconcerned parents know the legal rights of their children. When their children are injured in dorms or fraternity houses, parents want rigorous criminal investigations, not closed-door, internal disciplinary hearings.

College administrators, for their part, have tried to prevent hazing and binge drinking since the very start of fraternity life. Today, Greek organizations voluntarily submit to university regulations, but housing departments do not have as much control over fraternities as they have over dormitories.[10] (Of course, binge drinking occurs in both dorms and fraternities, but it is a standard part of the fraternity initiation process; a study published in the *NASPA Journal* in 2009 found that 86 percent of fraternity house residents engaged in binge drinking, compared to 45 percent of nonfraternity men.)[11] While a few places have banned all fraternities, most of these have been small private liberal arts colleges, like Colby, Bowdoin, Middlebury, and Williams.[12] At other universities, especially large, state-funded ones, fraternities are central to the history and life of the institution, and their removal is out of the question. Student life administrators contend that banning fraternities is a shortsighted and dangerous move. They argue that if fraternities are forced off campus and away from the watchful eye of deans, hazing rituals, sexual assaults, and (surprisingly common) accidental falls will increase in frequency and seriousness.[13]

Lawyers who specialize in fraternity crime note that there is a pressing need for legal support for victims. Attorney Doug Fierberg focuses on lawsuits involving fraternity rape, hazing injury, hazing death, wrongful death, sexual assault, and other crimes associated with Greek life. In one of his cases, a young man died of head injuries and a ruptured spleen. The story begins as a familiar one of rushing gone too far: a nineteen-year-old who attended bid acceptance night at Beta Theta Pi at Penn State in the fall of 2016 consumed a dangerous amount of alcohol in an initiation ritual. The events of that night were captured on security cameras and recounted in text messages. After falling down the stairs twice, the pledge was left writhing in pain. The brothers put a loaded backpack on top of him, so that he would not roll over and choke on his own vomit. While he drifted in and out of consciousness for twelve hours, two different men stepped over him, ignoring his bloodied face and bruises. The brothers Googled "cold extremities in a drunk person," but otherwise did nothing. When one fraternity member recommended calling 911, he was slammed against a wall. When the Beta brothers finally did call, they did not tell the 911 operator that the pledge had a head injury. The pledge subsequently died at the hospital.[14]

In order to paint a compelling picture of what is wrong with Greek life, Fierberg draws a hard-and-fast line between the fraternity and the dorm, noting that hazing does not exist in dormitories and that supervision of residence halls is far superior. Would an injured, drunken young man be left to lie on the floor of a dorm for twelve hours? To Fierberg, this scenario is unthinkable. As he puts it: "It doesn't happen outside a fraternity. Period."[15] The biggest problem, according to Fierberg, lies in the mismanagement of the Greek system, which is based on the assumption that fraternity men are competent to police themselves. The "Greek Industry," as he calls it, holds a peculiar place within the criminal justice system. Fraternity members are young adults, many of whom have demonstrated that they are not ready to be responsible for themselves or others. And yet no university employee is authorized to force his or her way behind the closed door of the fraternity house. Moreover, public universities do not report fraternity-related incidents of death, injury, or hazing in any systematic way. As Fierberg has observed, "Let's assume this is a public health issue. You would like to believe that everybody trying to solve the problem would have access to the information."[16] They do not.

Why do young people join Greek life? First of all, they tend to feel invincible, and many are likely not bothered by the litany of risks outlined above. Indeed, they sign up *for* the drinking, the fun, and the parties. Greek life gives new members ready access to older, popular students.[17] It provides a substitute family that offers companionship and esprit de corps. Fraternities and sororities do charity work, and their members offer each other daily and consistent support. Lifelong friendships come with the lifelong memberships. Among students who live in fraternity and sorority houses, "the affection felt for their brothers and sisters, the good times spent at parties and tailgates, and the unique experience of living with so many like-minded friends in such intimate settings [are] often cited as being far more influential and memorable than classes or professors."[18] Compared with nonmembers, fraternity members are less likely to drop out of school and more likely to get better jobs.[19]

Colleges also benefit from fraternities, because Greeks maintain closer ties to their alma maters and donate more money than do other graduates.[20] Sociologists

Elizabeth A. Armstrong and Laura T. Hamilton take universities to task for being complicit in maintaining class hierarchies through Greek life. They summarize the findings of their extensive research by identifying several pathways through college, the most prominent of which they call the "Party Pathway." For women on the "Party Pathway," the point of college *is* the social life. Studying is secondary and largely stands in the way of it. Armstrong and Hamilton observe that pledging a sorority at a large public university dominates interactions among first-year women. The price of belonging to a sorority—not just the fees, but also the costs of maintaining a fashionable image, with the proper hair and nails, handbags, dresses for formal events, and so on—makes entry into sorority culture nearly impossible for all but the wealthiest.[21] The researchers point out that affluent out-of-state students disproportionately aid the cash flow of large universities, because they pay double the tuition, make few demands on faculty, and tend to become loyal alumni who give generously.

Armstrong and Hamilton indicate that the experience of living in a dormitory also exacerbates class differences among hallmates.[22] The researchers embedded themselves on a hall in a women's dormitory known to be a "party dorm" at a midwestern state university where Greek life dominates the social scene. They chose this so-called party dorm, even though it was "not the prettiest, best resourced, or most comfortable residence," because they knew from family, friends, and Google searches that this particular dorm was the on-ramp to a high-profile social life.[23] The pressure to be accepted by a sorority completely overwhelmed the daily lives of all the young women who wanted to join, leaving no room for other associations. Rush was also damaging to schoolwork. Those who participated but did not get a "bid" were doubly disadvantaged because they had neglected their academics with no social payoff. Other women in the study chose easy majors to leave more time for sorority activities, which undercut their ability to get good jobs after graduation.[24] Sorority sisters tend to recruit women like themselves, thus narrowing the diversity of their living spaces. Armstrong and Hamilton conclude that the Greek system perpetuates class divides.

DIVERSITY AND CHARACTER

The ways in which diversity and difference have been constructed in American college life have changed over time. In the eighteenth century at Harvard, there was no doubt that the white Protestants considered themselves superior to the Native Americans. In the late 1800s, elite colleges were restricted to those who had attended prestigious private prep schools and passed Latin and Greek entrance exams. (These exams, like placement tests, also allowed teachers to slot boys into the appropriate academic levels, so they may not have served exclusively as vehicles for class sorting.) As Thelin and others have shown, there were class hierarchies within the colonial college. Urban men looked down on their rural peers, and fun-loving youths disparaged pious boys. As Catholics realized they were largely shut out of Ivy League schools, they built a parallel network of colleges with their own internal hierarchies. When Jews sought access to the highest ranks of Protestant universities, the leaders of those institutions did not take their arrival kindly. Convenient and ready at hand was a long-standing justification for keeping Jews and Catholics out. The prestigious colonial colleges, originally founded as religious institutions, claimed that the development of moral character had been their goal all along. Abbott Lawrence Lowell, president of Harvard from 1909 to 1933, proposed "a personal estimate of character on the part of the Admission authorities" as a selection device to control what he considered to be a dangerous increase in the proportion of Jewish students.[25] *Character* was a slippery term that thinly disguised discrimination against Jews, allowing admissions officers to choose the promising tennis player over the grocer's son even when the latter did better on his entrance exams. It allowed an elite school to admit an Old Stock Protestant based on his supposed character while rejecting a supposedly nouveau riche Jew.

The troubling history of exclusivity at the Ivies has recently come to the fore at Yale University. One of the residential colleges founded with the Harkness gift in the late 1920s (see chapter 3) was named Calhoun College, a name that was controversial even in 1933. New Haven was known for its large abolitionist population in the nineteenth century. Many people in the 1930s were aware that John C. Calhoun was an outspoken supporter of slavery; a Yale graduate (1804), he was also a legal theorist, the owner of a cotton plantation, a leading South Carolina statesman, and the seventh vice president of the United States. At the time of the residential college's naming, he was the first Yale graduate to have served in such a high-ranking national office. In 1933, that was the most important criterion, and thus he rose to the top of the list of Yale worthies.

In 2015, Yale students and faculty lobbied aggressively for a name change for Calhoun College. Together with a committee, Yale's president, Peter Salovey, decided not to change the name after a year of internal debate and discussion. Salovey's initial stance was that students needed to learn about the brutality of slavery and its aftermath, and learn how to argue against it, rather than "erase it from memory."[26] After his announcement that Calhoun's name would remain in place, Salovey put together a committee to devise principles for the naming or renaming of buildings at Yale going forward, and this committee reversed Salovey's earlier decision. Among the committee's recommendations was that a structure should be renamed if the historical person's primary legacy was antithetical to the principles of Yale. Since Calhoun was famous because of his promotion of slavery, rather than in spite of it, his name could be replaced. The Yale Corporation (now the board of trustees) agreed to the change: Calhoun College is now Grace Hopper College in honor of Grace Murray Hopper, a pioneering computer scientist who served as an admiral in the U.S. Navy. The debates about racial injustice have a material presence. The carved name of Calhoun remains on the residential college as a reminder and spur to discussion. The stained-glass windows of the college's dining room and common room have found a different fate. As late as 1983, in a book about the first fifty years of Yale's residential colleges, Thomas Bergin described the iconography of the stained-glass windows in Calhoun's common room as follows: "The college is noted for its pictorial windows. Those in the common room portray Calhoun as a statesman and farmer."[27] What Bergin neglected to mention is that one of the windows showed Calhoun looming over an enslaved black man. Later the part of the window depicting the slave was removed and replaced with clear glass, leaving the white supremacist all alone in the composition.

Another window (this one in the dining hall) showed slaves carrying baskets of cotton on their heads. A janitorial worker smashed this window in 2016, saying that he should not have to look at that image every day. He later apologized for destroying university property, and Yale reassigned him to a different job at the college without pressing charges.[28] Both of these windows have now been removed, and the college plans to exhibit them in a museum setting, where they will be contextualized with historical information. Several new windows for the dining hall will be designed by the artist and educator Faith Ringgold.

The removal of offensive imagery, the renaming of buildings, and the desire on the part of university administrators and faculty to create safe places for students of diverse backgrounds is frankly a work in progress. There is some cause for hope. David Halpern, a scholar who studies mutual trust among diverse peoples on a global stage and measures social trust, finds that universities are one of the few places where people learn to live with others who are different from them:

> People that go to university end up trusting much more than those who don't, particularly when they go away residentially. It doesn't look like it's explained by income alone. So there's something about the experience of going off as a young

Figure E.1. Portrait of John C. Calhoun in stained-glass window, with blank space where an enslaved man in chains was once depicted. This window was originally in the common room of Calhoun College (now Grace Hopper College), Yale University. Copyright Yale Daily News Publishing Company, Inc. All rights reserved; reprinted with permission.

Figure E.2. Stained-glass window showing slaves carrying baskets of cotton. This window was originally in the dining hall of Calhoun College (now Grace Hopper College), Yale University. Copyright Yale Daily News Publishing Company, Inc. All rights reserved; reprinted with permission.

> person in an environment where you have lots of other young people from different backgrounds and so on, hopefully, and different ethnicities. You learn the habits of trust because you're in an environment where you can trust other people; they are trustworthy. And you internalize these habits and you take them with you the rest of your life. So we tend to not think of [the reason for] going away to university as being . . . to build social capital and social trust, we think about learning skills and so on, but it may well be that it has as much, or even more value, in terms of [cultivating] social trust going forward.[29]

Social trust can be built among diverse students only if they are thrown into a bowlful of tired metaphors—the old "melting pot" or the newer "tossed salad." Now that many incoming frosh can choose their own roommates, the diversity of the dormitory may give way to more homogeneous meals. Facebook makes finding a like-minded roommate easy, given that most colleges set up pages for incoming classes. With a little snooping, teenagers can find those who drink (or don't), party (or don't), or mirror their own fashion choices, ethnicities, or skin colors. Websites like Roomsurf and Lifetopia, similar to online dating services, allow participants to enter personal preferences about music, sleeping, smoking, working, visitors, neatness, and so on, in order to match them to compatible roommates. One website suggests that those who intend to join a sorority should find a roommate who is doing the same, because rush is such a busy time of year.[30] It hardly needs stating that using participation in sorority recruitment as a preselection device will inevitably lead to greater uniformity among roommates. Undermining a hundred years of student affairs philosophy, a salesperson for Lifetopia says, "The kids are going to segregate themselves by likes and dislikes anyway, eventually."[31] It is too soon to know how such services will affect roommate choices, and it is possible that at least some first-year students will purposely choose roommates who are different from them to enhance their experience. As for the danger of promoting insularity, Steve Gilmore, assistant director of residence life at the University of Arizona, has noted that his office debated the point and ultimately decided that promoting diversity at a roommate level was less important than maintaining it at a facility level: "The roommate relationship seems to be this huge thing, and it may not be such a bad idea for some students to be able to room with someone who's a little bit more like them. We weren't as concerned about diversity within a room as diversity in our facilities on the whole."[32] On the one hand, this approach might be seen as a hypocritical dereliction of duty. On the other hand, it could lead to fewer demands for roommate changes.

DORMS AS RECRUITMENT DEVICES

In contrast to fifty years ago, many more of today's young people have grown up in America's exurbs, in giant houses where they have their own bedrooms and bathrooms. So it is a shock when they get to college to find that they are staying in a six-foot-by-nine-foot room with one window and two other people. Some are repulsed by the mere thought of sharing a bathroom with an entire hallway of classmates. Colleges—particularly elite private and flagship public schools—serve large numbers of affluent young people who are eager to benefit from the institutions' brand names and from the latest facilities and services the universities can offer. Wealthy families gladly pay higher-than-average rates to make sure their children are comfortable. And colleges in this tier compete with each other, aiming to outdo one another in pursuit of such students by installing desirable features such as recreation centers with climbing walls and residence halls with spa amenities and luxurious dining rooms.

Analysts have carefully tracked the extent to which amenities are a deciding factor when students are choosing a college. The authors of a National Bureau of Economic Research working paper titled "College as Country Club" explain that "more selective schools have a much greater incentive to improve academic quality since this is the dimension most valued by [their] marginal students. Less selective schools (particularly privates), by comparison, have a greater incentive to focus on consumption amenities, since this is what their marginal students value."[33] Another author notes that many of today's rising frosh have never shared a bedroom and will almost certainly want "more privacy than previous generations of dorm dwellers would have ever expected."[34] At less intellectually competitive schools, instructional spending achieves nothing for recruitment—research shows that "the vast majority of colleges appear to have a negative total enrollment response to increases in instructional spending."[35]

Many prospective students have no idea what they want to major in. For them, comfort will probably guide their choices. A student who does know what he or she wants to study will make a more focused choice, especially if he or she wants to major in something unusual. In the case of rare majors such as bowling industry management and technology (Vincennes), puppetry (University of Connecticut), and nautical archaeology (Texas A&M), a high school kid intent on a career in bowling, puppets, or shipwrecks will not be put off by masonry block dormitories. I was teaching a seminar on the history of higher education when the subject of recruitment came up. I asked the students, "How did you choose Rutgers?" And, more generally, "How did you make sense of the recruitment materials and websites from various colleges?" A business major replied nonchalantly, "You choose based on football and team spirit and the dorms, because, you know, the academics are all pretty much all the same." It was not exactly the pedagogical high point of my career. But if the academic offerings are similar (for example, business administration, education, or psychology), prospective students will choose based on their perception of what the quality of life will be like. Residence halls matter in that calculation. Certainly there are some outstanding and ambitious youth who choose a school primarily for its academics, but these tend to be those who are headed for the country's most competitive colleges.[36] If academics and job placement rates are about equal, students in the next-lower tier will choose a school based on the social scene and perceived contentment. As many incoming students find out, however, not everybody can be assigned to the brand-new residence hall, the one inevitably featured on the bus tour. At a midwestern state university, one student complained of being consigned to a low brick building with poor water pressure, cockroaches, and an odor reminiscent of "a mixture of mildew and old people."[37]

The Massachusetts Institute of Technology is among the most competitive universities in the United States and could probably attract high-quality students with run-of-the-mill dormitories. But even MIT boasts a cutting-edge residence hall, known as the Sponge, designed by the internationally known architect Steven Holl. Holl attracted attention by including in the Sponge a ball pit of the sort they have at Chuck E. Cheese's restaurants.[38] The playful imagery offsets MIT's reputation as a pressure cooker. More typical recruitment devices are fast Wi-Fi, air-conditioning, game rooms, cafés, and swimming pools. It is better for an institution's bottom line if students live on campus, thus amenities are important to attract those paying customers. As John Hitt, president of the University of Central Florida (which is eager to shed its reputation as a commuter school), has said: "They don't have to be the super-sexiest facilities you've ever seen, but there's a competitive market out there. . . . The schools that have the more modern arrangements, I think that makes a difference."[39] According to Laurie Girabola, the University at Albany's residential life director, "Students don't come to a campus because of housing, but if they're choosing between two campuses, housing plays a role." She concludes: "You have to wow the students and the parents."[40] In other words, schools cannot sit back and wait for students to come to them. Private schools are competing among themselves, and state universities are fighting over out-of-state students, who pay full freight.

Critics of the luxury campus, like former New Jersey governor Chris Christie, object to what they see as the coddling of students. In 2015, Christie claimed to have discovered an epidemic of climbing walls at universities. While speaking at the University of New Hampshire, nestled in the Green Mountains, he riled up the crowd: "What the hell do you need a rock climbing wall for? Tell the kids at the University of New Hampshire, 'Go outside and climb those rocks.'"[41] Christie identifies the climbing wall as an example of the kinds of wasteful and frivolous practices that drive up the cost of college.

The poor climbing wall. Once a flash point for attention, it has been superseded by the "lazy river." At the University of North Florida, a 200-foot lazy river swirls in front of the Osprey Fountains. Students in bathing suits float along in front of this splendid new residence hall, relaxing in their inner tubes.[42] The Osprey Fountains has one thousand student beds—and one thousand parking spaces. The University of Central Florida has a similar pool in front of its University House, and recreational centers at Auburn University in Alabama, North Dakota State, and Texas Tech all have signature aquatic facilities. The District on Apache, a private apartment building near Arizona State University in Tempe, designed by Humphreys & Partners, also has a lazy river (Plate 14). Missouri State has a lazy river, too, but the university does not call it that; as an assistant director of recreation put it, "We don't like to use the term lazy because we're not lazy in our institution."[43] At the University at Albany, housing officers believe that the new Empire Commons and Liberty Terrace (completed in 2012) serves to keep a higher percentage of upperclassmen living on campus. There are residence halls with tanning beds, cybercafés, putting greens, volleyball courts, and pet-washing stations.[44] John Eligon, a *New York Times* reporter, interviewed a student who was visiting a new residence hall and was impressed by the richness of its cultural offerings:

> He had seen the beach volleyball court, toured the game room equipped with billiards, Ping-Pong and air hockey tables, and learned with delight of the Friday pool parties with a D.J., free food and snow cones, spiked with rum for those of age. Now, as he and the three friends he was apartment hunting with stood peering at the pool, Mr. Heiland, 19, pondered what life might be like if he chose to live in . . . the Grove, when his sophomore year at the University of Missouri begins this fall. "It's like a vacation, almost," he said. "I'm not going to go to class—that's how I look at it."[45]

None of this necessarily means that students are accruing more debt than they would otherwise by living in flashy housing, but costly buildings probably do not help.

Even living off campus has gone up in price, because large corporate entities have taken over that market sector. As discussed in chapter 4, for centuries, off-campus housing consisted of boardinghouses, which were frequently operated by elderly neighbors, but boardinghouses slowly disappeared, for several reasons. After World War II, the economy roared. Students who could afford cars had new options: they could commute or drive from apartments that were not within walking distance of campus (proximity had been the boardinghouses' best advantage). Young men could cook and clean well enough to take care of themselves. The ladies who ran boardinghouses might have had other ways of earning money, too, as it became increasingly possible for women to enter the workforce. The sexual revolution might have put another nail in the boardinghouse's coffin: young people wanted privacy, which they could not get with a live-in supervisor of the stereotypical spinster persona. Today, off-campus housing is a big corporate undertaking, and there are companies with nationwide standing that construct private dorms just on the edges of college-owned land. These housing complexes tend to be competitive with the college residence halls in terms of price.

DISTANCE LEARNING

One might think that online learning would make the residence hall obsolete. Students can stay at home, studying in their bathrobes at their kitchen tables. But that does not sound like much fun, does it? If one enters the search term "distance learning" into Google Images, one finds stock photos: a young man with a laptop on a mountain precipice, a middle-aged woman in her jammies at home with a cup of coffee, and a single mortarboard resting on an Apple keyboard. These images inadvertently point to the fact that distance learning takes place *alone.* Some young people like to be by themselves, but most do not.

Of course, there are advantages to the use of distance learning technology: it minimizes or erases the cost of commuting and requires very little brick-and-mortar infrastructure on the part of universities. Online higher education is making advanced learning available to more students than ever before. In his alarmingly titled book *The End of College,* Kevin Carey explains the many ways that online education will make higher education increasingly accessible and democratic. Using himself as a subject (always a surefire method in the social sciences), Carey enrolled in a massive open online course, or MOOC, at the Massachusetts Institute of Technology. He took exactly the same course taken by a group of freshmen at MIT, with the same professor. He later visited MIT in order to physically attend one of the same lectures he had watched at home. After some consideration, he decided that he preferred watching the lecture online, because he appreciated being able to stop and go back to earlier points in the lesson. He got his online certificate, and he proved that the content of the online class was the same as the content of the course offered on campus.[46]

But even if the content was the same, the *experience* was not. In contrast to Carey's pro-democratic rhetoric, I would argue that MOOCs are not democratic at all, precisely because they lack the social aspect that has been a major theme of this book. One study found that the completion rate for MOOCs is 7 percent.[47] As reported by Steve Kolowich, very few students who start MOOCs actually finish them. In the sample he studied, only 5 percent of those registered for a course viewed at least half of the course materials, and 35 percent never viewed *any* of the materials.[48] Although there are chat rooms inside MOOC learning software platforms, such classes offer no real opportunity for networking. Is an MIT professor likely to write a letter of reference for a stranger who is one of ten thousand people taking a class online? Is an on-campus MIT student likely to strike up a friendship with a MOOC student? If so, would this unicorn-like MIT student prance up to the MOOC student in a chat room and say, "Hey, let's start a cool new disruptive company?" America's brightest young people go to MIT for the academics, surely, but they also go there to be surrounded by similarly ambitious, technologically minded go-getters. The networking must take place physically, in an embodied way, on the campus itself—in dining halls, recreation centers, dormitories, and pits full of multicolored plastic balls. MOOCs may not be doing any financial damage to low-income people, but they do create a false hope in the poor kid at the kitchen table that the gulf between him or her and the on-campus MIT student can be breached. It cannot.

We inhabit a world where distance learning could make the realm of brick-and-mortar universities a luxury for the few rather than an expectation of the many. But, as Blimling notes, no one has yet suggested how MOOCs will make money in the long term, and universities are likely to turn away from offering such courses once they start to actually lose money.[49] MOOCs may not be around for long, but the more generic category of online learning is here to stay. The proportion of students taking online courses increased from 10 percent in 2003 to 32 percent in 2011.[50] Blimling makes an interesting observation, which is that many people taking online courses are taking them while living on campus. He explains, "Course time conflicts, graduation requirements, work schedules, convenience, and learning styles contribute to students' decisions to take courses online."[51] Their schedules are packed. They are trying to graduate on time, and none of the required courses that meet in person fit their schedules. This creates an unexpected intersection between the residence hall and online learning. Rather than making the residence hall irrelevant, online courses reinforce the residence hall as the center of student life.

With the soaring costs of higher education, American students today take on more debt than ever before. In 2017, U.S. student debt was estimated at $1.3 trillion, more than double what it was in 2008. This level of debt is stymying the economy and causing young people to delay home ownership and marriage.[52] Not surprisingly, poor students are suffering disproportionately from skyrocketing debt, and the rate of default on student loans is increasing. The specter of insolvency has had a more insidious outcome: students cannot possibly use college as a time of exploration or to enhance their love of learning when they are anticipating a lifetime of student loan bills. What's a liberal arts college to do? Michael Roth, president of Wesleyan University in Connecticut, writes:

> As many in higher education succumb to fears of being left behind and choose vocational shortcuts for their curriculum, we who believe in the power of pragmatic liberal education must develop broad, contextual learning that enables our graduates to pursue meaningful work and lifelong learning. Yes, ours is a merciless economy characterized by deep economic inequality, but that inequality must not be accepted as a given; the skills of citizenship and the powers of creativity enhanced through liberal learning can be used to push back against it.[53]

And where will future students live? That is a difficult question to answer. As more classes are taught online, demand for residence halls might decrease, as students choose the inexpensive option of living at home. But the attraction of living on campus will endure. Some parents are relieved to become empty nesters, with their teenage children out of the house. Students are motivated to move out of their family homes, because that transition traditionally draws a sharp line between high school and college, between adolescence and adulthood. Residence halls solidify, even magnify, social differences. The gap between the rich and the poor is widening in American society at large, and this fact makes the in-person networking opportunities afforded to those who live on campus more valuable than ever. As I have argued throughout this book, living in a residence hall gives a student a boost up the social ladder and has done so since the earliest days of the colonial colleges. Residing on the physical campus, amid (if not in) stately, ancient, and hallowed halls will persist as a rite of passage, even if home is only a few miles away. Living on campus will remain essential for face-to-face networking, for both friendship and future careers, and the potential for making social connections will continue to serve as a major incentive for students to attend college at all. The architecture of dormitories, therefore, is an ever-changing manifestation of the social meaning of higher education.

Acknowledgments

To whom much is given, much is required. I start this way to remind the reader, indeed to remind myself, that writing a book is a gift. Admittedly, this was a gift about which I never ceased complaining. As my bellyaching son put it: "Mommie, you've been talking about your book for my whole life." A long gestation period leads to a very long list of thank yous.

Fortunately, architectural historians make good friends and excellent critics: Jeffrey A. Cohen, Marta Gutman, Sandy Isenstadt, and Aaron Wunsch have been especially generous. Many others (Emily Cooperman, Catherine Boland Erkkila, Sharon Haar, Kenneth Hafertepe, Will Moore, Susan Solomon, and Amber N. Wiley) intervened to assist me with a mind-boggling array of queries. Rachel Iannacone directed my attention toward an article in *Life*; Paul V. Turner and Christopher Drew Armstrong helped me solve a puzzle involving Claude-Nicolas Ledoux. Keith Morgan and Jack Quinan wrote letters of reference. Thomas Hubka assisted me with the Appendix. Jayne Merkel and Rejean Legault shared their knowledge of Eero Saarinen. Marc Treib allowed me to reproduce images from his collection. John Giganti made beautiful drawings that enhance the narrative. Joe Siry understood the key themes of the project from the beginning and invited me to speak at my beloved alma mater, Wesleyan. Alice Friedman and Martha McNamara included me in a wonderful symposium on the modern campus at Wellesley. The anonymous reader for *Buildings and Landscapes* and the editors of that journal, Anna Andrzejewksi and Cindy Falk, shaped chapter 2 in decisive ways. Alison Isenberg is the best of friends and readers. Seth Koven encouraged me to think expansively (and be funnier). After all these years, I don't compose a sentence without gratitude for David B. Brownlee.

My students at Rutgers participated in many ways, by studying campus architecture with me and by sharing their stories of spatial practice within the residence hall. They taught me that "dorming" is a verb, a lesson I chose to ignore. Coteaching with historian Paul Clemens brought out the best in our students, and I learned a great deal about the history of Rutgers from him. Paul also saved me from a contrived argument that I had nonetheless clung to for several years. I served as a low-level vice president in the central administration of Rutgers–New Brunswick for three and a half years, which amplified my understanding of how good universities inch their way toward greatness. President Emeritus Richard L. McCormick and Barry V. Qualls were always on hand to offer encouragement and perspective. At the Rutgers Libraries, I thank Caryn Radick, Tom Frusciano, Erika Gorder, and Jim Niessen. Art history students Anna Rogulina, Kathleen Pierce, Elijah Reiss, and Laura Leichtman attended to manuscript preparations. The "Deadline Divas," Belinda Davis and Judy Gerson, got me over the finish line.

Student affairs, as a profession, is a noble undertaking. Greg Blimling, Michael Coomes, Tony Doody, Amy Vojta, and Mark Schuster led me to appreciate the skills that are necessary for survival among students. Historians of education and college boosters also chipped in. Howard Schaffer gave permission for me to look at fraternity archives at Cornell; Margaret Leary generously shared her knowledge of Mr. Cook; and Howard Gillette's in-depth history of Yale was a great help.

No book of this scale could exist without archivists. Some of those who went above and beyond the call of duty were Ann Bowers, Christine Bunting, Michelle Drobik, Joellen ElBashir, James Gerencser, Ken Grossi, Kevlin Haire, Miranda Hanbro, Karen Jania, Waverly Lowell, Sandra "Miss Information" Markham, Malgosia Myc, and David Null. I visited archives at Harvard University, Oberlin College, the Ohio State University, New York University, the University of California at Santa Cruz, the University of Chicago, the University of Michigan, the University of Wisconsin–Madison, and Yale University, as well as the National Student Affairs Archive at Bowling Green State University and the Environmental Design Archives at the University of California at Berkeley.

I wish to recognize the Bentley Library for a research grant and the Rutgers Research Council for two grants. The Rutgers School of Arts and Sciences also supported me through a research account. The tireless folks at the University of Minnesota Press, especially Pieter Martin, supported this project from its early days. Judy Selhorst, a first-rate copy editor, earned my eternal gratitude. The reviewers for the University of Minnesota Press read the book with sharp eyes, making the final product much richer for its greater surfacing of student voices.

Since this book dates back to my son's babyhood, I must call attention to the world's greatest day care center, Yellow Brick Road, as well as to the YBR parents, who provided friendship, potlucks, and picnics at the pool. I am grateful for the unflappable Sarah Ayash, who turned out to be as patient a dog- and catsitter as she is a loving babysitter. The inspirational people at my dance studio, the perfectly named Inspira, keep my body and spirit fit. My sisters and brothers contribute in more ways than they know. Barbara was a cheerful companion on many an architectural adventure. Joan Kinney Yanni and Joseph A. Yanni, my witty, intelligent, and feisty parents, set high standards for everything, including longevity. Finally, I am sustained by Bill and Joseph, whose presence in my life has caused me to find new and exciting ways of working. My prefamily self would be shocked to learn that I am writing these acknowledgments in a cold church basement, waiting for the pinewood derby to start, as the cheerful shrieks of Cub Scouts seep through my noise-canceling headphones.

Appendix

From the time of America's earliest college dormitories, most students found the contrast between home and the institutional space of the dormitory to be drastic. In a freestanding family dwelling, the outdoors were only a step away, windows on all sides brought in light and air, and the kitchen was nearby. It is difficult to know if students had more or less privacy in the dormitory or the house, because bedrooms were shared in both types. In a home, the ratio of adults to children favored the oversight of the parents; in a dormitory, young people probably outnumbered the adults, but they were still under close watch.

Plans A.1 and A.2 show typical dormitory plans, the entryway type and the double-loaded corridor. The lower three plans are house types: the hall and parlor type (B.1), a worker's cottage (B.2), and a bungalow (B.3). B = bedroom; K = kitchen; Ba = bathroom; L = living room; D = dining room; and P = porch. The house plans are from Thomas C. Hubka, *Houses without Names: Architectural Nomenclature and the Classification of America's Common Houses* (Knoxville: University of Tennessee Press, 2013), 67; reprinted courtesy of Thomas C. Hubka and drawn to the same approximate scale by John Giganti.

A.1

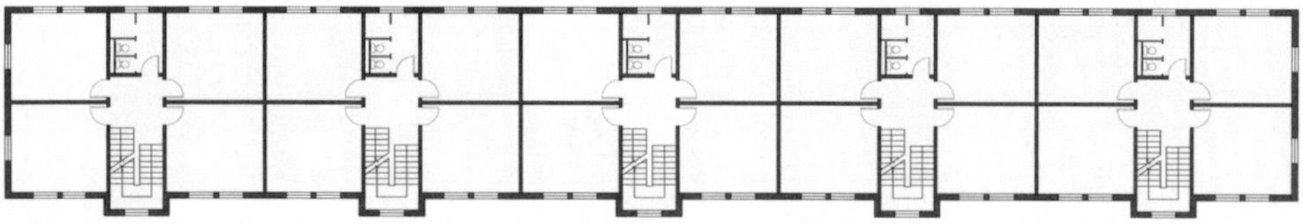

A.2

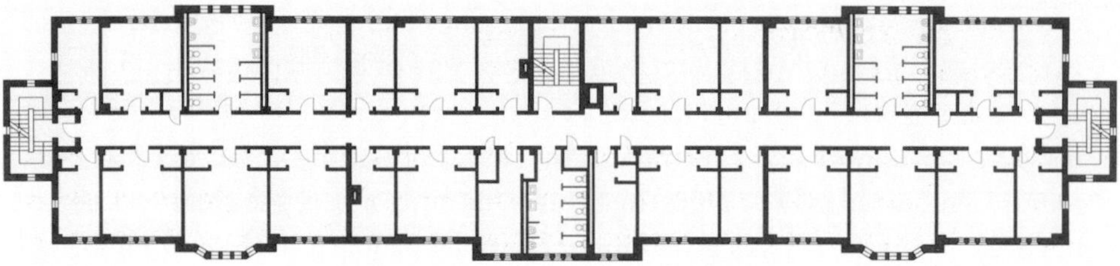

B.1
1–3 rooms
1800–1900

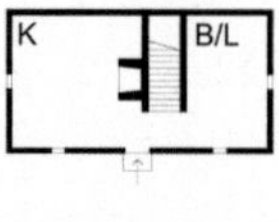

B.2
3–5 rooms
1860–1950

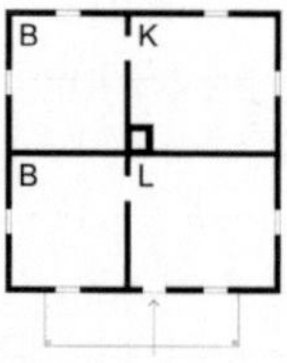

B.3
6–8 rooms
1940–2000

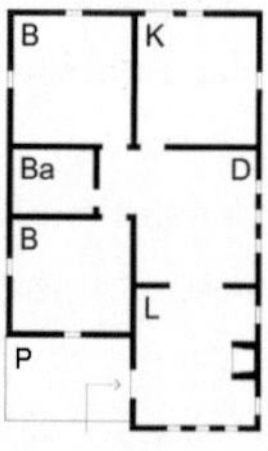

B = bedroom Ba = bathroom D = dining room
K = kitchen L = living room P = porch

Notes

INTRODUCTION

1. Philip Roth, *Indignation* (New York: Houghton Mifflin, 2008), 87.

2. Roth, 90.

3. Oxford, Cambridge, and Leuven were the exceptional medieval universities that had purpose-built housing. Philippe Ariès has described the difficult living situations for migrant students in France in the Middle Ages and the early modern period, but those students were not housed in university-sponsored buildings. See Philippe Ariès, *Centuries of Childhood* (Harmondsworth: Penguin, 1962).

4. See Carla Yanni, *The Architecture of Madness: Insane Asylums in the United States* (Minneapolis: University of Minnesota Press, 2007).

5. Steven Mintz, *Huck's Raft: A History of American Childhood* (Cambridge, Mass.: Belknap Press, 2006), 161.

6. Scholars of vernacular architecture find meaning in common buildings, and, indeed, many of the buildings discussed in this book are ordinary. I have benefited enormously from books such as the following: Annmarie Adams, *Medicine by Design: The Architect and the Modern Hospital, 1893–1943* (Minneapolis: University of Minnesota Press, 2008); Marta Gutman, *A City for Children: Women, Architecture, and the Charitable Landscapes of Oakland, 1850–1950* (Chicago: University of Chicago Press, 2014); Matthew Gordon Lasner, *High Life: Condo Living in the Suburban Century* (New Haven, Conn.: Yale University Press, 2012); Paula Lupkin, *Manhood Factories: YMCA Architecture and the Making of Modern Urban Culture* (Minneapolis: University of Minnesota Press, 2010); A. K. Sandoval-Strausz, *Hotel: An American History* (New Haven, Conn.: Yale University Press, 2007); and Abigail A. Van Slyck, *A Manufactured Wilderness: Summer Camps and the Shaping of American Youth, 1890–1960* (Minneapolis: University of Minnesota Press, 2006).

7. Charles Z. Klauder and Herbert C. Wise, *College Architecture in America and Its Part in the Development of the Campus* (New York: Charles Scribner's Sons, 1929), 120,

134. Klauder was a leading architect of academic campuses; he promoted Beaux-Arts planning and consistent, coherent style.

8. American Institute of Architects, *Building Type Reference Guide: College Residence Halls,* no. 6 (1948–49), 14, MS 218, folder "NAWE Pamphlets, NADW and National Association of Deans and Advisers of Men, 1949," National Student Affairs Archive (hereafter NSAA), Bowling Green State University (hereafter BGSU).

9. The University of Virginia has captured the attention of so many architectural historians that its details need not be repeated here. In basic outline, and looking only at the student bedrooms, Thomas Jefferson's innovation is visible in a plan in which the bedrooms open directly onto a walkway that is adjacent to the lawn. Jefferson did not utilize the internal double-loaded corridor, the single-loaded corridor, *or* the staircase plan. See Paul Venable Turner, *Campus: An American Planning Tradition* (Cambridge: MIT Press, 1984), 76–87; Mary N. Woods, "Thomas Jefferson and the University of Virginia: Planning the Academic Village," *Journal of the Society of Architectural Historians* 44, no. 3 (October 1985): 266–83; Richard Guy Wilson, ed., *Thomas Jefferson's Academical Village: The Creation of an Architectural Masterpiece* (Charlottesville: University of Virginia Press, 2009); Richard Guy Wilson, David J. Neuman, and Sara A. Butler, *University of Virginia: An Architectural Tour,* 2nd ed. (New York: Princeton Architectural Press, 2012).

10. To avoid introducing unneeded complexity, I did not look at housing for nurses, which is investigated in Adams, *Medicine by Design,* 71–88. I also chose not to write about housing designed for international students, cooperatives, and preparatory high schools.

11. In 2013–14, there were 3,039 degree-granting four-year colleges in the United States. National Center for Education Statistics, "Fast Facts: Educational Institutions," accessed August 20, 2018, https://nces.ed.gov/fastfacts/display.asp?id=84.

12. I do appreciate the relevance of retrofitted and repurposed buildings, which also carry the significant imprint of their makers. As Marta Gutman observes regarding the history of spaces intended for children: "Each establishment began in a repurposed house, intended to address the special needs of each group. Whether purpose-built or not, these institutions recorded human differences among the children." Marta Gutman, "The Physical Spaces of Childhood," in *The Routledge History of Childhood in the Western World,* ed. Paula S. Fass (London: Routledge, 2013), 261.

13. Questionnaire, Record Group Sections and Divisions, box 1, folder "Report on Housing Practices Survey," March 1963, MS 218, NAWE, NSAA, BGSU.

14. James W. Clark (university planner), "Re River Dorms," memo, July 8, 1963, RG 10/b/7, Ohio State University Archives.

15. In 1964, officials at OSU had a full-size mock-up of one suite in the proposed new dorms built in a warehouse near campus and solicited feedback from students who visited the installation. Thomas G. Buckham, "Skyscrapers to Rise Soon," *Lantern,* November 9, 1964.

16. Helen Lefkowitz Horowitz, *Alma Mater: Design and Experience in the Women's Colleges from Their Nineteenth-Century Beginnings to the 1930s* (New York: Alfred A.

Knopf, Inc., 1984); Helen Lefkowitz Horowitz, *Campus Life: Undergraduate Cultures from the End of the Eighteenth Century to the Present* (New York: Alfred A. Knopf, 1987).

17. Charles F. Frederiksen, "A Brief History of Collegiate Housing," in *Student Housing and Residential Life,* ed. Roger B. Winston Jr. and Scott Anchors and Associates (San Francisco: Jossey-Bass, 1993), 168.

18. Daniel J. Boorstin, *The Americans: The National Experience* (New York: Vintage Books, 2010), 153.

19. Boorstin, 154.

20. Phillip Lindley, president of the nondenominational University of Nashville in 1843, quoted in Boorstin, 154. I wish to thank Aaron Wunsch for helping me think about many aspects of nineteenth-century American colleges.

21. Nathaniel Hawthorne, *Fanshawe,* in *Collected Novels,* ed. Millicent Bell (New York: Library of America, 1983), 3.

22. Governing Board of Harvard, 1671, quoted in Turner, *Campus,* 23.

23. Benjamin Franklin, "A Proposal for Promoting Useful Knowledge among the British Plantations in America" (1744), in *Benjamin Franklin: The Autobiography and Other Writings,* ed. L. Jesse Lemisch (New York: Signet, 1961), 210–11.

24. Horowitz, *Campus Life,* 47.

25. See Blake Gumprecht, *The American College Town* (Amherst: University of Massachusetts Press, 2008), 74–83.

26. Nicholas Syrett, *The Company He Keeps: A History of White College Fraternities* (Chapel Hill: University of North Carolina Press, 2009), 18. In my discussion I focus on white fraternities because African American Greek organizations have not typically occupied purpose-built housing, and even today, many African American fraternities are nonresidential. The first Greek fraternity for African American men was a chapter of Alpha Phi Alpha founded at Cornell in 1904. Alpha Phi Alpha still exists. Another early African American fraternity, Alpha Kapp Nu at Indiana University, might have been founded earlier, but since it lasted only eleven months, it tends not to get as much attention as Alpha Phi Alpha.

27. Robert C. Clothier to Lansing P. Shield, Records of Lewis Webster Jones Administration, February 5, 1954, 10/9, Special Collections and University Archives, Rutgers University Libraries.

28. Klauder and Wise, *College Architecture in America,* 134.

29. *The Bison,* 1933, n.p.

30. Alex Duke, *Importing Oxbridge: English Residential Colleges and American Universities* (New Haven, Conn.: Yale University Press, 1996), 145.

31. Scott Carlson, "When College Was a Public Good," *Chronicle of Higher Education,* November 27, 2016. https://www.chronicle.com.

32. Kate Mueller et al., *The Residence Hall for Students,* pamphlet produced by the National Association of Women Deans and Counselors, MS 218, publications box 3, NSAA, BGSU.

33. "Dormies Cite Reasons for Exodus," *Daily Californian,* February 4, 1964, quoted in Page & Turnbull, "UC Berkeley Unit 3 Housing Historic Resource Evaluation," report prepared for University of California, Berkeley, April 19, 2013, 34.

34. Turner, *Campus,* 10.

35. Margaret Birney Vickery, *Buildings for Bluestockings: The Architecture and Social History of Women's Colleges in Late Victorian England* (Newark: University of Delaware Press, 1999), 13–14.

36. Duke, *Importing Oxbridge,* 50–51.

37. David J. Rothman, *The Discovery of the Asylum: Social Order and Disorder in the New Republic* (Boston: Little, Brown, 1971).

38. "Colleges in Colonial Times," *The Crimson,* April 20, 1883.

39. Gutman, *City for Children,* 7.

40. Gutman, "Physical Spaces of Childhood," 249.

41. As reported in the Dickinson College student newspaper the *Dickinsonian,* vol. 2 (1875–76), 3.

42. Sandoval-Strausz, *Hotel,* 36–37.

43. Elizabeth Collins Cromley, *Alone Together: A History of New York's Early Apartments* (Ithaca, N.Y.: Cornell University Press, 1990), 35.

44. A. Evelyn Newman, dean of women, State Teachers College, Greeley, Colorado, "Student Living Conditions and Their Effect on Character and Morals," *Thirteenth Yearbook,* 1926, MS 218, folder "National Association of Deans of Women," NSAA, BGSU.

45. Mark Jarzombek, "Corridor Spaces," *Critical Inquiry* 36, no. 4 (Summer 2010): 765.

46. American Institute of Architects, *Building Type Reference Guide.*

47. In 2014, there were about 12 million college students in the United States under age twenty-five and 8.2 million students who were twenty-five years old and older. National Center for Education Statistics, "Fast Facts: Enrollment," accessed August 17, 2018, https://nces.ed.gov/fastfacts/display.asp?id=98.

48. According to the National Center for Education Statistics, between 2002–3 and 2012–13, "the share of all bachelor's degrees conferred to U.S. residents earned by Hispanic students increased from 7 to 11 percent, and the share earned by Black students increased from 10 to 11 percent. In contrast, the share of bachelor's degrees earned by White students decreased from 76 percent in 2002–03 to 69 percent in 2012–13." Also, "across racial/ethnic groups, larger shares of undergraduate degrees and certificates were conferred to female students than to male students in academic year 2012–13." National Center for Education Statistics, "Fast Facts: Degrees Conferred by Race and Sex," accessed August 17, 2018, https://nces.ed.gov/fastfacts/display.asp?id=72.

49. Ariès, *Centuries of Childhood,* 264.

50. Thomas Hine, *The Rise and Fall of the American Teenager* (New York: HarperCollins, 1999), 58; John R. Thelin, *A History of American Higher Education,* 2nd ed. (Baltimore: Johns Hopkins University Press, 2011), 25.

51. Craig Steven Wilder, *Ebony and Ivy: Race, Slavery, and the Troubled History of America's Universities* (New York: Bloomsbury Press, 2013), 26. In 1823, Alexander Lucius Twilight was the first African American to receive a bachelor's degree; he graduated from Middlebury College in Vermont.

52. Ariès, *Centuries of Childhood,* 264.

53. Abigail A. Van Slyck, "The Spatial Practices of Privilege," *Journal of the Society of Architectural Historians* 70, no. 2 (June 2011): 237n30.

54. Thomas D. Snyder, ed., *120 Years of American Education: A Statistical Portrait,* NCES pub. no. 93442 (Washington, D.C.: U.S. Department of Education, Office of Educational Research and Improvement, 1993), 68, http://nces.ed.gov.

55. Robert A. Schwartz, "How Deans of Women Became Men," *Review of Higher Education* 20, no. 4 (Summer 1997): 419–36. For a fuller treatment of this subject, see Robert A. Schwartz, *Deans of Men and the Shaping of Modern College Culture* (New York: Palgrave Macmillan, 2010).

56. Charles F. Thwing, "What Becomes of College Women?," *North American Review* 161, no. 468 (November 1895): 546.

57. Thelin, *History of American Higher Education,* 169.

58. Thelin, 169.

59. Horowitz, *Campus Life,* 79.

60. Mintz, *Huck's Raft,* 196.

61. Don Romesburg, "Making Adolescence More or Less Modern," in Fass, *Routledge History of Childhood in the Western World,* 235.

62. Gail Bederman, *Manliness and Civilization: A Cultural History of Gender and Race in the United States, 1880–1917* (Chicago: University of Chicago Press, 1995), 92.

63. Mintz, *Huck's Raft,* 197.

64. Hine, *Rise and Fall of the American Teenager,* 199.

65. G. Stanley Hall, *Adolescence: Its Psychology and Its Relations to Physiology, Anthropology, Sociology, Sex, Crime, Religion and Education,* vol. 2 (New York: D. Appleton, 1905), 400.

66. Jerome Karabel, *The Chosen: The Hidden History of Admission and Exclusion at Harvard, Yale, and Princeton* (New York: Mariner Books, 2006), 51.

67. For an extended discussion of prostitution and college men, see Daniel Bluestone, "Charlottesville's Landscape of Prostitution," *Buildings and Landscapes* 22, no. 2 (Fall 2015): 36–61.

68. Mintz, *Huck's Raft,* 231.

69. *Hints Regarding the Residence Halls for Women,* n.d., pUA/1772, folder "Residence Halls: Information for Men Residents," University Archives and Special Collections, BGSU.

70. Page & Turnbull, "UC Berkeley Unit 3 Housing," 35.

71. Margaret A. Lowe, *Looking Good: College Women and Body Image, 1875–1930* (Baltimore: Johns Hopkins University Press, 2003), 104.

72. Horowitz, *Campus Life,* 289.

73. Gregory S. Blimling, *Student Learning in College Residence Halls: What Works, What Doesn't, and Why* (Jossey-Bass, 2015), 8.

74. Hine, *Rise and Fall of the American Teenager,* 8.

75. Hine, 12.

76. Mario Savio, quoted in Robert Cohen, *Freedom's Orator: Mario Savio and the Radical Legacy of the 1960s* (New York: Oxford University Press, 2009), 327.

77. S. Lipka, "Demographic Data Lets Colleges Peer into the Future," *Chronicle of Higher Education,* January 19, 2014, cited in Blimling, *Student Learning,* 279.

1. COLLEGE HOUSING FOR MEN

1. Owen Johnson, *Stover at Yale* (New York: Grosset & Dunlap, 1912), 13.

2. This chapter is focused on small schools for boys aged approximately fourteen to eighteen who lived in close proximity to one another; these schools had narrower curricula than did universities, and faculty were not expected to conduct research. Many such institutions still exist today in the form of boarding high schools intended to prepare students for college. These were (and are) casually called prep schools, and some of those still in operation date back to the colonial period, including the prestigious Phillips Exeter Academy and Phillips Academy Andover. Many prep schools have dormitories that were built during the same period as those discussed here and resemble them closely. From today's vantage point, it would be difficult to tell early nineteenth-century Exeter from Williams College in the same period, in terms of either architecture or curriculum. Prep schools maintain the faculty-to-student relationship that was typical of nineteenth-century colleges. For example, Wilbraham & Monson Academy, founded in 1804, had 425 students enrolled in 2016, approximately 200 of whom lived on campus. With seventy-two faculty members, the student–teacher ratio was six to one. (The school is now coed and integrated, both significant changes from its earlier status.) Prep school teachers are involved in the moral development of their students. Since prep schools have never felt the need to turn themselves into universities, their faculty members do not need to do research, and they are rewarded for focusing on teaching. Given this book's primary focus on postsecondary educational institutions, the architecture of boarding preparatory schools is beyond the scope of this chapter.

3. Thelin, *History of American Higher Education,* 27. Thelin noted that there were few divinity schools in the United States; therefore, most young men preparing to be Anglican ministers went to Britain for their training and ordination. While I have relied on Thelin for much of the history of higher education, in terms of curriculum, student class, and the growing professoriate, his scholarship is much like other history of education in lacking precise or in-depth discussions of space.

4. Thelin, 36.

5. Thelin, 67.

6. Horowitz, *Campus Life,* 11.

7. Thelin, *History of American Higher Education,* 67.

8. Turner, *Campus,* 23. This building is also referred to as the Old College or Harvard Hall I.

9. Samuel Eliot Morison, *Harvard College in the Seventeenth Century* (Cambridge, Mass.: Harvard University Press, 1936), 12.

10. Wilder, *Ebony and Ivy,* 27.

11. "Burning of Harvard Hall, 1764," *Publications of the Colonial Society of Massachusetts* (1911): 36–37. The building was occupied by the state government when it burned, which is why the legislature agreed to reimburse the students for their destroyed belongings.

12. Colonial Society of Massachusetts, "Harvard College Records Part I—Corporation Records 1636–1750," *Publications of the Colonial Society of Massachusetts* 15 (1925): 260.

13. Stephen Peabody, *Pedagogues and Protesters: The Harvard College Student Diary of Stephen Peabody, 1767–1768,* ed. Conrad Edick Wright (Amherst: University of Massachusetts Press, 2017), 51–52.

14. Conrad Edick Wright, the editor of Peabody's diary, underscores this point. See Peabody, 52.

15. Colonial Society of Massachusetts, "Harvard College Records Part I," 260.

16. The rough sketch of Stoughton Hall drawn by Holyoke circa 1763–64 shows two hallways cutting across the building the short way (transversely). The dimensions are noted on the sketch, which was reproduced in Colonial Society of Massachusetts, 260.

17. Bainbridge Bunting, *Harvard: An Architectural History,* ed. Margaret Henderson Floyd (Cambridge, Mass.: Belknap Press, 1985), 21.

18. Rick Kennedy, "Thomas Brattle, Mathematician-Architect in the Transition of the New England Mind, 1690–1700," *Winterthur Portfolio* 24, no. 4 (Winter 1989): 233. Kennedy attributes the building to Thomas Brattle.

19. Samuel Eliot Morison, *Three Centuries of Harvard, 1636–1936* (Cambridge, Mass.: Harvard University Press, 1936), 311.

20. Bunting, *Harvard,* 21.

21. Edward A. Chappell, "Architecture, Archaeology, and the Revolution in Williamsburg," *Colonial Williamsburg Journal* (Summer 2014), http://history.org/foundation/journal.

22. "Wren Building," Colonial Williamsburg Foundation, http://www.history.org. The Wren Building appears today much as it looked in 1732, based on research conducted at the time of the restoration in the 1930s.

23. Turner, *Campus,* 28. See also James Kornwolf, *So Good a Design: The Colonial Campus of the College of William and Mary—Its History, Background, and Legacy* (Williamsburg, Va.: College of William and Mary, Joseph and Margaret Muscarelle Museum of Art, 1989), 50.

24. Turner, *Campus,* 27.

25. Douglas Shand-Tucci, *Harvard University: The Campus Guide* (New York: Princeton Architectural Press, 2001), 11.

26. For an illustration of Jefferson's design, see Kornwolf, *So Good a Design,* 48; or Turner, *Campus,* 78.

27. Turner, *Campus,* 28.

28. Turner, 47.

29. Turner, 23.

30. Ezra Stiles, sketch of Nassau Hall, 1754, reproduced in *Proceedings of the Massachusetts Historical Society* 7 (1892): 343.

31. W. Barksdale Maynard, *Princeton: America's Campus* (University Park: Pennsylvania State University Press, 2012), 13–14; Kenneth Hafertepe, "Princeton and the

Presbyterian Plain Style" (unpublished manuscript, 1993); Henry Lyttleton Savage, ed., *Nassau Hall, 1756–1956* (Princeton, N.J.: Princeton University Press, 1956), 17.

32. Deborah Yaffe, "Princeton and Slavery: Our Original Sin," *Princeton Alumni Weekly*, November 8, 2017, n.p.

33. Samuel Blair, *An Account of the College of New Jersey* (Woodbridge, N. J.: James Parker, 1764), n.p.

34. Phyllis Vine, "The Social Function of Eighteenth-Century Higher Education," *History of Education Quarterly* 16, no. 4 (1976): 411.

35. Vine, 410–11. The nine colonial colleges (that is, those schools of higher learning founded before the American Revolution) developed into different types of institutions. Seven remained private. Cornell is partly private and partly state funded, and Rutgers and William and Mary are state affiliated. In terms of undergraduate enrollment, Dartmouth is the smallest with 4,300, and Rutgers is the largest with 35,000.

36. John Witherspoon, *Letters on the Education of Children and on Marriage* (Andover: Flagg and Gould, 1817), 17.

37. Vine, "Social Function of Eighteenth-Century Higher Education," 412.

38. Margaret Sumner, *Collegiate Republic: Cultivating an Ideal Society in Early America* (Charlottesville: University of Virginia Press, 2014), 4.

39. Vine, "Social Function of Eighteenth-Century Higher Education," 409.

40. Syrett, *The Company He Keeps*, 15.

41. Francis Henshaw Dewey to the Hon. Charles T. Dewey (his father), September 19, 1836, Williams College Archives. Also published in Francis Henshaw Dewey, *From My End of the Log: Francis Henshaw Dewey's Letters from Williams College, 1836–1840*, ed. Jane Kenah Dewey (Worcester, Mass.: Commonwealth Press, 1982), 7–8. I thank Margaret Sumner for directing me to this source.

42. Wilder, *Ebony and Ivy*, 158–59.

43. Ulysses Hobbs, diary, November 1849, Special Collections, Dickinson College.

44. Benjamin Henry Latrobe, quoted in Turner, *Campus*, 67.

45. Benjamin Henry Latrobe, *The Architectural Drawings of Benjamin Henry Latrobe*, ed. Jeffrey A. Cohen and Charles E. Brownell (New Haven, Conn.: Yale University Press, 1995), pt. 2, 425.

46. In asylums, single-loaded corridors were sometimes used for refractory wards, where the most violent patients were housed. The potential danger such patients posed to the staff justified the additional expense. Yanni, *Architecture of Madness*, 60.

47. Hobbs, diary, November 1849.

48. Sumner, *Collegiate Republic*, 105. See also Merrit Caldwell to the Dickinson Board of Trustees, July 29, 1836, Durbin Presidential File, Special Collections, Dickinson College.

49. "A Noble Gift to Rutgers: Mr. Winants Presents a New Dormitory Building," *New York Times*, February 18, 1889.

50. Cromley, *Alone Together*, 20.

51. Preston H. Sessoms to Penelope E. White (sister), September 27, 1861, in "True and Candid Compositions: The Lives and Writings of Antebellum Students at the University of North Carolina in Chapel Hill," ed. Erika Lindemann, Documenting the

American South, University Library, University of North Carolina at Chapel Hill, http://docsouth.unc.edu.

52. Ulysses Hobbs, diary, January 2, 1850, Special Collections, Dickinson College. As Dickinson's size increased, students lived off campus in boardinghouses because the two on-campus dormitories could not hold them all. The town of Carlisle grew up around the college.

53. Alfred B. McCalmont, diary, December 2, 1842, Special Collections, Dickinson College.

54. McCalmont, diary, December 2, 1842.

55. Thelin, *History of American Higher Education,* 66.

56. Arthur Latham Perry, *Williamstown and Williams: A History* (Williamstown, Mass.: Norwood Press, 1904), 196.

57. Perry, 198.

58. Horowitz, *Campus Life,* 23.

59. Syrett, *The Company He Keeps,* 17.

60. Perry, *Williamstown and Williams,* 266.

61. Horowitz, *Campus Life,* 29.

62. Ulysses Hobbs, diary, January 9, 1849, Special Collections, Dickinson College.

63. See William D. Moore, *Masonic Temples: Freemasonry, Ritual Architecture, and Masculine Archetypes* (Knoxville: University of Tennessee Press, 2006).

64. Thelin, *History of American Higher Education,* 78. Federal funds could not be spent on architecture, thus the states were required to invest in infrastructure and buildings.

65. Board of Trustees, minutes, January 3, 1872, Record of Proceedings of the Board of Trustees of the Ohio Agricultural and Mechanical College and The Ohio State University from May 11, 1870, to June 25, 1890, Ohio State University Archives. For more on OSU's early dormitories, see "Born in Adversity: The Founding of the Ohio State University," online exhibit, University Libraries, Ohio State University, accessed July 22, 2015, https://library.osu.edu/blogs/founding.

66. Board of Trustees, minutes, April 23, 1872, Record of Proceedings of the Board of Trustees of the Ohio Agricultural and Mechanical College and The Ohio State University from May 11, 1870, to June 25, 1890, Ohio State University Archives. The architect of North Dorm seems to have been Jacob Snyder of Akron.

67. John H. Herrick, "The OSU Oval" (unpublished manuscript, July 15, 1982), http://www.horizonview.net/~beeryb/ref. Herrick was the longtime head of university planning. Old North dormitory was razed in 1908, and Old South was razed in 1924. Old South was briefly used as a hospital and then as a nurses' dormitory.

68. Board of Trustees, minutes, January 3, 1877, Record of Proceedings of the Board of Trustees of the Ohio Agricultural and Mechanical College and The Ohio State University from May 11, 1870, to June 25, 1890, Ohio State University Archives.

69. James Ellsworth Boyd, "A Note on the Old North Dormitory," *Ohio State University Quarterly* 2, no. 2 (October 1910): 35–36.

70. Horowitz, *Campus Life,* 45.

71. Horowitz, 131.

72. Horowitz, 45.

73. Syrett, *The Company He Keeps,* 162.

74. Syrett, 162.

75. Thomas Hubka, *Houses without Names: Architectural Nomenclature and the Classification of America's Common Houses* (Knoxville: University of Tennessee Press, 2013), 37, 44, 55.

76. Board of Trustees, minutes, June 24, 1890, Record of Proceedings of the Board of Trustees of the Ohio Agricultural and Mechanical College and The Ohio State University from May 11, 1870, to June 25, 1890, Ohio State University Archives.

77. Although generally fraternity rituals are secret and passed down only through the spoken word, in 2001 Wikileaks published a 136-page document detailing the rituals of Sigma Chi. The document's first page describes it as a "reprint of 1983 text with adopted revisions." *The Ritual,* 2001, Wikileaks, https://file.wikileaks.org/file/sigma-chi-ritual-2002.pdf.

78. Syrett, *The Company He Keeps,* 162.

79. Syrett, 163, quoting a description of a new house at Amherst College.

80. Psi Upsilon Fraternity, *The Phi Chapter of the Fraternity of Psi Upsilon in the University of Michigan* (Ann Arbor, Mich., 1906), 45–46, Bentley Historical Library, University of Michigan.

81. Psi Upsilon Fraternity, 52.

82. Psi Upsilon Fraternity, 52.

83. Psi Upsilon Fraternity, 51.

84. Dorothy Parker, *Not So Deep as a Well* (New York: Viking Press, 1937), 70.

85. Syrett, *The Company He Keeps,* 168.

86. Blake Gumprecht, "Fraternity Row, the Student Ghetto, and the Faculty Enclave: Characteristic Residential Districts in the American College Town," *Journal of Urban History* 32, no. 2 (January 2006): 237. See also Gumprecht, *American College Town,* 78–83.

87. Charles Thompson, *Halfway down the Stairs* (New York: Harper, 1957), quoted in Gumprecht, *American College Town,* 83.

88. Gumprecht, *American College Town,* 78–83.

89. Although early plans and the *Cornell Daily Sun* refer to the structure as a lodge, the brothers called it the Chapter House, the Temple, or the Goat House.

90. For a compendium of jokes, stories, and poems about goats in fraternities, see James Pettibone, *The Lodge Goat: Goat Rides, Butts, and Goat Hairs* (Cincinnati: James Pettibone, 1902).

91. William D. Moore, "Riding the Goat: Secrecy, Masculinity, and Fraternal High Jinks in the United States, 1845–1930," *Winterthur Portfolio* 41, nos. 2–3 (Summer–Autumn 2007): 168.

92. According to Howard Schaffer, Alpha Delta Phi brother, the Goat House was used for solemn ceremonies and serious meetings. Howard Schaffer, interview by author, August 18, 2016.

93. Alpha Delta Phi Records, self-published document, box 1, 37/4/2101, Cornell University Archives. This document refers to the Goat House as the Chapter House.

94. Alpha Delta Phi Records, self-published document, box 1, 37/4/2101.

95. *The Ritual,* 19.

96. As recently as 2006, fraternity members at Western Kentucky University in Bowling Green were arrested for cruelty to animals when a goat was found in the basement of their dwelling. According to a police spokesman, the fraternity brothers brought the animal into the house to make pledges believe they would be forced to have sex with it. Elizabeth F. Farrell, "Alleged Hazing Incident That Involved a Goat Threatens a Fraternity's Future at Western Kentucky U," *Chronicle of Higher Education,* February 20, 2006, https://www.chronicle.com.

97. The third Alpha Delta Phi House (which is still standing) is a Gothic Revival stone building from the early twentieth century that copies the plan of the one from 1900.

98. Paulette Singley, "The Anamorphic Phallus within Ledoux's Dismembered Plan of Chaux," *Journal of Architectural Education* 46, no. 3 (February 1993): 179.

99. Roxanne Williamson, *American Architects and the Mechanics of Fame* (Austin: University of Texas Press, 1991), 66.

100. Sigma Phi House, drawer 8, folder 3, Albert Kahn Collection, Bentley Historical Library, University of Michigan.

101. Syrett, *The Company He Keeps,* 151.

102. David Potts, *Wesleyan University, 1831–1910: Collegiate Enterprise in New England* (Hanover, N.H.: Wesleyan University Press, 1999), 199.

103. Syrett, *The Company He Keeps,* 164–65. In 1960, according to Harold Riker's estimate, 15 percent of undergraduates lived in fraternity chapter houses, or about 300,000 students. Harold C. Riker with Frank G. Lopez, *College Students Live Here: A Study of College Housing* (New York: Educational Facilities Laboratories, 1961), 18.

104. *Michiganensian,* 1907, ix–lxxv, Bentley Historical Library, University of Michigan.

105. *Cornellian,* 1909, 186–254, Cornell University Archives.

106. Henry Tappan, *A Discourse Delivered by Henry P. Tappan, D.D. at Ann Arbor, Mich., on the Occasion of His Inauguration as Chancellor of the University of Michigan, December 21st, 1852* (Detroit: Advertiser Power Presses, 1852), 20.

107. Julie A. Reuben, *The Making of the Modern University: Intellectual Transformation and the Marginalization of Morality* (Chicago: University of Chicago Press, 1996), 268.

2. THE COED'S PREDICAMENT

1. Olive San Louie Anderson, *An American Girl, and Her Four Years in a Boys' College,* ed. Elisabeth Israels Perry and Jennifer Ann Price (Ann Arbor: University of Michigan Press, 2006), 58. The book was originally published by D. Appleton in 1878, under Anderson's pseudonym Sola.

2. Anderson, 65.

3. On the use of *coed,* see Lowe, *Looking Good,* 63.

4. John Coolidge describes workers' housing in Lowell: "The boarding houses of the farm girls could be arranged in pairs, or in long strings. . . . Each unit would hold at least thirty girls. . . . Their design would be controlled entirely by accepted practice in domestic architecture." John Coolidge, *Mill and Mansion: A Study of Architecture and Society in Lowell Massachusetts, 1820–1865* (New York: Russell & Russell, 1967), 34. Lowell's ladies' houses resembled two- or three-story duplexes or row houses, each with a room for the matron on the first floor; on the upper floors, four to six female mill workers shared each room. The physical form of these houses, therefore, does not seem to have been a model for the dormitories discussed here. See also Margaret Crawford, *Building the Workingman's Paradise: The Design of American Company Towns* (London: Verso, 1995), 24.

5. Snyder, *120 Years of American Education,* 68.

6. Schwartz, "How Deans of Women Became Men," 419.

7. Horowitz, *Alma Mater,* 65.

8. Lowe, *Looking Good,* 73.

9. Syrett, *The Company He Keeps.*

10. Edward H. Clarke, *Sex in Education; or, A Fair Chance for the Girls* (Boston: J. R. Osgood, 1875), 126.

11. Henry Maudsley, a well-known British psychiatrist, quoted Clarke approvingly when he described the ill effects of educating girls and boys together. Maudsley went so far as to predict that the men in the New World would lose wives altogether, as the Romans found themselves without wives when the Sabines were abducted. See Angelique Richardson, *Love and Eugenics in the Late Nineteenth Century: Rational Reproduction and the New Woman* (Oxford: Oxford University Press, 2003), 41.

12. Schwartz, "How Deans of Women Became Men," 419. See also Jana Nidiffer, *Pioneering Deans of Women: More Than Wise and Pious Matrons* (New York: Teachers College Press, 2000), 158.

13. Lowe, *Looking Good,* 21.

14. Lowe, 73.

15. James H. Fairchild, *Oberlin: The Colony and the College, 1833–1883* (Oberlin, Ohio: E. J. Goodrich, 1883), 112, cited in Cally L. Waite, "The Segregation of Black Students at Oberlin College after Reconstruction," *History of Education Quarterly* 1, no. 3 (Autumn 2001): 355.

16. Geoffrey Blodgett, *Oberlin Architecture, College and Town: A Guide to Its Social History* (Oberlin, Ohio: Oberlin College, 1985), 2.

17. "Talcott Hall Celebrates Its Tenth Anniversary," *Oberlin News,* October 23, 1896.

18. *Alumni Catalogue 1833–1936* (Oberlin, Ohio: Oberlin College, 1937), 18, 20.

19. Berea College built Fairchild Hall in imitation of Second Ladies' Hall, and Fairchild Hall has an L-shaped plan. Shannon H. Wilson, *Berea College: An Illustrated History* (Lexington: University Press of Kentucky, 2006), 53.

20. The exteriors of nineteenth-century women's dormitories followed the fashions of other collegiate building types. One can find dormitories in every mainstream style,

from Italianate and Richardsonian to Gothic and Colonial Revival. The women's dormitories at the University of Chicago were nestled within the gray-stone Gothic Revival quadrangles and, given that they looked like every other part of the college, would not have been visible as dormitories. The specific styles of individual dormitories did not carry much meaning. At Michigan, there were plans for a mock Tudor dormitory, but these were superseded by the Martha Cook Building, which was Tudor Gothic (or Elizabethan), as can be seen in the diaper patterning in the brickwork and the square-headed windows.

21. Harriet L. Keeler, *The Life of Adelia A. Field Johnston Who Served Oberlin College for Thirty-Seven Years* (Cleveland, Ohio: Britton Print, [1912?]), 133.

22. For more on the uneven development of Sage College, see Charlotte Williams Conable, *Women at Cornell: The Myth of Equal Education* (Ithaca, N.Y.: Cornell University Press, 1977), 100–104; and Lowe, *Looking Good,* 70–72. Henry W. Sage was not related to Russell Sage, husband of the philanthropist Olivia Sage.

23. Keeler, *Life of Adelia A. Field Johnston,* 138.

24. Horowitz, *Alma Mater,* 65. In the context of dormitory design, the adjective *congregate* refers to many students under one roof, not many people in one bedroom.

25. Horowitz, 65.

26. Horowitz, 75.

27. Horowitz, 87.

28. Horowitz, 87.

29. Horowitz notes the trend toward the oxymoronic large cottage, observing that at Smith College, as "the cottages swelled in size, a certain level of fantasy prevailed, in design language, as well as in words." Horowitz, 214.

30. Blodgett, *Oberlin Architecture,* 20. Almost all male students lived in boardinghouses, although twenty-four men lived in Walton Hall, a frame house on the main street. For a clear indication that the men at Oberlin saw themselves as having no real dormitory, see Edward A. Miller, "The Men's Building," in the Oberlin yearbook *Hi-O-Hi,* 1911, 8.

31. The rule book was for Lord Cottage, Baldwin Cottage, and Talcott Hall. Rule Book, "Residences: Miscellaneous," Record Group: Student Life, box 6, Oberlin College Archives.

32. Miller, "Men's Building," 8.

33. Letter to the editor, unsigned, written by "negro students who love their Alma Mater and revere her principles," *Oberlin Review,* March 3, 1883, quoted in Waite, "Segregation of Black Students," 354.

34. Waite, 348.

35. Waite, 355.

36. Waite, 360.

37. Jay Pridmore, *University of Chicago: The Campus Guide* (New York: Princeton Architectural Press, 2006), 1.

38. Ruth Bordin, *Women at Michigan: The "Dangerous Experiment," 1870s to the Present* (Ann Arbor: University of Michigan Press, 2002), 20. Bordin explains that the first

president of the University of Chicago was reluctant to admit women on an equal basis with men, but he did so to appeal to popular sentiment.

39. William Rainey Harper, *The President's Report* (Chicago: University of Chicago Press, 1903), xxxv.

40. Minutes, meeting of the Conference of Deans of Women of the Middle West, 1903, NSAA, BGSU.

41. Robin F. Bachin, *Building the South Side: Urban Space and Civic Culture in Chicago, 1890–1919* (Chicago: University of Chicago Press, 2004), 43.

42. Edward W. Wolner, *Henry Ives Cobb's Chicago: Architecture, Institutions, and the Making of a Modern Metropolis* (Chicago: University of Chicago Press, 2011), 209.

43. Mary Beecher, the donor, was the wife of Jerome Beecher from upstate New York. She was not related to the Beechers of Connecticut (Catharine Beecher, Harriet Beecher Stowe, and Henry Ward Beecher).

44. Wolner, *Henry Ives Cobb's Chicago,* 208. Wolner's illustration 7.16A appears to have the wrong caption; it is a plan of the second, third, and fourth floors of Beecher Hall, not the men's graduate dormitory.

45. For a description of a suite of rooms off a corridor at Vassar, see Horowitz, *Alma Mater,* 39.

46. Marion Talbot to William Rainey Harper, September 11, 1898, Office of the President, Harper, Judson and Burton Administrations, box 41, folder 7, University of Chicago Archives.

47. Talbot to Harper, September 11, 1898.

48. Bachin, *Building the South Side,* 46.

49. Ellen Richards and Marion Talbot, *Food as a Factor in Student Life: A Contribution to the Study of Student Diet* (Chicago: University of Chicago Press, 1893), 7.

50. Alice Freeman Palmer to William Rainey Harper, March 16, 1893, Office of the President, Harper, Judson and Burton Administrations, box 66, folder 16, University of Chicago Archives.

51. Cromley, *Alone Together,* 121.

52. See also Delores Hayden, *Grand Domestic Revolution: A History of Feminist Designs for American Home, Neighborhoods, and Cities* (Cambridge: MIT Press, 1981), chaps. 3 and 4.

53. Hayden, 151.

54. Lowe, *Looking Good,* 18–20.

55. Richards and Talbot, *Food as a Factor,* 7.

56. Richards and Talbot, 7.

57. Conable, *Women at Cornell,* 65.

58. Minutes, meeting of the Conference of Deans of Women of the Middle West, 1903, n.p. (third page).

59. "Housing of Women Students at College: An Investigation Conducted by the Housing Committee of the American Association of University Women" (1921), NSAA, BGSU. The report, which was printed in the *Journal of the American Association*

of University Women 15, no. 4 (July 1922), did not reveal the names of the respondents or their home schools.

60. Richards and Talbot, *Food as a Factor,* 7.

61. "Integrating the Life of the Mind: African Americans at the University of Chicago, 1870–1940," web exhibit, September 1, 2008, Special Collections Research Center, University of Chicago Library, https://www.lib.uchicago.edu.

62. "Integrating the Life of the Mind." The web exhibit says that the Simpson incident took place in Green Hall, but Breckinridge herself later recalled Kelly Hall as the site. See Sophonisba Breckinridge, draft of memoirs, 1919, box 1, folder 8, Breckinridge Papers, University of Chicago Archives.

63. Wolner and Bachin disagree about whether the architecture shuts the city out or whether "the articulate walls raised row house urbanity to an institutional scale." See, respectively, Bachin, *Building the South Side,* 54; and Wolner, *Henry Ives Cobb's Chicago,* 209.

64. Bachin, *Building the South Side,* 54–55.

65. John F. Moulds to Ernest DeWitt Burton, March 19, 1923, Office of the President, Hutchins, Burton and Judson Administrations, box 41, folder 8, University of Chicago Archives.

66. Hedwig and Hannah were not related to Richard Albert Loeb, the infamous child murderer, although all three attended the University of Chicago. Richard Loeb was born in 1905 to Anna (née Bohnen) Loeb and Albert Henry Loeb.

67. Horowitz, *Alma Mater,* 63; Lowe, *Looking Good,* 33.

68. Hedwig Loeb's photo album, 1899–1900, Hedwig L. Loeb Papers, Special Collections Research Center, University of Chicago Library.

69. Deborah L. Miller, "'The Big Ladies' Hotel': Gender, Residence, and Middle-Class Montreal—A Contextual Analysis of the Royal Victoria College, 1899–1931" (master's thesis, McGill University, 1998), 3.

70. Henry Tappan, *First Annual Report to the Board of Regents, 1853,* 11–12, quoted in Frederiksen, "Brief History of College Housing," 169. Tappan brushed over some historical details in this comment. In the nineteenth century Oxford and Cambridge were bastions of Anglicanism, not Roman Catholicism. On the other hand, the oldest colleges at Cambridge and Oxford traced their roots to the period before the Reformation, and their quadrangular form was derived from monastic cloisters.

71. Tappan, 11–12, quoted in Frederiksen, 169.

72. Wilfred B. Shaw, ed., *The University of Michigan: An Encyclopedic Survey* (Ann Arbor: University of Michigan Press, 1941), 1802. According to Shaw: "The first fraternity clubhouse especially erected as living quarters for the student members was that built by Psi Upsilon on the corner of South University and State Street, where the Lawyers' Club now stands. It was a large, rather ungainly brick building, erected in the college year 1879–80, and reconstructed and greatly enlarged twelve years later" (1803).

73. Syrett, *The Company He Keeps,* 129.

74. Syrett, 221.

75. Syrett, 226. At Cornell, female students were not admitted to fraternity parties until the 1920s.

76. Before the term *sorority* came into wide usage, Greek organizations for women were called *women's fraternities.*

77. Bordin, *Women at Michigan,* 28.

78. Myra Beach Jordan to James Angell, box 5, folder "Correspondence July–Sept 1902," Papers of James Angell, Bentley Historical Library, University of Michigan.

79. Records indicate that the number of female students increased from 34 in 1870 to 1,584 in 1919. Shaw, *University of Michigan,* 1791–94.

80. For a fictional account of the life of an early coed at the University of Michigan, see Anderson, *An American Girl.* The author was among the first women to study at UM, and the novel reflects the difficulties she and her friends encountered.

81. The first gymnasium at UM was constructed in 1894 for the use of both sexes, but it soon was dominated by men. In 1895, two university regents, Charles Hebard and Levi Barbour, donated a portion of the funds for a gymnasium exclusively for women, with fund-raising assistance from the Women's League. Bordin, *Women at Michigan,* 28.

82. Quoted in "Secretary Pays Visit to Ann Arbor—Says Campaign Has Been Successful—All Are Enthusiastic," *Michigan Daily,* February 29, 1911.

83. Myrtle White Godwin, "Interview Catches W. W. Cook's Attention," *Michigan Alumnus* 36, no. 35 (August 16, 1930): 716.

84. Zachariah Rice to Myrtle White, November 24, 1910, Michigan University Women's League, box 1, folder "Correspondence 1905–1929," Bentley Historical Library, University of Michigan. For more detail, see Margaret A. Leary, *Giving It All Away: The Story of William W. Cook and His Michigan Law Quadrangle* (Ann Arbor: University of Michigan Press, 2011), 88–93.

85. Zachariah Rice to Frieda Kleinstuck, May 29, 1911, Michigan University Women's League, box 1, folder "Correspondence 1905–1929," Bentley Historical Library, University of Michigan.

86. Zachariah Rice to Josephine Rankin, July 7, 1911, Michigan University Women's League, box 1, folder "Correspondence 1905–1929," Bentley Historical Library, University of Michigan.

87. Rice was married to the daughter of Thomas Palmer, an important U.S. senator, and was therefore well connected in the state. Thomas Palmer was not related to the dean of women at the University of Chicago, Alice Freeman Palmer, who was married to the Harvard-trained scholar George Palmer.

88. Agnes P. Parks to Josephine E. Rankin, January 4, 1912, Michigan University Women's League, box 1, folder "Correspondence 1905–1929," Bentley Historical Library, University of Michigan. Parks was secretary of the Women's League and Rankin was president.

89. William Cook to Regents of the University of Michigan, February 10, 1914, box 1, "William C. Cook Files," Martha Cook Building Records, Bentley Historical Library, University of Michigan.

90. Cook to Regents, February 10, 1914.

91. Leary, *Giving It All Away,* 94.

92. Leary, 90. The Martha Cook Building eventually cost $400,000, quite an increase from Cook's first gift of $10,000. According to his biographer, Margaret Leary, Cook was highly competitive and probably knew about another women's dormitory at Michigan that was intended to house fifty girls. This other dormitory, Newberry Hall, opened in the same year as the Martha Cook Building but was more modest and not considered a model.

93. William Cook to Harry B. Hutchins, June 5, 1911, box 3, folder 4, Papers of Harry B. Hutchins, Bentley Historical Library, University of Michigan.

94. Montgomery Schuyler, "Architecture of American Colleges, V: University of Pennsylvania, Girard, Haverford, Lehigh and Bryn Mawr Colleges," *Architectural Record* 28, no. 3 (September 1910): 183–212.

95. William Cook to Mrs. Frederick B. Stevens, July 8, 1925, box 1, Martha Cook Building Records, Bentley Historical Library, University of Michigan.

96. Leary, *Giving It All Away,* 94.

97. Cook to Stevens, July 8, 1925.

98. Cook to Stevens, July 8, 1925.

99. William Cook to Walter Hume Sawyer, May 5, 1925, box 1, Martha Cook Building Records, Bentley Historical Library, University of Michigan.

100. Adams, *Medicine by Design,* 80.

101. Potts, *Wesleyan University, 1831–1910,* 199.

102. Adams, *Medicine by Design,* 88.

103. *The Cook Book: Martha Cook Annual* (1918), n.p., Bentley Historical Library, University of Michigan.

104. Leary, *Giving it All Away,* 50.

105. Cook to Stevens, July 8, 1925.

106. Bachin, *Building the South Side,* 46.

107. Miller, "'The Big Ladies Hotel,'" 126.

108. Lowe, *Looking Good,* 109.

109. York & Sawyer to William Cook, June 20, 1917, box 1, folder "Correspondence with Architects, 4," Martha Cook Building Records, Bentley Historical Library, University of Michigan. The letter is signed "York & Sawyer," therefore it is difficult to know which individual wrote it.

110. William Cook to York & Sawyer, June 20, 1917, and June 29, 1917, box 1, folder "Correspondence with Architects, 4," Martha Cook Building Records, Bentley Historical Library, University of Michigan.

111. Horowitz, *Alma Mater,* 311.

112. The law students, however, were older than the women students who occupied the Martha Cook Building, because being at least twenty-one years of age was an admission requirement for the law school. This might be another reason, in addition to gender, that the men were afforded greater mobility. Horowitz notes that "men's college buildings, such as those at Amherst, had multiple entries which allowed doors to open off stairways." She claims that the residence halls planned for Smith College between 1919

and 1921 "broke the pattern" for dormitories at both men's and women's colleges; she does not provide an illustration of a plan. Horowitz, 311. There are some errors in this particular argument. Horowitz identifies three planning innovations at Smith: first, the placement of semipublic rooms on the ground floor; second, single rooms on double-loaded corridors above; and third, a single structure with few doors to the outside. Since the Martha Cook Building opened in 1915, four years earlier than the Smith dorm Horowitz describes, and since Martha Cook demonstrates all three of those characteristics, the pattern could not have been broken at Smith. Horowitz's main theme about administrators' fears of close female friendships seems to be overdetermined in this particular chapter. She argues that cell-like single rooms were not conducive to intimacy (314), but one could argue the opposite: the total privacy offered by a single bedroom could allow lesbian relationships to flourish more easily than they could in double bedrooms.

113. Vickery, *Buildings for Bluestockings,* 13.

114. E. R. Holme, *The American University: An Australian View* (Sydney: Angus & Robertson, 1920), 143–45. The correct name is the Martha Cook Building, not Hall. William Cook to Grace Greenwood, October 21, 1921, box 1, "William C. Cook Files," Martha Cook Building Records, Bentley Historical Library, University of Michigan.

115. *Michiganensian,* 1916, 40.

3. QUADRANGLES IN THE EARLY TWENTIETH CENTURY

1. Charles Richard Van Hise, "Inaugural Address of Charles Richard Van Hise, June 7, 1904," *Science,* August 12, 1904, 198.

2. Van Hise, 199.

3. See Turner, *Campus,* 27. Turner's conceptualization of the quadrangle relies heavily on an essay written by Ashton Willard in 1897; Willard complained that America's Puritan ancestors avoided the "severe, calm, and tranquil idea of the cloistered college built around its quadrangles" because that form was Anglican. Ashton Willard, "The Development of College Architecture in America," *New England Magazine* 16, no. 5 (July 1897): 513. While it is probably not necessary to argue with a critic who published in 1897, since Willard's article features prominently in Turner's book, it seems worth noting that Willard was not correct in drawing this hard line between quadrangles (Anglican) and everything else (Puritan).

4. John S. Brubacher and Willis Rudy, *Higher Education in Transition: A History of American Colleges and Universities,* 4th ed. (London: Routledge, 2017), 331.

5. Reuben, *Making of the Modern University,* 260.

6. Michael S. Hevel, "Toward a History of Student Affairs: A Synthesis of Research, 1996–2015," *Journal of College Student Development* 57, no. 7 (October 2016): 847.

7. Hevel, 847.

8. Hevel, 847. See also Carroll L. L. Miller and Anne S. Pruitt-Logan, *Faithful to the Task at Hand: The Life of Lucy Diggs Slowe* (Albany: State University of New York Press, 2012).

9. Schwartz, *Deans of Men,* 25.

10. Nidiffer, *Pioneering Deans of Women,* 148.

11. E. G. Williamson et al., "The Student Personnel Point of View" (American Council on Education Studies, Series VI—Student Personnel Work, no. 13, September 1949), n.p.

12. Minutes, meeting of the Conference of Deans of Women of the Middle West, 1903, n.p. Miss Evans was the dean at Carleton College in Minnesota; it is unclear if she had firsthand knowledge of the housing in California.

13. Minutes, meeting of the Conference of Deans of Women, Colorado Springs, Colorado, October 24, 1910, 8, NSAA, BGSU. This was the first national meeting of deans of women, although there had been earlier regional meetings; Miss Potter of Northwestern presided.

14. S. H. Goodnight to Lydia L. Brown, April 9, 1926, UW Student Affairs, Division of Dean of Student Affairs, General Correspondence A–K, S. H. Goodnight 19/2/1–4, box 1, University of Wisconsin Archives.

15. Schwartz, *Deans of Men,* 65.

16. Quoted in Schwartz, 4.

17. MS 391, folder "NASPA Conference Proceedings & Secretarial Notes," 1930, 39, NSAA, BGSU.

18. MS 391, folder "NASPA Conference Proceedings & Secretarial Notes," 1930, 41.

19. J. L. Rollins, "Effective Housing and the Deans of Men," second session, annual meeting of the Association of Deans and Advisers of Men, 1930, 38, MS 391, folder "NASPA Conference Proceedings and Secretarial Notes," NSAA, BGSU.

20. Rollins, 38.

21. Rollins, 36.

22. O. A. Stolen to S. H. Goodnight, September 21, 1923, Goodnight, Speeches and Articles, 1923, UW Student Affairs, Division of Dean of Student Affairs, General Correspondence, University of Wisconsin Archives.

23. "Secretarial Notes on the Seventh Annual Conference of Deans and Advisers of Men," Chapel Hill, N.C., 1925, 59, MS 391, folder "NASPA Conference Proceedings & Secretarial Notes," NSAA, BGSU.

24. Hevel, "Toward a History of Student Affairs," 849.

25. Louise Nardin to S. H. Goodnight, 1920, Papers of the Dean of Student Affairs, S. H. Goodnight, 19/2/1/4, box 3, University of Wisconsin Archives.

26. "Judge Assails Morals in University Quarter," *Washington Post,* January 28, 1925.

27. VP of Business and Finance, General Correspondence, 1911–49, Mc–Me 1926–27, series 24/1/1, box 31, University of Wisconsin Archives.

28. L.S.W., "Some Early University and North Hall History," *Wisconsin Alumni Magazine* 5, no. 5 (February 4, 1904): 146.

29. Jim Feldman, *The Buildings of the University of Wisconsin* (Madison: University Archives, 1997), 11.

30. Barry Teicher and John W. Jenkins, *A History of Housing at the University of Wisconsin–Madison* (Madison: UW History Project, 2006), 3.

31. Teicher and Jenkins, 6.

32. Teicher and Jenkins, 8.

33. In 1905, to relieve crowding on campus, the university encouraged girls to live in sororities. See Feldman, *Buildings of the University of Wisconsin,* 35.

34. Van Hise, "Inaugural Address," 198. This speech is quoted extensively in Teicher and Jenkins, *History of Housing.*

35. Van Hise, "Inaugural Address," 198.

36. Van Hise, 199.

37. Van Hise, 199.

38. Warren Laird to Charles R. Van Hise, December 20, 1906, President Van Hise, General Correspondence, Miscellaneous I, 1906, 4/10/1, box 6, folder 82, University of Wisconsin Archives.

39. The Wisconsin Union was an administrative unit at UW that oversaw student life outside the classroom, offering recreational, cultural, and musical programs. Dollard's job was akin to what today would be that of director of student life.

40. John Dollard, secretary, "Report to the Faculty Committee on the Social Needs of Wisconsin Undergraduates," 1924, 11, UW Chancellor and President Edward A. Birge, General Correspondence, series 4/12/1, 1924–25, C–D, University of Wisconsin Archives.

41. Dollard, 10.

42. Arthur Peabody to J. D. Phillips, UW business manager, September 11, 1924, VP of Business and Finance, series 24/1/1, 1924–25, A–D, box 16, University of Wisconsin Archives.

43. Dollard, "Report to the Faculty Committee," 3.

44. "Men's Dormitories to Provide Attractive Homes—Halverson," *Daily Cardinal,* April 23, 1926.

45. *Tripp Hall, Its Answer to Seven Needs,* undated (1926), series 25/00/4, box 1, folder "Tripp Hall," UW Residence Halls, Division of Publications, University of Wisconsin Archives.

46. Meeting of the Faculty Committee on Dormitories, April 1, 1925, VP of Business and Finance, series 24/1/1, 1924–25, A–D, box 16, University of Wisconsin Archives.

47. Arthur Peabody to J. D. Phillips, February 27, 1923, VP of Business and Finance, series 24/1/1, 1924–25, A–D, box 16, University of Wisconsin Archives. The refectory was originally named for Van Hise, until another structure at UW was named in his honor; at that time, the refectory's name was changed to Carson Gulley Hall.

48. "Men's Dormitories to Provide Attractive Homes."

49. Adams Hall has its original porter's lodge, whereas the porter's lodge at Tripp Hall was redesigned and expanded in 1968.

50. "U.W. Dormitories to Be Open for Fall Semester," *Wisconsin State Journal,* August 1, 1926.

51. Papers of the National Association of Student Personnel Administrators, MS 391, folder "NASPA Conference Proceedings & Secretarial Notes," 1927, NSAA, BGSU.

52. *Tripp Hall,* 5.

53. "Men's Dormitories to Provide Attractive Homes."
54. *Tripp Hall,* 9.
55. *Tripp Hall,* 3.
56. *Tripp Hall,* 5.
57. "Adams and Tripp Halls," in *The Badger,* 1929, n.p.
58. "Dormitory Life," *Daily Cardinal,* December 7, 1926, 4.
59. H. C. Bradley to D. L. Halverson, September 30, 1926, VP of Business and Finance, General Correspondence, 1911–49, Mc–Me, 1926–27, series 24/1/1, box 31, University of Wisconsin Archives.
60. Alex L. Trout, "Some Basic Problems in Dormitory Planning," annual meeting of the Association of Deans and Advisers of Men, 1930, 46, NSAA, BGSU.
61. Kendrick Ian Grandison, "Negotiated Space: The Black College Campus as a Cultural Record of Postbellum America," *American Quarterly* 51 (September 1999): 570.
62. Ellen Weiss, *Robert R. Taylor and Tuskegee: An African American Architect Designs for Booker T. Washington* (Montgomery, Ala.: New South Books, 2012), xvi.
63. Weiss, xvi.
64. Weiss, xix.
65. Weiss, xix.
66. *Student Manual,* Howard University, 1922, 6, box 90-12, folder 224, Lucy Diggs Slowe Papers, Howard University Archives.
67. Hevel, "Toward a History of Student Affairs," 850.
68. Lucy Diggs Slowe, "The Administration of Personnel Work at Howard University," draft, n.d., box 90-6, folder "The Administration of Personnel Work at Howard University," Lucy Diggs Slowe Papers, Howard University Archives.
69. "Howard U Student Manual, 1922," 8, box 90-12, folder 225, Lucy Diggs Slowe Papers, Howard University Archives.
70. Lucy D. Slowe, "The Dormitory—A Cultural Influence," *Journal of the National Association of College Women* (1931–32): 11.
71. Slowe, "Administration of Personnel Work," n.p.
72. Slowe, "The Dormitory." See also Linda M. Perkins, "Lucy Diggs Slowe: Champion of the Self-Determination of African-American Women in Higher Education," *Journal of Negro History* 81 (1996): 89–104.
73. Slowe, "Administration of Personnel Work," n.p.
74. James W. Hammond, "The Purpose and History of the Association of College and University Housing Officers," Association of College and University Housing Officers (hereafter ACUHO), First Annual Meeting, 1949, 17, MS 487, box 1, NSAA, BGSU.
75. Hammond, 17.
76. Harriet Hayes, *Planning Residence Halls for Undergraduate Students in American Colleges and Universities* (New York: Teachers College, Columbia University, 1932), 84.
77. Hayes, 83.
78. Hayes, 84.

79. Slowe, "The Dormitory," 13.

80. Thomas G. Bergin, *Yale's Residential Colleges: The First Fifty Years* (New Haven, Conn.: Yale University Press, 1983), 19.

81. Bergin, 19.

82. Turner, *Campus,* 216.

83. Turner, 216.

84. "Council of the Heads of College," Yale College, emphasis added, accessed August 21, 2018, http://chc.yalecollege.yale.edu.

85. Bergin, *Yale's Residential Colleges,* 58.

86. Bergin, 58.

87. The first universities in the United States to establish residential colleges were Harvard and Yale, in the 1930s. Harvard's was called the "house system" and Yale's was known as "the college system," but both were based on the same housing principles. In this chapter I focus on Yale as preparation for the discussion in chapter 5 of the remarkable Yale residential colleges designed by Eero Saarinen.

88. In today's parlance, *living-learning community* is the term more frequently used in reference to the concept that in the 1920s and 1930s was called a residential college. Living–learning communities can be created within any type of building. They may have academic themes (such as science, pre-med, or social justice), or the students may be assigned randomly.

89. Duke, *Importing Oxbridge,* 7–8.

90. Edward Harkness also funded the residential colleges at Harvard, which were every bit as influential as those at Yale.

91. Dollard, "Report to the Faculty Committee."

92. Brooks Mather Kelley, *Yale: A History* (New Haven, Conn.: Yale University Press, 1974), 374.

93. Susan Ryan, "The Architecture of James Gamble Rogers at Yale University," *Perspecta* 18 (1982): 27.

94. Kelley, *Yale,* 373.

95. Bergin, *Yale's Residential Colleges,* 17.

96. Princeton's Woodrow Wilson had proposed what he called a "quadrangle plan" in 1907 in a bid to defeat the university's exclusive and discriminatory eating clubs; it failed. The idea perished because the dining clubs at Princeton served some of the same social purposes as fraternities, and the loyalty that alumni felt toward their clubs could not easily be shaken. Brubacher and Rudy, *Higher Education in Transition,* 337; Karabel, *The Chosen,* 65. President Harper at the University of Chicago repeatedly promoted residential colleges, starting in 1892 and up to 1905.

97. Kelley, *Yale,* 374.

98. Bergin, *Yale's Residential Colleges,* 25.

99. Kelley, *Yale,* 388.

100. Bergin, *Yale's Residential Colleges,* 136.

101. Patrick L. Pennell, *Yale University: The Campus Guide* (New York: Princeton Architectural Press, 1999), 64. After Branford and Saybrook, seven more colleges were

added, thanks to the Harkness gift, for a total of ten by 1940. See Bergin, *Yale's Residential Colleges,* 144. The names and founding dates of the colleges up to 1940 were as follows: Berkeley College, 1934; Branford College, 1933; Calhoun College, 1933; Davenport College, 1933; Timothy Dwight College, 1935; Jonathan Edwards College, 1933; Pierson College, 1933; Saybrook College, 1933; Silliman College, 1940; and Trumbull College, 1933.

102. Aaron Betsky, *James Gamble Rogers and the Architecture of Pragmatism* (New York: Architectural History Foundation, 1994), 139.

103. Bergin, *Yale's Residential Colleges,* 41.

104. With all due respect and gratitude, I differ with Turner on the broad-brush outlines of the history of dormitory planning during this period. See Turner, *Campus,* 244. He presents a circular path from entryways, which were replaced by corridors, then replaced again by entryways. I find this to be overly simplified. The two types overlapped in time, and there were hybrid forms as well as cottages. In most respects, this is a minor quibble, since Turner addresses campuses as a whole, not dormitories.

105. Charles Seymour to Samuel H. Fisher, September 28, 1933, box 4, folder 61, Yale Manuscripts and Archives. In this letter, Seymour noted that seven colleges were ready on September 25, 1933.

106. Turner, *Campus,* 240.

107. Kelley, *Yale,* 361, 364.

108. MS 391, folder "NASPA Conference Proceedings & Secretarial Notes," 1930, 45.

109. Hayes, *Planning Residence Halls,* iii.

110. Hayes, 17.

111. Donald L. Halverson, quoted in Robert Moser, "Educational Philosophy in Residence Halls," 14, ACUHO, Conference Proceedings, Second Annual Conference, 1950, MS 487, box 1, NSAA, BGSU.

4. DORMS ON THE RISE

1. Riker, *College Students Live Here,* 6.

2. Carlson, "When College Was a Public Good."

3. According to Alex Duke, "In 1946, one million veterans enrolled in colleges and universities, almost doubling the size of the American college student population." Duke, *Importing Oxbridge,* 145.

4. Lloyd Morey, Association of College and University Housing Officers (hereafter ACUHO), First Annual Meeting, 1949, 2, MS 487, box 1, NSAA, BGSU. The meeting, which was held at the University of Illinois at Urbana–Champaign, was attended by sixty-two delegates representing thirty-three colleges.

5. Some colleges did not accede to modernist hegemony, among them the University of New Mexico and the University of Colorado Boulder. Almost every U.S. campus has a few buildings that are modernist in every way except for cladding materials (such as brick or stone) that refer to the existing context.

6. Hammond, "Purpose and History," 7.

7. Workshop, ACUHO, Conference Proceedings, Second Annual Conference, 1950, 37, MS 487, box 1, NSAA, BGSU.

8. Workshop, ACUHO, Conference Proceedings, Second Annual Conference, 1950, 19. For a thorough investigation of the costs of elevators, economic height, and skyscraper design, see Carol Willis, *Form Follows Finance: Skyscrapers and Skylines in New York and Chicago* (New York: Princeton Architectural Press, 1995), 45–46.

9. Thelin, *History of American Higher Education,* 287.

10. Thelin, 287.

11. Small liberal arts colleges remained relatively unaffected by these changes, because their class sizes stayed the same, but at the most competitive small colleges, professors still had to publish at the same rate as professors at research universities.

12. Rutgers became the state university in stages, through a complicated set of legislative maneuvers that are not relevant here. After the war, Rutgers was, by and large, the flagship state university for New Jersey, although it was still influenced by its roots as a small religiously affiliated men's liberal arts college.

13. Paul G. E. Clemens, *Rutgers since 1945: A History of the State University of New Jersey* (New Brunswick, N.J.: Rutgers University Press, 2015).

14. Elijah Reiss, "Colonial Conformity and Historic Roots: Analyzing Rutgers University's Demarest Hall" (term paper, April 2015). I thank Elijah Reiss for this paper (and several others, including his honors thesis), which fills in large gaps in the history of Rutgers, especially in relation to land acquisition and the early destruction of much of the college's historic fabric.

15. *The Scarlet Letter,* 1957, 84, Special Collections and University Archives, Rutgers University Libraries.

16. I thank Rutgers graduates Cristina Toma and Eric Kaplan for their research papers on the River Dorms.

17. Cornelius Boocock to Lewis Webster Jones, June 10, 1953, 10/9, Jones Papers, University Archives, Rutgers University Libraries.

18. Minutes of Joint Committee Meeting on Buildings and Grounds, Finance and School of Law, March 25, 1954, Building and Grounds Papers, box 1, folder "Buildings and Grounds, Committee Meeting Minutes, October 1952–December 1957," University Archives, Rutgers University Libraries.

19. Clothier to Shield, February 5, 1954.

20. Clothier to Shield, February 5, 1954.

21. Richard L. Atkins, "New Dorms to Be Erected by 1956," *Daily Targum,* Office of the President, box 10, University Archives, Rutgers University Libraries.

22. Cornelius Boocock to Lewis Webster Jones, June 3, 1954, 10/9, Jones Papers, University Archives, Rutgers University Libraries.

23. Cornelius Boocock to Lewis Webster Jones, August 31, 1954, 10/9, Jones Papers, University Archives, Rutgers University Libraries.

24. Boocock to Jones, August 31, 1954.

25. Boocock to Jones, August 31, 1954.

26. Cornelius Boocock to B. Sumner Gruzen, December 2, 1954, Office of the President, RG 04/A15/01, box 10, University Archives, Rutgers University Libraries.

27. Boocock to Jones, August 31, 1954. The canal was later filled in with a highway, which disrupted the view from the classrooms.

28. Page & Turnbull, "UC Berkeley Unit 3 Housing."

29. Martin Beck, "Distinctive Dormitories for Rutgers," *Rutgers Alumni Monthly* 34 (February 1955): 2.

30. Frederick Sibley, "New Dorm Club," in *The Scarlet Letter,* 1957, 87.

31. *Report from Rutgers* 8, no. 5 (September 1954): n.p., University Archives, Rutgers University Libraries.

32. "Coed College vs. Girls' College," *Life,* May 9, 1949, 72.

33. "Coed College vs. Girls' College," 79. I wish to thank Rachel Iannacone for introducing me to this wonderfully evocative source.

34. Thomas J. Frusciano and Marilyn H. Pettit, *New York University and the City: An Illustrated History* (New Brunswick, N.J.: Rutgers University Press, 1997), 133.

35. The *New York Times* reported that "the university also plans to construct a dormitory with separate quarters for men and women." "N.Y.U. to Be Co-ed in Bronx in Fall," *New York Times,* December 5, 1958. Coeducation was introduced gradually. The first female students were commuters, and then women moved into the dorm.

36. "College Buildings," *Architectural Record* 126 (September 1959): 187.

37. "Milestones in Higher Education: The Introduction of Coeducation at University Heights," internal fund-raising document, 1960, "Development Office," Office of the President, 1951–65, box 4, folder 12, New York University Archives.

38. Hammond, "Purpose and History," 17.

39. Hammond, 17.

40. "NYU University Heights Center: Handbook for Students," 1963–64, 8, group no. 1, series no. 10, folder 8-25, New York University Archives.

41. Quoted in Cranston Jones, *Marcel Breuer: Buildings and Projects, 1921–1961* (New York: Praeger, 1962), 25.

42. Robert F. Gatje, *Marcel Breuer: A Memoir* (New York: Monicelli Press, 2000), 76–77.

43. Terry Ferrer, "NYU on Heights Goes Coed in Fall: Men and Women Will Be Housed in the New $4,400,000 Dormitory," *New York Herald Tribune,* December 1959, clipping, frame 1209, Marcel Breuer Papers, Archives of American Art, Smithsonian Institution.

44. "The Proceedings of the Dedication of the Julius Silver Residence Center," Buildings Collection, folder 9-5, "Silver, Julius, Residence Center," New York University Archives. The building was dedicated on September 25, 1963.

45. John H. Herrick, campus planner, to William E. Linch, university architect, December 28, 1962, RG 6/e/7, box 054-375-1, folder 6416, "River Towers: Planning, Developers' Proposals," Papers of the Architect's Office, Ohio State University Archives.

46. Thomas. G. Buckham, "Skyscrapers to Rise Soon," *Ohio State Lantern,* November 9, 1964, 1.

47. University planner James Clark noted that "John [Bonner] seemed quite upset with the situation." Clark, "Re River Dorms."

48. Charles W. Lerch & Associates, elevator construction engineers, "River Towers: Planning: Developers' Proposals," RG 6/E-7, folder 6416, Ohio State University Archives.

49. For more on the social engineering of students after World War II, see Clare Robinson, "Student Union: The Architecture and Social Design of Postwar Community Centers in California" (PhD diss., University of California, Berkeley, 2012).

50. Buckham, "Skyscrapers to Rise Soon," 2.

51. Walter A. Taylor and Paul Merrill, "Current Trends on Residence Hall Architecture," May 3, 1954, Office of the President, RG 04/A15/01, box 10, University Archives, Rutgers University Libraries.

52. John T. Bonner, executive dean of student relations, "Report to the Board of Trustees, River Residence Halls," November 15, 1963, Exec Dean, Deans of Men and Women—River Dormitories, 1963–64, RG 9/a/10, Papers of the Office of Student Affairs, Ohio State University Archives.

53. Bonner, "Report to the Board of Trustees."

54. Maude A. Stewart to John T. Bonner, executive dean of student relations, November 29, 1963, RG 9/a/10, folder "Office of Student Affairs, Exec Dean, 1963–64," Papers of the Office of Student Affairs, Ohio State University Archives.

55. Martin Krumlauf to Gordon Carson, March 14, 1968, "Office of Student Affairs Executive Dean," RG 9/a/21, folder "M. W. Overholt, Associate Dean," Papers of the Office of Student Affairs, Ohio State University Archives.

56. John T. Bonner to Martin Krumlauf, March 22, 1968, "Office of Student Affairs Executive Dean," RG 9/a/21, folder "M. W. Overholt, Associate Dean," Papers of the Office of Student Affairs, Ohio State University Archives.

57. Roberta Katherine Jones, "A Study of the Physical Facilities at Morrill Tower, The Ohio State University, as Assessed by the Students and Resident Staff" (master's thesis, Ohio State University, 1967), 7. Jones's thesis adviser was Maude A. Stewart.

58. Jones, 74.

59. Memo from Men's Housing Office (M. W. Overholt) to the Parents of Franklin County Male Students, January 1965, RG 9/a, box 10, folder "Student Affairs: Dean of Men, Dean of Women: Housing Crisis, 1964–65," Papers of the Office of Student Affairs, Ohio State University Archives.

60. Memo from Men's Housing Office, January 1965.

61. Jack Hicks, "State Arson Investigators Probe Fire Damaged Lincoln Tower at OSU, One of Two High Rise Buildings Which State Inspectors Term 'Unconventional,'" *Columbus Dispatch,* May 22, 1968, 1A.

62. R. R. Fling to President Novice G. Fawcett, April 3, 1965, RB 3/I, box 44, folder "Office of the President—Student Housing, Dec 1964 to Dec 1965," Ohio State University Archives. Mr. Fling was correct, in the sense that residence halls were paid for with initial loans, followed by the income from rents to amortize the debt. Many state universities built residence halls with loans rather than with private funds.

63. C. Carney Strange and James H. Banning, *Designing for Learning: Creating Campus Environments for Student Success* (San Francisco: Jossey-Bass, 2015), 146. The work that Strange and Banning cite is Robert Gifford, "The Consequences of Living in High-Rise Buildings," *Architectural Science Review* 50, no. 1 (2007): 2–17.

64. Strange and Banning, *Designing for Learning*, 147.

65. Clark Kerr, "The Worth of Intellect" (inaugural address delivered at University of California, Berkeley, September 29, 1958), 8–9, http://bancroft.berkeley.edu/CalHistory/inaugural.kerr.html. See also "Residence Halls: University of California, Berkeley Campus," *Architectural Record* 127 (March 1960): 159.

5. REJECTING THE HIGH-RISE

1. Horowitz, *Campus Life*, 220.

2. Tony Judt, *Postwar: A History of Europe since 1945* (New York: Penguin Books, 2006), 409. The events that took place in Paris in May 1968 were a turning point in European history, and several of those uprisings were sparked by students objecting to the sudden enforcement of parietal laws in their rough-and-tumble student housing complexes. At that time, residence halls were relatively new in the French university system.

3. Riker, *College Students Live Here*, 43–44.

4. "Dormies Cite Reasons for Exodus," cited in Page & Turnbull, "UC Berkeley Unit 3 Housing."

5. Michael H. Carriere, "Between Being and Becoming: On Architecture, Student Protest, and the Aesthetics of Liberalism in Postwar America" (PhD diss., University of Chicago, 2010), 112.

6. For more on the architecture of student centers in this period, see Robinson, "Student Union."

7. Riker, *College Students Live Here*, 7.

8. Hermann Schlimme, "The Mediterranean Hill Town: A Travel Paradigm," in *Travel, Space, Architecture*, ed. Jilly Traganou and Miodrag Mitrašinović (Aldershot, England: Ashgate, 2009), 148. The Smithsons, Candilis, and Van Eyck traveled to hill towns; De Carlo lived in Urbino.

9. Schlimme, 148.

10. John McKean, *Giancarlo De Carlo: Layered Spaces* (Stuttgart: Edition Axel Menges, 2004), 58.

11. Eero Saarinen, "Saarinen Explains: An Architecture for Individuals," *Yale Daily News*, February 17, 1959.

12. A. Whitney Griswold, "A Proposal for Strengthening the Residential College System at Yale University," March 21, 1958, 6, Record Unit 22, YRG 2-A, ACCN 1963-a-002, box 212, folder 1958, A. Whitney Griswold Papers, Yale Manuscripts and Archives.

13. Griswold, 7. Antonio Román refers to this document using the phrase "shortly after its publication," but it was not actually published in the usual sense of the word; rather, it was circulated widely around Yale. Antonio Román, *Eero Saarinen: An Architecture of Multiplicity* (New York: Princeton Architectural Press, 2003), 78.

14. A. Whitney Griswold, quoted in Michael Rey, "The David S. Ingalls Hockey Rink: Eero Saarinen and A. Whitney Griswold at Yale," in *Eero Saarinen: Shaping the Future,* ed. Eeva-Liisa Pelkonen and Donald Albrecht (New Haven, Conn.: Yale University Press, 2006), 245.

15. A. Whitney Griswold, quoted in Kelley, *Yale,* 440.

16. *New Haven Register,* November 26, 1962, Group No. 593, series III, box 56, Scrapbooks and Clippings, Yale Manuscripts and Archives.

17. Sam Callaway, interview by author, August 30, 2017.

18. Callaway.

19. Charles Remmel, interview by author, August 23, 2017.

20. Rejean Legault, "Masonry without Masons: Saarinen's Morse and Stiles Colleges" (paper presented at the annual meeting of the Society of Architectural Historians, New Orleans, April 17, 2011).

21. Basil Duke Henning to A. Whitney Griswold, September 5, 1958, Record Unit 22, YRG 2-A, ACCN 1963-a-002, box 212, folder 1955, A. Whitney Griswold Papers, Yale Manuscripts and Archives. Griswold asked each of the college masters to suggest programming ideas for the new colleges. Several commented that they preferred the entryway system over corridors.

22. Paul Mellon, quoted in clipping, original source unknown, Group No. 593, series III, box 56, Scrapbooks and Clippings, Yale Manuscripts and Archives. Half of Mellon's donation of $15 million was spent on the construction of these new residential colleges. The remainder of the money was spent on other undergraduate educational endeavors at Yale.

23. Michelangelo Sabatino, *Pride in Modesty: Modernist Architecture and the Vernacular Tradition in Italy* (Toronto: University of Toronto Press, 2010), 19.

24. Terry Ferrer, "2 New Yale Colleges Will Have Butteries," *New York Herald,* November 13, 1959.

25. A. Whitney Griswold to Paul Mellon, May 26, 1958, Record Unit 22, YRG 2-A, ACCN 1963-a-002, box 212, folder 1956, A. Whitney Griswold Papers, Yale Manuscripts and Archives.

26. A. Whitney Griswold, quoted in Kelley, *Yale,* 441.

27. A. Bartlett Giammati, preface to Bergin, *Yale's Residential Colleges,* 15. There was also a dean of students for all undergraduates, and he dealt with disciplinary issues and matters of life and death; he reported directly to the centralized office of the dean of Yale College.

28. Deans of men were not as powerful at Yale as they were at state universities, because the level of supervision that came from having a master and a dean in each residential college made a central office of student affairs redundant. In 2016, the title "master" was abolished and replaced with "head of college." Monica Wang and Victor Wang, "'Master' to Become 'Head of College,'" *Yale Daily News,* April 28, 2016, http://yaledailynews.com/blog/2016/04/28/master-to-become-head-of-college.

29. Clark Kerr, *The Uses of the University,* 5th ed. (Cambridge, Mass.: Harvard University Press, 2001).

30. Under Kerr's supervision, UC Berkeley constructed twelve high-rise dorms that were much disliked by students.

31. Duke, *Importing Oxbridge,* 159.

32. "California's New Campuses: Building Big While Seeming Small," *Architectural Record* 136 (November 1964): 175–91; Kerr's comments are on p. 175; McHenry's are on pp. 176–85.

33. Virginia Jansen, *The First 20 Years: Two Decades of Building at UCSC* (1968), 2, pamphlet, collection of the author.

34. Jansen, 3. See also "Designing the Colleges," in "An Uncommon Place: A Digital Companion," digital exhibit, University of California, Santa Cruz, University Library, accessed August 24, 2018, http://exhibits.library.ucsc.edu/exhibits.

35. Duke, *Importing Oxbridge,* 159.

36. Jansen, *First 20 Years.*

37. Richard P. McCormick, *The Black Student Protest Movement at Rutgers* (New Brunswick, N.J.: Rutgers University Press, 1990), 30.

38. Kimbro Frutiger, "Architecture for the New Left: Benjamin Johnson Associates' Kirkland College," *Mod* 2 (2017): 20–25. Kirkland College, a women's school associated with Hamilton College, included some of the same design principles employed at Livingston, including C-shaped residence halls adjacent to an academic center. Benjamin Thompson of TAC was hired in 1967, after Cowell College opened at UC Santa Cruz.

39. Dean E. McHenry to Ernest A. Lynton, January 21, 1965, Records of the Office of the Dean of Livingston College, EAL, 1965–1973, RG 21/A0/04, box 17, folder 12, University Archives, Rutgers University Libraries.

40. "Summary of Progress on New College," undated (circa 1965), 1, RG 04/A16, box 62, folder 2, Mason W. Gross Papers, Special Collections and University Archives, Rutgers University Libraries. This was among Lynton's earliest statements about the ideas behind the new colleges; the document includes references to meetings with architects as well as faculty from the existing colleges within Rutgers. The statement probably dates from spring 1965.

41. "Rutgers to Start Work at Kilmer Tract," *Home News Tribune* (formerly *New Brunswick Daily Home News*), March 16, 1966, R-Vert Buildings and Grounds R-36, folder "Livingston Acquisition and Development," University Archives, Rutgers University Libraries.

42. "Summary of Progress on New College," 4.

43. "Summary of Progress on New College," 4.

44. "Summary of Progress on New College," 2.

45. "Program for the Raritan Campus," February 19, 1965, 2, RG 02/C4, Board of Governors' Buildings and Grounds Committee, box 2, folder 3, University Archives, Rutgers University Libraries.

46. Bonner, "Report to the Board of Trustees." The student life deans who contributed to this report paraphrased a document put together by the National Association of Student Personnel Administrators.

47. "Annual Report, Livingston College, 1965–66," Annual Reports, Livingston College, RG 21, University Archives, Rutgers University Libraries.

48. Ernest A. Lynton, quoted in *Daily Targum,* April 20, 1965, 3.

49. Ernest A. Lynton, quoted in "New Rutgers Unit Seeks Relevance: College Emphasizes Urban Studies and Student Role," *New York Times,* June 8, 1969, 50.

50. Peter Klein, interview by Sandra Stewart Holyoak and Paul Clemens, June 6, 2011, Rutgers Oral History Archives, https://oralhistory.rutgers.edu.

51. Ricki Sablove, "Building for the 1960s Generation: Livingston College at Rutgers University" (master's thesis, Rutgers University, 2007), 16. I especially want to thank Sablove for calling my attention to the similarity between Cowell College and the Livingston Quads. In contrast to Santa Cruz, which did not have any tall buildings, Livingston had two towers. Square in outline, these towers contained all the services in the center and did not have any long corridors. Although the towers were eight stories tall, they were distinctly different in plan from the last large dormitories built at Rutgers, the River Dorms (discussed in chapter 4). The plan of the towers was a complete circuit around each floor.

52. Bert Kaplan, quoted in Gerald Grant and David Reisman, *The Perpetual Dream: Reform and Experiment in the American College* (Chicago: University of Chicago Press, 1978), 265.

53. Charles Moore, in "Campus Planning Committee Special Meeting, College No. 6," August 28, 1967, box 35, folder V. 204, William Turnbull/MLTW 2000–9, Environmental Design Archives, University of California, Berkeley. The following people were present at the meeting: McHenry, Church, Moore, Turnbull, Jack Wagstaff, Theresa Yuen, and Charles Wheelock.

54. Sabatino, *Pride in Modesty,* 202.

55. Schlimme, "Mediterranean Hill Town," 148. Schlimme traces the roots of architectural interest in Mediterranean hill towns back to the nineteenth century (Karl Friedrich Schinkel and Camillo Sitte) and to Bernard Rudofsky in the 1930s (148–49).

56. David Littlejohn, *Architect: The Life and Work of Charles Moore* (New York: Holt, Rinehart and Winston, 1984), 226.

57. [Robert S. Edgar?], "Kresge College: Progress Report December 1971," box 39, folder 2, Campus Planning, University of California, Santa Cruz, Archives. The report went on: "The groups are composed of about 60% resident students who live together in a cluster of neighboring apartments. The rest are commuters who hopefully see those apartments as their campus-home."

58. Steve Menagh, interview by author, August 9, 2009.

59. Robert S. Edgar, provost, Kresge College, "Kresge College the Early Years (1970–74): An Appraisal for the Ford Foundation," 1974, Appendix A, LD 781 S52 K73, Special Collections, University of California, Santa Cruz, Archives.

60. Minutes of meeting held October 28, 1972, box 39, folder 10, University of California, Santa Cruz, Archives.

61. Selene Vega, interview by author, July 21, 2009.

62. Minutes of meeting held October 28, 1972.

63. Menagh, interview, August 9, 2009. Menagh took the class Creating Kresge College.

64. The students' desire to prepare their own food was related to the trend against in loco parentis. Even at schools far less radical than UCSC, students rebelled against curfews and other parietal rules. They demanded that administrators relinquish control of where students went, whom they socialized with, what they ate, what time they came home, when their laundry was done, and who visited whom in the bedrooms.

65. Plan of sauna, April 22, 1974, William Turnbull/MLTW Collection, 2000-9, box 35, folder V. 190, UC Santa Cruz Kresge College, Environmental Design Archives, University of California, Berkeley.

66. "Palaset Order," handwritten page, January 5, 1973, William Turnbull/MLTW Collection, folder V. 199, UC Santa Cruz Kresge College, Environmental Design Archives, University of California, Berkeley.

67. Heikki Kiviluoto, marketing manager for Treston Oy, to University of California, Santa Cruz, December 12, 1972, William Turnbull/MLTW Collection, 2000-9, box 35, folder V. 199, Environmental Design Archives, University of California, Berkeley.

68. Menagh, interview, August 9, 2009.

69. Menagh; and Marc Treib, interview by author, December 2, 2009. For possible mention of attendance at such meetings, see also Bob Edgar to Bill Turnbull, handwritten note, September 22, 1972, William Turnbull/MLTW Collection, 2000-9, box 35, folder V. 190, Environmental Design Archives, University of California, Berkeley. In March 1970, Turnbull was referred to in documents as "the Executive Architect," leading me to conclude that Moore was out of the picture by then. Box 39, folder 2, Campus Planning, University of California, Santa Cruz, Archives.

70. Treib, interview, December 2, 2009.

71. At UCSC, the cluster college was an idealistic notion that could not stand up against the real forces at a research university—academic departments. Scientists need laboratories, researchers need libraries, and, to recruit good graduate students, the UC schools needed strong departments, not colleges aimed at undergraduate community building. The Santa Cruz colleges were essentially dismantled in 1978. Although they still exist as dormitories and places for students to live, they are not places for reinventing higher education. The dichotomy between achieving research excellence and serving the needs of undergraduates persists, as the competing demands are difficult, maybe impossible, to balance.

EPILOGUE

1. "Living on Campus: Live with Us," in "Residence Life & Student Housing," University of New Mexico, accessed February 11, 2018, https://housing.unm.edu.

2. Strange and Banning, *Designing for Learning,* 146.

3. Susan Painter, quoted in Piper Fogg, "Dorm Therapy," *Chronicle of Higher Education,* October 7, 2008, https://www.chronicle.com.

4. Gregory S. Blimling, "Residence Halls in Today's Compartmentalized University," in *Increasing the Educational Role of Residence Halls,* ed. Gregory S. Blimling and

John H. Schuh (San Francisco: Jossey-Bass, 1981), 6. The ideal progression for on-campus living, according to Blimling, is a stepped process. For students in their first year of college, a traditional dorm is most appropriate; for those in their second year, suites are appropriate; and for juniors and seniors, apartments are developmentally correct. Blimling, *Student Learning,* 131–32.

5. "Graduate Program Directory," National Association of Student Personnel Administrators, accessed August 27, 2018, https://www.naspa.org.

6. Tim Pierson, quoted in Allie Grasgreen, "Challenging the Role of Student Affairs," Inside Higher Ed, March 31, 2011, https://www.insidehighered.com. Pierson serves as Vice President for Student Affairs at Longwood University in Virginia.

7. *Animal House,* directed by John Landis; written by Harold Ramis, Douglas Kenney, and Chris Miller (Universal City, Calif.: Universal Studios, 1978).

8. Caitlin Flanagan, "The Dark Power of Fraternities," *The Atlantic,* March 2014, https://www.theatlantic.com. See also John Hechinger, *True Gentlemen: The Broken Pledge of America's Fraternities* (New York: Public Affairs, 2017).

9. Flanagan.

10. Gumprecht, *American College Town,* 71–93.

11. Cited in Jon Marcus, "The Decline of the Greek Empire: US Fraternities," *Times Higher Education,* May 28, 2015. See also Jake New, "Banning Frats?," Inside Higher Ed, September 30, 2015, https://www.insidehighered.com.

12. New, "Banning Frats?"

13. New.

14. Commonwealth of Pennsylvania, Office of the District Attorney, "Beta Theta Pi Fraternity and 18 Brothers Charged in Death of Timothy Piazza; 8 Facing Manslaughter Charges," press release, May 5, 2017. The district attorney's notification of criminal charges is available online in Mike Deak, "The Shocking Final Hours of Timothy Piazza's Life," *Courier News and Home Tribune,* May 5, 2017, updated May 8, 2017, http://www.mycentraljersey.com. See also Christina Caron, "Ex-Penn State Fraternity Member Sentenced to House Arrest in Hazing Death," *New York Times,* July 31, 2018. Ryan Burke, who was in charge of rushing and recruitment, pleaded guilty to nine misdemeanor charges and was sentenced to twenty-seven months' probation under house arrest. Penn State banned its chapter of Beta Theta Pi.

15. Doug Fierberg, interview by Marty Moss-Coane, *Radio Times,* WHYY, May 16, 2017.

16. Fierberg.

17. Alan D. DeSantis, *Inside Greek U.: Fraternities, Sororities, and the Pursuit of Pleasure, Power, and Prestige* (Lexington: University Press of Kentucky, 2007), 218.

18. DeSantis, 221.

19. Marcus, "Decline of the Greek Empire." Apparently this study controlled for race and family history.

20. Marcus.

21. Elizabeth A. Armstrong and Laura T. Hamilton, *Paying for the Party: How College Maintains Inequality* (Cambridge, Mass.: Harvard University Press, 2013), 40.

22. Armstrong and Hamilton, 125.

23. Armstrong and Hamilton, 67.

24. Armstrong and Hamilton, 59, 70.

25. Abbott Lawrence Lowell, quoted in Karabel, *The Chosen,* 107.

26. "Slavemaster Still Honored; 'Master' Bites the Dust," *New Haven Independent,* April 28, 2016.

27. Bergin, *Yale's Residential Colleges,* 130. This book was published in 1983, 120 years after the Emancipation Proclamation, and yet the author referred to Calhoun as a "farmer" rather than a plantation owner.

28. Daniela Brighenti, Qi Xu, and David Yaffe-Bellany, "Worker Smashes 'Racist' Panel, Loses Job," *New Haven Independent,* July 11, 2016; Zoe Greenberg, "Yale Drops Case against Worker Who Smashed Window Depicting Slaves," *New York Times,* July 12, 2016.

29. David Halpern, in discussion with Stephen Dubner, "Trust Me" (transcript), *Freakonomics Radio,* podcast, November 10, 2016, http://freakonomics.com. Halpern is the author of *The Hidden Wealth of Nations* (Cambridge: Polity Press, 2010).

30. Megan Landau, "Choosing Your First College Roommate," *USA Today,* April 19, 2012, http://college.usatoday.com. The website promoter explains: "Are you planning on going through [sorority] recruitment? You may be very busy for a few weeks during recruitment and it could be nice to be living with someone who is going through the same thing."

31. Quoted in Steve Kolowich, "Match at First Site," Inside Higher Ed, August 26, 2009, https://www.insidehighered.com.

32. Quoted in Kolowich.

33. Brian Jacob, Brian McCall, and Kevin M. Stange, "College as Country Club: Do Colleges Cater to Students' Preferences for Consumption?" (Working Paper 18745, National Bureau of Economic Research, January 2013), 37.

34. Matt Zalaznick, "Five-Star Accommodations on Campus," *University Business,* November 2014, https://www.universitybusiness.com.

35. Jacob et al., "College as Country Club," 32.

36. Jacob et al., 37.

37. Quoted in Vivian Yee, "Dumpy Dorms," *New York Times Education Supplement,* August 2, 2015, ED20.

38. Dawn Wotapka, "Resort Living Comes to Campus," *Wall Street Journal,* December 6, 2012.

39. Quoted in Wotapka.

40. Quoted in Zalaznick, "Five-Star Accommodations."

41. Steve Casimiro, "Jersey Governor Decries 'Rock Climbing Wall Epidemic,'" *Adventure Journal,* September 8, 2015.

42. I wish to thank Daniel Toren, a student in a class on collegiate architecture, for research on the subject of residence halls as recruitment devices in 2016.

43. Brandon Eckhardt, quoted in Courtney Rubin, "Making a Splash on Campus," *New York Times,* September 19, 2014, http://www.nytimes.com.

44. Wotapka, "Resort Living Comes to Campus."

45. John Eligon, "In Student Housing, Luxuries Overshadow Studying," *New York Times,* June 14, 2013, http://www.nytimes.com. The residential complex mentioned in this article, the Grove, is actually just off campus, not on campus.

46. Kevin Carey, *The End of College: Creating the Future of Learning and the University of Everywhere* (New York: Riverhead Books, 2015).

47. Blimling, *Student Learning,* 292.

48. Steve Kolowich, "Completion Rates Aren't the Best Way to Judge MOOCs, Researchers Say," *Chronicle of Higher Education,* January 22, 2014, https://www.chronicle.com, cited in Blimling, *Student Learning,* 292.

49. Blimling, *Student Learning,* 292.

50. I. Elaine Allen and Jeff Seaman, *Changing Course: Ten Years of Tracking Online Education in the United States* (Babson Park, Mass.: Babson Survey Research Group, 2013), cited in Blimling, *Student Learning,* 291.

51. Blimling, *Student Learning,* 293.

52. "Student Debt's Grip on the Economy," *New York Times,* May 20, 2017.

53. Michael Roth, "'Hamilton' and Liberal Education," Huffington Post, June 15, 2016, https://www.huffingtonpost.com/michael-roth/hamilton-and-liberal-educ_b_10465636.html.

Index

Page numbers in italics refer to figures.

CARLA YANNI is professor of art history at Rutgers, The State University of New Jersey. She is author of *Nature's Museums: Victorian Science and the Architecture of Display* and *The Architecture of Madness: Insane Asylums in the United States* (Minnesota, 2007).